Acne

Acne

A Memoir

Laura Chinn

New York

Hachette Books
Hachette Book Group
1290 Avenue of the Americas
New York, NY 10104
HachetteBooks.com
Twitter.com/HachetteBooks
Instagram.com/HachetteBooks

First Edition: July 2022

Published by Hachette Books, an imprint of Perseus Books, LLC, a subsidiary of Hachette Book Group, Inc. The Hachette Books name and logo is a trademark of the Hachette Book Group.

The Hachette Speakers Bureau provides a wide range of authors for speaking events. To find out more, go to www.hachettespeakersbureau.com or call (866) 376-6591.

The publisher is not responsible for websites (or their content) that are not owned by the publisher.

Print book interior design by Amy Quinn.

Library of Congress Cataloging-in-Publication Data

Names: Chinn, Laura, author.
Title: Acne : a memoir / Laura Chinn.
Description: First edition. | New York, NY : Hachette Books, an imprint of
    Perseus Books, LLC, a subsidiary of Hachette Book Group, Inc., 2022.
Identifiers: LCCN 2021048400 | ISBN 9780306828881 (hardcover) | ISBN
    9780306828904 (ebook)
Subjects: LCSH: Chinn, Laura. | Chinn, Laura—Family. | Television
    Writers—United States—Biography. | Television producers and
    Directors—United States—Biography.
Classification: LCC PN1992.4.C495 A3 2022 | DDC 818/.603
    [B]—dc23/eng/20220301
LC record available at https://lccn.loc.gov/2021048400

ISBNs: 9780306828881 (hardcover), 9780306828904 (ebook)

Printed in the United States of America

LSC-C

Printing 1, 2022

For Max and Jaz

Toxins

I WAS TEN YEARS OLD WHEN I DISCOVERED MY FACE. IT'S NOT LIKE I DIDN'T know what a face was; I had just never once thought about my own face. Much like not being aware of your stomach until it hurts, I wasn't aware of my face until there was something suddenly wrong with it. A small, white ball popped out of my right cheek and then, like magic, I realized I had a face. I stared at that little ball in the mirror and thought about my face for the first time and have not been able to stop thinking about my face since.

At that moment, I had no clue how much that little zit was going to change my life. I didn't realize it was a pus-filled canary warning me that a shitstorm of acne was on its way. My self-esteem was about to be ravaged. My identity was about to be transformed from a confident, plucky kid to an anxious, insecure adult. If you have never suffered the wrath of acne, you may think that this sounds a little extreme. It's a nonfatal disease after all, and if you have always had clear skin, it's almost impossible to understand what it really feels like to live with *Cutibacterium acnes* bacteria attacking your face all day and night.

It was as if some unseen force was making me wear a raw, red, swollen mask. The mask felt ugly and terrifying and people stared at it with disgust or, even worse, with pity. I didn't know how the mask got on my face, but I knew I couldn't take it off. After genocide, nuclear war, famine, slavery, and child abuse, acne is the absolute worst thing that can happen to a person. Okay, fine, maybe cancer is worse, and probably a bunch of other stuff, but acne is challenging, really challenging, and if you haven't lived through it then . . . honestly, go fuck yourself.

Some people only have to wear that tragic acne mask for a few years, and then they get to rejoin society and rebuild their self-worth. I, however, have had to wear the mask for most of my life. I have had some form of acne from mild to Freddy Krueger for over twenty years, and I have the scars to prove it. Oddly enough, my childhood was filled with so many heartbreaking events that my obsession with the whole acne thing seems wildly vain and ridiculous in comparison. But that's how psychologically impactful this skin disease is. Out of all the other tragedies of my childhood, the acne was the loudest and most obnoxious. It was constantly screaming at me, "You look different than everyone! You should kill yourself because of that!"

But as painful as this skin disease is, it ultimately saved my life. My winning combination of cystic acne and above-average narcissism forced me to seek help from doctors, dermatologists, psychologists, healers, hypnotherapists, inner child specialists, acupuncturists, chiropractors, Reiki masters, angel channels, and shamans. My numerous attempts to cure the skin condition made me look deeper and learn more about myself than I ever would have cared to otherwise. That first little white bastard that introduced me to the concept of hating myself was foreshadowing intense suffering and inevitable growth and transformation, but all I could do was stare at it in the mirror, like a goddamn moron.

After I questioned what was suddenly sprouting on my cheek, my mom explained that it was "toxins" coming out of my skin. This terrified me because although I didn't have a super firm grasp on what toxins were, I knew my parents were always desperately trying to avoid them. Our family was an organic, free-range, humanely sourced kind of family. The kind of family who uses plant-based cleaners that aren't strong enough to actually degrease anything so every pot and pan has a sort of waxy sheen on it forever. My parents were hippies and didn't do anything according to the status quo. I'm pretty sure my father still wakes up every morning, checks in on what the entire world is doing, and then does the opposite.

Our diet was always fluctuating. Sometimes we were raw vegans, meaning we only ate vegetables that were never heated over 118 degrees. Sometimes we were Indian-tarians, meaning my dad tried Indian food once and liked it so much that he paid the Indian woman who owned the 7-Eleven around the corner to come over and teach my mom to cook Indian food, and my dutiful mother cooked it for us every day for months. We were always following the rules of some new kick of my dad's, and that kick was never the American standard.

Currently, my dad is on a raw meat diet: raw chicken, raw beef, and the occasional raw goat testicle. Yes, my father has eaten the raw balls of a goat. He started this diet after he read a book written by a guy named Aajonus Vonderplanitzk, whose real name is John.

Aajonus claimed that raw meat and raw dairy are the healthiest things you can eat and apparently that was different enough from conventional thinking to have my dad fully convinced. If I went to my dad's house right now, he would sit in front of me and eat what he calls "raw chicken curry," which is exactly what it sounds like. He would slurp up little, slimy chunks of raw bird while attempting to convince me to switch to his rawsome lifestyle.

Growing up, whenever I asked my parents why we were eating a room temperature vegan loaf or dal makhani instead of hot dogs and Bagel Bites like my friends, I was told my friends' parents were sheep who blindly followed the SAD (standard American diet) and their food was full of toxins. Okay, but here I was watching toxins pop out of my face? Where were these mysterious facial toxins coming from? I was eating clean food and using clean detergents and soaps. I was taking my vitamin supplements every day and drinking my calcium-magnesium powder every night. I was eating my mom's home-ground, organic, non-GMO grains. And I wasn't doing anything insane like taking a shower without a chlorine filter, or brushing my teeth with fluoridated toothpaste, or eating store-bought mayonnaise.

I didn't understand what could've caused that zit. But after it went away and nothing else popped up, I forgot all about it. I just went back to having that deliciously creamy, poreless, little-kid skin that makes me wonder if God hates adults. I had no clue there was something more precious than diamonds wrapped around my skull. I just naïvely played with my Barbies and swam at the local YMCA with *stunningly perfect* skin and didn't even think about it, because no one told me it was about to change forever.

Moving

AROUND THE TIME OF THAT FIRST DERMAL ERUPTION, MY MOM SAT MY older brother and me down to tell us "wonderful, exciting news!" We were relocating to Clearwater, Florida. Apparently, my mom, my brother, and I were going to drive to Florida with all of our belongings in a U-Haul and our father was going to join us in a few months, after he finished his latest computer programming contract. She said all this with a huge smile, like she was announcing that we had just won ten thousand dollars on a scratcher.

We were currently living in La Crescenta, California, a small suburb north of Los Angeles, in an 827-square-foot house, and I was reasonably happy there. Our neighborhood was overflowing with kids and there seemed to always be a blockwide game of cops and robbers going on. My best friend, Samantha, lived four blocks away. Samantha's mom homeschooled my brother and me along with fifteen other extremely sheltered children. Every morning, my brother and I would walk to our nontraditional little school, stopping to chew lemon grass or inspect a slug's slow migration across a hot sidewalk. Sometimes we would pour salt on the slug and watch it dehydrate to death, because darling neighborhoods can still house devilish children.

Within those four blocks, our whole lives were contained. Within those four blocks, all of our stories occurred. Our childhood was simple and small just like our quiet suburb and I always believed it would stay that way. So my mom's lame attempt to manipulate me into thinking that moving across the country to this completely foreign and exotic Florida place was "wonderful, exciting news" . . . actually worked right away because children are gullible idiots.

She told us we were moving right near a beach, into a bigger, better house, and we'd spend all day building sandcastles and swimming with dolphins. I bought it like a sucker. I was nervous and excited to go on the adventure, but when we arrived in Florida, I quickly discovered I had been conned. Our supposedly beachfront property was at least fifteen minutes away from that sandcastle and dolphin-stuffed beach we were promised and the "bigger, better house" we were going to live in for the rest of our lives was condemned.

There were actual "condemned" stickers on all of the windows. The previous, highly negligent tenants had owned several German shepherds and the walls were basically painted with dog hair. All of the windows were rusted shut. The air conditioning had stopped working years ago. And there was no kitchen. Truly. The kitchen was just an empty room that smelled like food had once been cooked inside of it. There was an old, abandoned doghouse in the overgrown, lizard-infested backyard and we were greeted by a possum that had lived and died inside of that doghouse.

Since our new house was unlivable, we had to stay in the studio apartment that was attached to the garage. The three of us slept crammed onto one mattress on the floor of that tiny studio for months while the house was becoming less condemned next door. And we did it all during *a Florida summer.*

You know that moment when you open your hot oven to check on your turkey or whatever and scorched air blasts you in the face, making you worry for your eyebrows? A Florida summer feels like that moment all day long. I'm amazed Floridians have eyebrows. But the biggest twist to my mom's wonderful, exciting news was that my father actually would not be joining us. After a year of our new, humid Florida life, my parents decided it would be best if my dad just stayed in Los Angeles forever because . . . they were getting divorced.

I didn't know this at the time, but it turns out divorce can be extremely traumatizing to children. On a particularly awkward day in middle school, I was sitting next to an adorable, plump girl with curly red hair and we were making a list of our likes and dislikes. Our teacher had forced every student to partner up with someone they didn't know and we were asking each other things like "Do you like eggs?"

"Oh, um, not really."

"Oh, okay. I do . . ."

"Oh . . . cool."

The teacher was encouraging us to get to know each other in this stilted, robotic way and it wasn't really working. In the middle of this agonizing assignment, the girl I was getting to know started peeing. Our desks were scooted close to each other, so I heard the sound of dripping water. I looked down and she was just peeing all over herself, down her legs, onto the floor. A large, dark puddle was forming underneath her on the cheap, public school–blue carpet.

We made eye contact while she peed. She looked like a cornered gazelle: *Are you going to eat me?* her eyes seemed to say. I don't know why the gods of kindness shined down on me that day; I was eleven, I easily could've had a gut reaction of "ew!" or "What the fuck are you doing?!" but I said nothing. *I'm not going to eat you, you're safe*, my eyes responded.

The whole room started to smell like pee. Some oblivious kids started whispering about the mysteriously strong smell in the room. Our teacher seized this opportunity to tell us all to start wearing deodorant. Then the bell rang and the girl looked at me one more time to make sure I wasn't going to pounce when her back was turned. *Run free little gazelle*, I nodded at her. She wrapped her sweatshirt around her waist and fled. No one ever found out what happened to that deeply embarrassed, well-hydrated little girl that day. Years later, she told me her parents had just gotten divorced and the trauma of their divorce made her lose control of her bladder.

So knowing how devastating divorce is to children, telling them that you're getting a divorce should obviously be handled with extreme delicacy. But my mom did this instead: I was ten years old, sitting on the couch with my thirteen-year-old brother while my mom yelled on the phone with my dad. She hung up on him and threw the phone across the house. After it shattered on the wall, my brother asked what was wrong and our mom yelled back, "Ask your fucking father! He's divorcing me!" Then she stormed into her room and slammed the door.

That's how I learned my father was never going to live with me again. That's how I learned my silly, funny dad who always made sure I was taking my vitamins, doing my homework, and eating unconventional food was never going to do any of those things again.

Thankfully, my brother and I did not lose control of our bladders, but we were very rattled. After twenty years of a seemingly happy marriage, our parents were breaking up forever? But my mom confessed that throughout those twenty years our father had been having extramarital affairs and she had finally reached her breaking point. My mom, being a *very* untraditional mother, didn't believe in silly concepts like boundaries or protecting a child from sensitive information, so she talked us through their divorce in vivid and intimate detail. Supposedly, the original marital plan had been to allow my father to have these affairs, but at some point, my mom changed her mind.

My father believes men are not capable of being monogamous and he has told me this since I was barely old enough to understand the concept of monogamy.

"If you ever do get married, just know that your husband will never be satisfied unless you allow him to have sexual partners outside the marriage," my father informed me when I was twelve.

"Thanks for the advice. I'm excited to grow up—men seem great."

My mom says the divorce happened because she was afraid my dad was going to get AIDS from one of the women he was sleeping with and infect us all with it. She told me this when I was barely old enough to understand the concept of AIDS. But I think their marriage ended because it got too hard on my mom's ego. He was having sex with and giving his attention to different women and they were all much younger than my mom. When she signed up for the marriage, I think she fancied herself a free wheelin', free lovin' hippie who could easily be in an open relationship. But when reality set in, she was a mother of two, in her fifties, legally bound to a man who was fucking nineteen-year-old girls.

To his credit, when the divorce first happened, my father visited us every other weekend. He flew from California to Florida so often that Delta always upgraded him to first class, a detail I was weirdly proud of. He was also very generous with his child support payments as sort of a *sorry I can't be there to tuck you in ever again, but enjoy yourself at the mall!* However, he did not pay my mother any alimony, so, what initially felt like a copious amount of child support wasn't actually enough for my mom, my brother, and me to live on forever, but we didn't know that at the time, so we spent those monthly checks like they were an endless geyser of cash flow and a few years later . . . we were poor.

Those post-divorce mall trips did wonders for my self-esteem though. Sure, I was a girl whose father loved extramarital affairs more than living with her, *but look at all of my new clothes!* A year after the divorce, I was still making it rain at Limited Too on a weekly basis. I began to suspect that maybe I was a supercool, eleven-year-old, high fashion goddess. Not only did I have a chic tween wardrobe, complete with cutoff jean shorts, white Adidas crew socks, and K-Swiss sneakers, I also had fresh blonde highlights.

The highlights were a little wonky because my mom did them herself with hydrogen peroxide, but I loved them. My mom feared real hair dye would have soaked into my skull and caused brain cancer, so peroxide was my only option. My hair was extremely curly, which was unique and therefore frowned upon, but my new blonde highlights were basic and therefore celebrated! On the first day of sixth grade, I strutted into Dunedin Middle School not giving one shit about my recently broken home; I felt gorgeous, fashionable, and confident . . . and that's exactly when the zits returned.

BFF

WHEN THE PIMPLES SHOWED UP AGAIN, IT WAS KIND OF NORMAL; A LOT of my friends had some blemishes here and there. Except, of course, my best friend, Tori. Tori's skin looked fake, like smooth plastic—no pores, no scars, just ear-to-ear silk. People with skin like that should all just go live on an island together.

When we learned about menstrual cycles in health class, all the videos explained that after young ladies get their periods, their hormones change and the dreaded acne could occur. Meanwhile, I hadn't gotten my period yet, but I was somehow freckled with zits. So the day Tori got her first period, I remember thinking, *Yes, here we go. Now she's going to start breaking out too and we'll be blister sisters.*

Tori called me into the bathroom and casually said, "Damn, I just bled on the floor." She pointed to a dot of blood near the toilet. That's how she told me she'd just got her first period. How cool was she?! Any other prepubescent loser would've been excited or scared, but not Tori. She played everything very low-key. I was a constant ball of anxiety, but she was always so calm that she seemed like she could fall asleep at any second. Probably because she smoked so many cigarettes; that habit kept her pretty chilled out.

Tori grew up in a house that was similarly broken, and she started drinking Budweiser and smoking Camels at eleven years old. When I first learned Tori smoked, I thought maybe smoking would chill me out too, but it just gave me more anxiety. Trying to buy cigarettes when you're eleven but look like you're seven is a pretty anxiety-inducing undertaking. The corrupt gas station near my house, which the entire town referred to as "the ghetto store," would always eventually let me buy the cigarettes, but they would hassle me and ask when my fake birthday was and who the current president was. They made me sweat for my smokes.

A week before my twelfth birthday, my mom asked me what I wanted and I responded, "A carton of Marlboro Lights." That was my preferred brand and there are ten packs of cigarettes in a carton, so I hoped that they would last me until I looked a little older. Instead of grounding me or sending me away to a school for troubled youth, my mom went to the store and bought me a carton of Marlboro Lights.

I remember gleefully unwrapping the cellophane around my shiny, new toy. I couldn't wait to get my tiny child hands on all those cigarettes. When I recently asked my mom why she gave a twelve-year-old, who just hours before had been an eleven-year-old, so many cigarettes, she said, "Because that's what you asked for." Hey, she's not wrong. I did ask for them. That's on me.

A year after Tori's first period, I was patiently waiting for her face to explode, but she still didn't have a single breakout. Meanwhile, my face was looking more and more like the surface of Mars, but my vagina was still just a stupid, bloodless hole. I was painfully jealous of my fertile friend. I longed for the menstruation fairy to touch me with her magic wand. I couldn't wait to strut down the so-called feminine hygiene aisle like a goddamn rock star and confidently buy one of those pink boxes that only grown-ass adult women buy.

What was inside the boxes was still a mystery to me, but I knew it was probably something very chic. I smoked a half a pack of cigarettes a day but still didn't fully comprehend what tampons were. Eventually, Tori started complaining about monthly menstrual cramps—which was the coolest thing a twelve-year-old could complain about—but her skin was still as smooth as a rose petal. I was mystified. Those health class videos had *promised* me that Tori would start breaking out, but she had somehow cheated the system . . .

The mystery was finally solved during one of our classic sleepovers. Since there was no real family structure at Tori's house, she always spent the night at my house, which also had no structure, but she thought my mom was nicer than hers. Our sleepovers revolved around marijuana. We had recently discovered it and quickly became huge fans. We smoked it whenever we needed to soften the pain of our existence, which was every night. We would smoke a blunt filled with low-grade, cheap weed and then demand my mom drive us to the grocery store where we would buy potato chips, sour cream, a block of cheddar cheese, and olives. This is what we ate when we were high, and nothing else would suffice.

My mom would spend the drive ranting about what a selfish monster my father was and how the divorce had ruined her life. Tori and I were so stoned we would just laugh or try to change the subject. But my mom would not allow that; there was no other subject. For several years, my mom would prattle on about the ways in which my dad had robbed her of her youth and then abandoned her with two shitty kids. She didn't say the "shitty" part, but I always added it in my mind.

She would blame my father for anything that ever went wrong. After months of being single, she stormed through the house screaming, "Well, thanks to your dad I have to masturbate again tonight!" That particular display happened in front of five of my shocked friends. Her fault-finding with my dad wasn't always logical, but it worked for her. Sometimes her hatred toward him would get so overwhelming she would just start smashing plates on the kitchen floor, then she'd sweep them up, go buy more plates at the thrift store, and eventually smash those too.

After Tori and I returned home with our munchies, we locked my bedroom door and sat in my open window, smoking more weed and some of my birthday Marlboro Lights. A very stoned Tori stumbled into the bathroom and then came back minutes later with wide eyes. My perpetually relaxed friend suddenly seemed ill at ease. She looked, for the first time ever, like an anxious twelve-year-old girl.

When I asked her what was wrong, she quietly confessed that she had just started her first period. I was confused, didn't her period start a year ago? She admitted that it was actually her older sister's period blood on the bathroom floor that day. She had lied and said it was hers. But hadn't she been complaining about menstrual cramps? She breezed past all of these lies like she wasn't basically a lunatic who had just long-conned me for a year and swore that this time it was real, this time she really was bleeding! And my first thought, like that of any deeply supportive best friend, was *Yes! This asshole is finally gonna break out!* But alas, she didn't. She actually never broke out in her entire life. But I did get one of my wishes . . .

Three days later, when Tori and I were again very high and again wandering around the grocery store looking for munchies while my mom complained that my dad didn't give her enough money for groceries, I went to the bathroom and there it was: a tiny dot of dried blood in my underwear. I got my first period, three days after Tori, in a Kash n' Karry bathroom, and I raced to the feminine hygiene aisle to collect my prize.

Puberty

Tori and I were extremely close. She was my absolute best friend and my feelings toward her were 80 percent deep unconditional love and 100 percent jealousy. That math doesn't check out, but that's how it felt. It was like Tori was born to make everyone around her jealous. She fit the late-nineties impossible beauty standards perfectly. She was skinny with clear, white skin, straight blonde hair, wide blue eyes, the slightest hint of a nose, and puffy little bow lips.

She had a very childlike face, and in our pedophiliac culture, looking like a child is every woman's beauty goal. But she grew up in a tough environment, so to offset her cherubic face, she intentionally deepened her voice and cursed more than any adult I knew. She looked like an American Girl doll and talked like a crusty old war veteran who had seen too much. She had the worldly confidence of a much older girl and she got even more confident when her full pubic bush grew in.

One humiliating afternoon, Tori and I were in my backyard smoking cigarettes with my brother and his friends, all of whom I had crushes on, and they were making fun of us for being younger than them. They were calling us "jits" and "*ten*-agers" and one of them said, "I bet y'all don't even have pubic hair yet." My acne-covered face turned even redder. I wanted to yell, "Shit! He knows we're bald down there, Tori! Run!" But she just looked at him, with all of her glorious preteen swagger, and pulled down her pants, revealing her full, luscious bush. She was covered in thick, dark hair; some of it was even creeping up to her belly button. A bush *and* a happy trail?! I was stunned! When did that happen? My vagina looked like a naked mole rat, and I'd thought Tori and I were on the same bald page.

I was mortified. Everyone turned to me and I was like, "Um, I would totally show you guys my thick, lustrous pubic hair but I think instead I'm gonna go cry under my bed—" But before I could bolt, one of my brother's friends yanked my pants down and my tiny, hairless cat just stood there squinting in the sudden sunlight. The look on my face must've made them all realize what they had just done. They seemed immediately ashamed and my brother looked at me like, *I'm sorry for your loss.* As if he was at a funeral for my dignity.

I tried to run away but my pants were around my knees. I tripped and flashed my buttery smooth vagina in new and exciting angles to all the people whose opinions I valued the most. Then I collected myself, pulled up my pants, and took off. I ran out into the street and began searching maniacally for a hiding place. Eventually, I climbed a tree and sat huddled on a branch, tucking myself behind the leaves. I remained there cursing my hairless body for hours.

To his credit, my brother's pants-yanking friend circled the neighborhood on his bike, calling my name. But I decided I could never go home again. There had to be some kind of shelter for women with hairless pussies. A place where they could be hidden from the world and, in turn, the world could be spared the awful sight of their fleshy vagina lips shivering in the cold.

Long after dark, I finally decided to head home. If I hadn't been covered in mosquito bites and starving, I would still be hiding in that tree to this day. On my walk home, I came up with a plan. I asked my mother to take me to Kash n' Karry so I could buy a box of black hair dye. She was hesitant. She was still worried hair dye was going to soak into my brain and cause brain cancer, until I explained that the dye wasn't going to touch my head because I was only going to dye my three wispy blonde pubes. I think this explanation was so bizarre that she just said, "Fine, whatever."

My mom is the least judgmental person I have ever met. She has this superpower of being able to picture herself in another person's situation, no matter how insane the situation is. I think the real reason she bought me a carton of cigarettes for my twelfth birthday is that she felt bad for me. She put herself in my shoes. I really wanted cigarettes but couldn't buy them, because the government and pretty much every rational adult had agreed on laws that prevented it, so she decided to help me out. She is incredibly empathetic toward everyone except my father. I could just feel her trying to imagine being a weird twelve-year-old girl who, for some reason, really wanted black pubic hair.

She drove me to the store without another question, but while she drove, she couldn't help but blame my lack of pubic hair on my father's side of the family. Dying my pubes gave me some much-needed confidence. I waited for someone, anyone, to ask me if I had pubes, and I was ready to whip out my three newly dark hairs with all of Tori's bravado. But no one ever asked me again. I mean, it's actually super fucking weird that someone had asked me in the first place. Several years later, when I finally grew an adult bush, I learned our pedophiliac culture had decided pubic hair was disgusting and all women should be as hairless as a five-year-old, so I shaved it off immediately.

Scieno

AFTER A YEAR OF MY FACE BEING ENGULFED IN WHITEHEADS AND CYSTS, my mom finally began to notice my skin condition. To be fair, she was busy dating Tori's uncle, Fred, whom we all called "Uncle Fred." Calling a man Uncle Fred while your mom is banging him is odd, but I didn't mind 'cause Uncle Fred did cool stuff like give us cigarettes for doing menial tasks. It turns out a carton of cigarettes goes pretty fast when you're basically a chimney in a training bra, so Tori and I would take out the trash and sweep the floor and Uncle Fred would fill our twelve-year-old coffers with fresh cigarettes.

But I don't think Uncle Fred was the only reason my mom didn't notice my skin condition right away. She also didn't notice because she doesn't really comprehend our society's definition of beauty. My mother has never worn a drop of makeup or dyed her hair, and she has never understood why I wanted to do those things. She has always viewed me and the entire world through rose-colored-beauty glasses.

It's like she missed that moment that the rest of us all went through, that moment when we were all brainwashed by impossible beauty standards and forced to see the world divided into pretties and uglies. If we walk past a woman whose face is decidedly not destined to hock beauty products on a billboard, my mom will say something like, "Wow, that woman is *gorgeous*." And she'll genuinely mean it. My mother sees beauty everywhere, so she never felt a need to artificially enhance her own and was always perplexed when I was desperately trying to enhance mine.

My mother naturally fits the beauty standards; she has perfectly symmetrical features and creamy, smooth, freckled skin. She is what I like to call a "poolside beauty." You know the girls who still look amazing even after they swim for an hour? They get out of the chlorine and their wet hair somehow dries perfectly and their make-up-free skin glows in the sunlight. I never felt like a poolside beauty. My coarse, curly hair would never actually get wet in the pool. It was like duck feathers; water just ran off of it without saturating the shafts, but then, for some reason, it would poof into a ball, casting a large shadow over my potholed skin.

But my mom was always telling me how gorgeous I was, even when my face looked like it had permanent diaper rash. She also *loved* my unruly hair and encouraged me to wear it wild and free. "Don't put gel in it! Just let it be natural," she would say. And the night I straightened it with a hot iron on an ironing board, she had to look away. "I can't believe you would do that to your amazing hair," she whined. She somehow missed all the billboards, commercials, TV shows, and music videos jam packed with straight-haired, clear-skinned models and actresses. She somehow avoided the horrifically destructive, false programming that I lived by: Textured hair is wrong. Smooth hair is right. Textured skin is wrong. Smooth skin is right.

She is thankfully not one of those image-obsessed mothers who constantly nitpick their daughters' looks. I have some friends whose mothers are jealous of their daughters' beauty. They make snarky comments to try and diminish their daughters' self-esteem. I have other friends whose mothers simply cannot tolerate any unique traits in their offspring. One mother would tape her daughter's ears back when she was a toddler in the hope that they would someday lie flat against her head.

My mother was the opposite of these mothers. She seemed to look through my ravaged skin and just see a pretty girl. She has never made one negative remark about my looks or told me to change anything about myself. When I would cry about my skin, she would say, "Oh, Laura, no one notices, I promise you. Your skin is beautiful." If I had been unlucky enough to be the daughter of an image-obsessed mother, it would've destroyed me. I hated my looks enough for the both of us.

But when my mom finally did realize my skin was getting worse and worse, she did the only thing she knew how to do: she took me to a Scientologist chiropractor. The dermatologist might seem like a logical choice, but it isn't when you enjoy bucking tradition and you've been a Scientologist for thirty years. My parents had been Scientologists since the seventies. They credited Scientology with helping them quit using drugs, and they always told us that Scientology saved their lives.

My brother and I were raised exclusively in the Los Angeles Scientology community until we moved to Clearwater. Clearwater is actually the mecca for Scientology, but ironically, as soon as we arrived in the mecca, my brother and I lost interest in the religion. My mom was too distraught over the divorce to keep pushing us to go to private Scientology schools. We said we wanted to try public school and she gave us her blessing / was too tired to fight with us.

After starting my new Florida public school, I learned that although there were a lot of Scientologists in Clearwater, their kids went to private Scientology schools and they were all thoroughly despised by the local non-Scientologist population. So I decided to never tell any of my public school friends that I was an L. Ron Hubbard–loving, E-meter can–squeezing, full-blown "Scieno," as they were not so lovingly called by the locals. When other kids were insulting Scientology and saying things like "My dad says Scienos are buying up all the property in Clearwater tax-free" or "My mom says they're building a spaceship to go live in a volcano," I would just nod along and hope no one noticed how nervous I looked.

In my teens, I was at a house party hanging out in the front yard when a drunk fascist, whom everyone appropriately called "Nazi Pete," threw a beer bottle at a passing Scientology bus. I watched the bottle fly through the air and dramatically shatter on a side window, no doubt terrifying all the passengers inside, and I just stood there. While everyone was laughing and yelling, "You fuckin' Scienos!" I just stood there.

I fantasized about yelling at Nazi Pete, "Hey! Scientologists are people too! They don't deserve to be treated that way!" Instead, I just looked at the ground. I was basically the opposite of a hero. But that's slightly unfair because heroes are supposed to stand up for what they believe in and I never really believed in Scientology. But I guess I *did* believe in not assaulting innocent strangers for participating in their religion, so I could have said something, but

I wasn't willing to blow my cover. I pretended like I wasn't a Scientologist out in the world, and I pretended like I was a Scientologist at home.

In front of my parents, I participated in all the rituals and customs of Scientology. If anything went wrong, there was always a Scientology solution. If you fell down and banged your knee, you had to "touch it back," which meant you had to slowly reenact the fall over and over again until the "engram" or traumatic event was released from your "reactive mind" or subconscious. Scientology parents say "touch it back" to their child after they experience any injury, no matter how big or small, and the Scientology child has to then repeat the event, slowly touching their knee to the spot they fell on. Even if my brother and I fell down a flight of fucking stairs, we would not share it with our parents, lest we would have to slowly reenact that stair fall over and over again.

But even worse than injuring yourself and having to touch it back was yawning while reading. In Scientology schools, the teachers are trained to watch for yawning or bored-looking kids. This is a sure sign that the kid has read a word they don't understand. It's called a "misunderstood word" or "MU." Several times a day, I would yawn while reading and a teacher would appear over my shoulder. "Let's find that MU, shall we?" She would then go over every single word I had just read, doing a spot check to find out which word was foreign to me and causing all those tricky yawns.

After scanning my book, she would look at me with cocky eyes, knowing she'd found the MU, and ask, "What does the word 'the' mean?" To which I would reply, "Denoting one or more people or things already mentioned or assumed to be common knowledge." 'Cause I wasn't a fucking fool. I obviously knew the dictionary definition of "the" and so did all of my classmates. But she would always eventually find something. "Okay, what does 'then' mean?" *Dammit*. I would have to look up "then" and build the meaning of the word "then" out of clay. This is called a "clay demo," and you don't know shit until you've modeled the definition of a word with clay.

Looking up so many words every day taught me a lot, but above all, it taught me to suppress a yawn better than anyone. I can sense a yawn coming from minutes away and with just a slight tightening of the jaw and flare of the nostrils, I can swallow that yawn, sending it back from whence it came, saving myself hours of looking up words and building their definitions out of clay.

If you ever have an issue with another Scientologist, you can officially tattle on them by writing a "Knowledge Report," though if you're in the know you call it a KR because that sounds cooler. If a Scientologist does anything "out-ethics" (general bad behavior or anything harmful to Scientology), you write a long report about what they did and give this report to an "Ethics Officer." (If you're picturing a stern woman in a military-style uniform with a furrowed brow and a tight bun, then you're picturing correctly.) But the best part is, you also have to give a copy of the KR to the person you tattled on. So if you don't have the courage to just talk to this person face-to-face about their bad behavior, you better have the courage to mail them a copy of your angry document that shit-talks them for four pages.

I have never written a KR in my life; even when I was a kid, I was like, *that seems childish*. But I have received several Knowledge Reports, all from the same person, who will not be named. This person would even go so far as to leave my copy of the KR on my car in the middle of the night. In the morning, I would walk out to my car and find an envelope stuffed with horrific and shameful facts about me like I dated a guy who smokes weed or I asked too many questions during a Scientology informational presentation. Because of all these complicated rules and rituals, I always kept my distance from Scientology, but when my mom mentioned that a Scientologist chiropractor might be able to fix my skin, I was instantly back on board with the whole religion.

The chiropractor examined my oily, infected pores and seemed to feel confident that she could help. Most people know chiropractors as *that doctor that cracks your bones*, and that's not wrong, but chiropractors also do many other hippie-dippy-crunchy forms of healing. This woman did something called applied kinesiology or "muscle testing."

She had me hold a glass vial with a small piece of wheat grain in it. Then she told me to hold my arm up strong and she pressed down on it; if she pressed down on my arm easily, then I was allergic to wheat gluten! But if I was able to keep my arm strong while holding the wheat, that meant I was gluten tolerant and could keep eating gluten. To a true atheist or lover of science, this might sound irrational, but I have had some weirdly wonderful breakthroughs with this healing modality.

She tested all kinds of foods on me and told us my skin was breaking out because I was allergic to gluten, dairy, chocolate, and sugar. We left there thinking my acne would be a cinch to heal! All I had to do was give up those four things! I didn't realize those four things were pretty much in all food.

Meanwhile, my mom got busy again. She broke up with Uncle Fred and started dating Joe, a profoundly introverted Scientologist with a very serious drinking problem. While my mom was navigating that, I was attempting to stick to my new diet. I would go to the Dodge's Store gas station and get chicken fingers and pick the breading off. That's technically "no gluten," right? Then I would get pizza sticks and eat the pizza goo out of the inside and leave the crust behind! This was going to be easy!

Being thirteen, I didn't realize pizza goo was filled with dairy. I also didn't realize beer was filled with gluten and I was consuming at least four of those a night. The days of my mom making her own home-ground flour were long over. For most meals, my brother and I had to fend for ourselves while my mom was off piecing together a love life in her fifties. She also signed a two-year contract with the Church of Scientology of Tampa. Tampa was thirty minutes away from Clearwater and she volunteered there for over fifty hours a week, so there was truly no adult in my home for several years. But my parents always made sure we had money for food, and my mom always made sure there was plenty of food in the fridge. We were fortunate enough to never ever go hungry, but the food choices my brother and I were making were not wise ones.

Needless to say, my skin did not improve at all. My dad would chime in from Los Angeles over the telephone, saying things like, "I read that cooked tomatoes make you break out." So I cut out all tomato sauce, including the pizza goo, but I kept eating ketchup because I didn't know ketchup was 100 percent cooked tomatoes. I did the best I could, which wasn't great. And I continued to wake up every morning with raw, red skin. And my mom continued to tell me it was beautiful.

Max

M Y FATHER WOULD TRY TO COMFORT MY ACNE ANGUISH BY SAYING IT was genetic. He explained that he had the same skin condition when he was a teenager. It seemed like he felt responsible for my skin disease. The sight of me in so much pain agonized him and he would reassure me that it eventually goes away. But if it was genetic, I wondered, then why did my sixteen-year-old brother, Max, who shared my genetics and my diet, have such beautiful skin? I used to look at his face and naïvely think that if I had skin like his, I would be intensely happy all the time. Which is why it baffled me that he was severely depressed.

He would sit in front of his TV, playing video games, in his dark bedroom all day long. His walls were decorated with sexy posters (Carmen Electra in a wet bra and Jenny McCarthy in a dry bra) and funny posters (the best one was "NEVER SNEEZE AND FART AT THE SAME TIME" over an image of a cartoon dog whose anus and mouth had exploded), but the objectification of women and humiliation of cartoon dogs wasn't enough to cheer him up. He kept his curtains shut tight and only went outside a few times a day to smoke weed. I would watch him chug a forty-ounce beer by himself every night, right before he yelled at me to get out of his room so he could entomb himself for the evening.

My brother wasn't always depressed and grumpy though. He was a pretty happy kid, and I'm told he was a very happy baby. Max was born three years before me, on February 26, 1983. Our father is Black and our mother is a freckle-faced, white brunette; Max was a beautiful combination of them both. His complexion was the color of coffee ice cream and his hair was straight and dark. If you didn't know the races of his parents, you would assume he was Mexican or Hawaiian. And people constantly did.

He was strikingly handsome, and the story goes that he was born with muscle tone beyond his years. My dad proudly claims, "My son came out of the womb doing push-ups." Max was extremely physically gifted and excelled at anything that required hand-eye coordination or strength or flexibility. He could do a backflip off a wall, he could throw a football what seemed like miles, and he could drop from a handstand into the splits. And he was completely baffled as to why I was incapable of doing any of the aforementioned feats.

I was born on March 24, 1986. Although my father is Black and my mother has very dark hair and eyes, I was born with fair skin, a pile of bright blonde curls, and blue eyes. I looked nothing like either of my parents or my brother. There are no legends of me coming out of the womb doing push-ups.

According to my parents, the story of my entry into the world goes something like this: "We really wanted you to be a boy and so did Max. We just *loved* the idea of having two boys that could play together. When you came out, we were so . . . not disappointed but surprised that you were a girl. Also, you looked very red and small and odd. You were very weak and never smiled and we were so . . . not disappointed but worried something was developmentally wrong with you for several months. Max was *very* unimpressed with you. He kept looking inside your crib, holding a soccer ball and wondering when you would be big enough to play with him." The answer to that question was never.

Even though I eventually developed average human muscle tone and learned how to smile, I never came close to keeping up with my brother's athleticism. He would spend hours with me in the front yard trying to teach me a back handspring, but after I fell on my head a dozen times, I would shamefully try to give up, and he would say, "Come on, Laurie. It's so easy." But it wasn't easy for me. All I wanted to do was read and write and play pretend. Where he was a physical god, I was a reading god, and my thing wasn't nearly as cool as his.

But for some reason, my parents were always worried about Max's self-esteem, even though he was frequently winning karate trophies and gymnastics medals. That didn't seem to be enough for them. To their dismay, he seemed insecure about his less than impressive academic achievements, so they came up with a plan: they decided to downplay my academic achievements. They thought if they didn't make too big a deal about my straight As, then my brother would never have to feel a moment of humility.

When my brother was six, my parents hired a special tutor to come to our house and teach him how to read. He was struggling with reading at school, so they wanted to offer him some extra support. I would sit in the back of the living room and watch this woman hold up giant, multicolored reading charts in front of my brother, and that's how, at three years old, I learned to read. My brother continued to struggle, but I took to it instantly. I read voraciously and quickly graduated to higher and higher reading levels.

When I was nine, I had far surpassed my brother's reading level and my mom told me I had to read in the bathroom in secret from then on because she didn't want Max to see how advanced my books were. He didn't have to hide his athletic trophies and medals from me, but for some reason I had to hide my talents from him. This all seemed perfectly normal to me, so I started reading my Dean Koontz books while locked in the bathroom.

Dean Koontz was my absolute favorite author. His dark and terrifying books are recommended to readers who are sixteen and older, but no one told me that. His best book, in my nine-year-old opinion, was *Intensity*, about a woman named Chyna who watches her best friend get raped and murdered by a serial killer and then exacts her revenge, by lighting him on fire. It was novels like these that were undeniably the inspiration behind one of my finest short stories, *Vioant*, which I think was supposed to be *Violent*:

Vioant

One day I walked to school and I got stolen by this really big man and I egged him bad and he started to run but I cot up with him and socked him with my marculay biseps. and cut off his dick and put it in his mouth: I mean the nerve of him to try to steal me and rape me I mean he tryed to rape me! I know you think it is vioant but if I didnt cut off his dick he would rape so many other kids,

The toilet wasn't the most comfortable place to read, but I didn't want my brother to find out about my IQ, so I spent hours in the bathroom locked away from his fragile ego, consuming adult horror thrillers and writing Dean Koontz fan fiction. Although, in retrospect, I don't think his ego was that fragile. I think it was something my parents had convinced themselves of because he was a boy and therefore his self-esteem took precedence over mine, but I think Max and I balanced each other out nicely and we would've been fine left to our own devices. We were a team. When we played video games, he held the controller and did all the action while I read the entire game manual cover to cover. Then I would tell him all the secret moves and cheats and together we would win the game. It didn't particularly bother me that he was an incredible athlete. If anything, I was proud to be related to someone who was that good at everything.

Max was kind and ridiculously funny and always made me feel like he had my back. When a neighbor kid threw a rock at me, my brother ran to his house, called him outside, and threatened to beat him up. Moments like that made me feel incredible. It was like all my messed-up ideas about how men have to protect women were unfolding before my little eyes. My brother was my knight in shining armor. I hid my intelligence from him and he threatened my attackers with physical violence. It was a perfect male-female dynamic, inspired by our parents, who were raised during a time when this was exactly how males and females were supposed to interact. But gender brainwashing aside, I adored him.

He eventually started skateboarding and that is when he was able to put all of his physical gifts into one endeavor. I would sit outside and watch him for hours as he ollied and 180ed his way through an afternoon. His body moved weightlessly, easily manipulating that piece of wood like it was glued to his sneakers.

He would quickly surpass anyone he skateboarded with and then would move on to older and older crowds of long-haired, baggy-pantsed, Vans-wearing skater dudes. He dominated the skate park and was always looking for bigger half-pipes. When we first moved to Florida, no one was skateboarding. My brother brought skate-boarding to that small beach town, and all the Clearwater kids who started skateboarding because of him have told me so many times what an important influence he was on them. For years, everyone in town only knew me as "Max's little sister"; it was like being related to a movie star or, even better, Tony Hawk.

When my brother stopped skateboarding seemingly for no rea-son, that's when I knew he was officially depressed. At the time, I didn't understand why. My mom thought it was the divorce, the loss of a father figure, and the anger that had taken over our house-hold. She figured all that pain caused him to swap his skateboard for a self-medicating bong. His depression and alcohol and drug use eventually became too intense and he announced that he needed a life change. He decided that moving back to Los Angeles and living with our dad, who was much more strict than our mom, would be just the thing that could help him get his life together; a very wise and mature decision to make at sixteen years old.

My brother moving away triggered the feelings of abandon-ment I'd experienced when my dad left a few years earlier, and as I watched Max pack up his beat-up gray Acura on twenty-inch chrome rims, I felt anxious and angry. But I masked my feelings with weird jokes, and I wrote him a goodbye letter filled with pan-icked awkwardness: "Are you ever gonna call me again or are you just gonna pretend you don't have a sister? Ha ha! I'll miss you but you probably won't miss me! Ha ha! JK! But seriously keep in touch or I'll drive out there and force you to! Ha ha ha ha!" I wanted to hold him close and shove him across the country at the same time. As scared as I was to live without him, I also believed the move could really help him get his life together, so I resisted the strong urge to chase after that cheap old car on expensive new rims as it drove him away from me.

In one of those strange curveballs the universe sometimes tosses out, while on his drive to better his life, Max's vision started failing him. He would go through brief periods where he couldn't see anything except blackness. Thankfully, a friend was driving with him and they got to Los Angeles safely. When Max called and told me what was happening to his vision, I made fun of him. I told him he was going to have to wear glasses and called him a nerd. I had no idea how serious this was. I knew a lot at thirteen. I knew Mommy and Daddy could get divorced. I knew Captain Morgan and weed could create several hours of anxiety-free numbness. I knew a cop could pepper spray you in the face if you were in a rowdy crowd in Tampa on Mardi Gras. But I had no idea someone I loved could get very sick. That was a true impossibility in my mind.

It was a completely normal school day when my life changed forever. My mom struggled to wake me up, like any other morning. I immediately thought about my skin and wondered how aggressive the new breakouts would be, like any other morning. But before I could run to the mirror and obsess about myself, my mom informed me that my brother had a brain tumor and was going into emergency surgery in Los Angeles at that very moment. I knew my mom was terrified, but I only felt confusion. I had no clue what she was talking about. I knew it was serious, but my mind couldn't even conjure up images of my brother and "brain tumor" or "emergency surgery." It was truly unimaginable.

My mom explained that my father brought Max to an eye doctor who found nothing wrong with his eyes, but after a CAT scan, they discovered a large tumor growing on his ocular nerve. So on that very normal morning, my mom and I were frantically packing our bags to get on a last-minute flight to Los Angeles to see my brother. Earlier that day, before Max went into surgery, the doctor informed my father that there was a chance that Max wouldn't survive the surgery, so my mom and I ran through the Tampa airport and buckled ourselves into that plane knowing we might already be too late.

Hospital

CHILDREN'S HOSPITAL LOS ANGELES IS THE WORST PLACE I'VE EVER BEEN. The buildings are modern, sleek, and well kept. The giant colorful wooden blocks that spell out "CHLA" on the front lawn are just delightful. Most of the doctors and nurses are kind and attentive. But none of that makes up for the bleeding three-year-old girl, covered in tubes, whizzing past you at top speed on a gurney pushed by frantic EMTs who just rescued her from a horrific car accident. Nothing can prepare someone for the intensive care unit of a children's hospital. Nothing. And I was less than prepared. I was a thirteen-year-old girl, who truly only cared about herself, suddenly thrust into this world of suffering, and it forced me to briefly think . . . *huh, maybe there are worse things than acne?*

My stressed-to-her-absolute-limit mother and I waited outside Los Angeles International Airport for our ride to the hospital. When my father pulled up in his midlife-crisis car, my mom rolled her eyes so hard I could hear them scraping the inside of her brain. My dad's car was so on the nose middle-aged-man-clinging-to-his-youth it was breathtaking. We piled into his bright red Mustang Cobra convertible, top down, and drove in windblown silence. That's probably not true. There was probably a conversation, but I have no memory of it. I bet it was short and curt. Those two hadn't necessarily been chummy since the divorce three years earlier, and if it were up to my mom, she would've gladly never driven in a car with him again.

At some point, my father told me he'd had a breakdown earlier, before my brother went into brain surgery. He said he'd lost control of his legs and collapsed in the hospital hallway. He was somehow even less prepared for this situation than I was. My father adored my brother. Max was his son, his boy, and he related to him in ways that I don't think he ever could have with a daughter.

My father sees women as "other." To this day he emails me jokes about how unbearable wives are when they're on their periods, and even though my dad did a decent job of not treating me as other, I still grew up feeling in a class below my brother's. My brother was the fruit of my father's loins; it was as if my father *was* my brother, and he reacted to this tragedy as if he himself were going through it. He even said on several occasions how much he wished everything was happening to him instead of my brother and he meant it.

Walking through the ICU felt like a nightmare that I wished so badly I could wake up from, back in my bed in Clearwater, listening to my brother's skateboard grinding and cracking on the pavement outside, but part of me knew I would never hear those sounds again. As I took in all the sick and injured babies around me, I could feel empathy being forced upon me and I did not like it.

The nurse informed us that Max had survived the surgery. *Oh, thank God that's over, let's get the hell outta here*, I thought. She said he wouldn't be awake for a while, but we were welcome to go in and sit with him. *Oh, right, we should probably do that, then let's get the hell outta here*, I thought. Then she lowered her voice, which told me this next piece of information was going to be serious. "We got his results back and his tumor was cancerous," she said gravely. I didn't understand why a cancerous tumor was worse than just a regular Joe tumor until my mom explained that cancerous meant it could come back. Come back?! Meaning, we'd have to return to this devastating place and do this shit all over again? I wasn't thrilled. Also, I wondered why my mom had been so worried that I was going to get a brain tumor from dying my hair, but my brother got one without using even a drop of hair dye.

When we arrived in Max's glassed-in room, the very first thing I noticed was the vein on his right temple. It was huge, bulging and pulsing with the beat of his heart, and I stared at it for a very long time. That was all my eyes could handle, just a little bit at a time. *Okay, eyes, you've stared at that bulging vein, now let's move on to the IVs jammed into his wrist, holy shit that sucked. Now, let's glance at his unconscious face, wow, that was really depressing. Now, let's check out that bloody bandage on his head and that one visible stitch sticking out from under it. Jesus, that looks disgusting and incredibly painful. Okay, we did it. We have officially looked at the worst thing ever, inside the worst place ever. Well done, eyes.*

After hours of that, my mom and I arrived at the motel room my brother had been living in. My brother came to Los Angeles to live with my dad, but he was temporarily living in a motel room by himself. I think my father was waiting to move Max in with him once he got a bigger apartment or something—this all made sense to everyone at the time. My mom and I entered to find dirty clothes, loose joint roaches, liquor bottles, and pizza boxes strewn around the room. I guess letting a teenage boy live by himself in a motel isn't a great idea. My mom and I halfheartedly cleaned it up and then passed out on the hard mattress.

We then began a routine of visiting Max in the ICU all day and coming back to that motel room at night, with temporary breaks to go visit the nearby Scientology center. When my brother woke up from surgery, we learned he was going to be blind for the rest of his life. He had what's called a pinhole of vision, which meant he could kind of see if he moved his head around a bunch and if the object he was trying to look at was enormous. The doctor was like, "Welcome back! Now say goodbye to any job you thought you were going to have when you grew up and say hello to a really tight neck from moving your head around a billion times just to see the parked car that you're about to walk into. That'll be one hundred thousand dollars."

He also woke up with difficulty speaking. And apparently, the surgeon cut out the part of his brain that had learned how to read and do math, so he couldn't do those things anymore either. I probably heard all this information and then went to the bathroom to inspect my skin in the mirror. It was quite possibly a little too much for my young heart to handle. But my mom, like a goddamn hero, just rolled up her sleeves and got to work. She almost immediately started teaching him how to read and do math again. While he still had a catheter in his penis, she was holding those same giant, multicolored reading charts from our youth in front of his tiny pinhole of vision and forcing him to sound out words. On one of these desperately sad days, I asked my dad if I could use his cell phone to call Tori.

I went outside the hospital, paced around, and then dialed. I was nervous to call her. I felt like I had changed; I didn't understand how, but I knew I was different and, to me, different was bad. Her voice on the other end of the phone was like warm milk and honey. Tori was a tough, preteen badass and quite honestly scared the hell out of me, but she was mine. She was *my* best friend, and after spending weeks doing nothing but talk about my brother, it was so delicious to talk to someone who was all mine. Someone was giving *me* attention. For the first time since Max got sick, I felt like I still existed. Maybe not to my parents, but to Tori I was real.

She filled me in on the latest drama back in Clearwater: who lost their virginity, who got genital warts, whose dad stopped paying child support. We were both in eighth grade at the time. I ached to be back in school. Even though the acne made me withdraw from my social groups, I still loved Dunedin Middle School. And now more than ever I wanted to be there in that brick building with my friends, and my teachers, and my books.

Before we got off the phone, Tori surprised me with the best news of all. Our entire class had voted for eighth-grade superlatives while I was gone, and I had won . . . Most Popular. Most Popular?! Suddenly, the greatest moment of my life and the worst moment of my life were happening simultaneously. Now I know winning a superficial award in eighth grade doesn't sound like that big of a deal, but at the time it was *everything*. It was a life preserver. It was God saying, "Don't kill yourself today. Not today, because a lot of people like you."

Sometimes those things that seem so trivial can greatly uplift a person who needs it. And I needed it immensely. I had never won anything in my entire life (again, not an athletic person). And this wasn't just any award, this was the "you are loved" award, and at that moment that award was more necessary than oxygen and water. I relished this news. It was my Lifetime Achievement Award and I wanted to savor it. But now Tori, much like everyone else, wanted to talk about my brother.

Tori said no one at our school knew about what happened yet, but Max was a beloved member of the teenage community of Clearwater and word would travel fast. I gave her the facts to share with people and I could tell she felt deputized with an important task. Tori had been in love with my brother since the first moment she met him. She was mostly my friend because she liked me, but partly my friend because she wanted to marry my brother.

She used to come over to my house, play Mariah Carey at top volume, press her body against the wall between our bedrooms, and cry along to "Always Be My Baby." She would actually cry real tears. She longed for him. She would sometimes randomly shout, "I love you!" through the wall, but he would ignore it. He thought she was a "little grom" who would be "hot one day" but he never took her seriously as a prospect. She had not taken the news of his brain tumor well, but to her credit she really made me feel like I was the priority and I was thankful for that. Eventually my dad appeared outside, gently saying I was using up all of his cell phone minutes, so I reluctantly got off the phone.

My dad wasn't at the hospital as much as my mom. Everyone grieves in different ways. My mother's way was to fix my brother as fast as possible. My father's way was to shower my brother with love during each visit but keep the visits short and sweet. After all, the man had to work. Someone had to keep paying for our motel room. He also had to fund Chardonnay's chicken nugget addiction. Chardonnay was my father's girlfriend. Chardonnay, though named after a wine varietal, wasn't legally allowed to drink alcohol yet since she was only nineteen years old. Six years older than me at the time and over thirty years younger than my dad. She was smoking hot and fun and, according to my father, loved McDonald's chicken nuggets. She couldn't get enough of them.

Thankfully, my father had the sense not to bring young Chardonnay to the hospital in front of my grieving mother. Just kidding, he definitely did bring Chardonnay to the hospital and it absolutely destroyed my mom. I wish I could've been in Chardonnay's bedroom while she was getting dressed for those hospital visits. *So my fifty-year-old boyfriend is picking me up in his dope convertible and taking me to the hospital to visit his newly blind son, his lonely, acne-ravaged daughter, and his sad ex-wife. I think I'll wear wedge sandals, a miniskirt, and a neon green tube top.*

Chardonnay would awkwardly stand in the outskirts of my brother's recovery room while my mom went over my brother's multiplication tables with him, while my dad held back tears and told my brother he loved him, and while I pretended I was somewhere else and caked more Clinique makeup on my already three-layer-caked face. She must have been really hard up for chicken nuggets to put up with this scene.

Well, she didn't fully put up with it. She was very jealous of my mom and she told my dad, "I'm not comfortable with you spending so much time with your ex-wife." She didn't seem to take into account that they were "spending so much time" together in a children's ICU. I guess she thought the romantic sounds and smells of dying babies were going to rekindle my parents' relationship, or maybe the size of the throbbing scar on their son's freshly shaved head was going to make them want to rip each other's clothes off.

Instead of keeping this information to himself, my father told my mother. While my mom was tending to her son's new disabilities, my father said, "Hey, just so you know, Chardonnay is uncomfortable with you being here." And instead of keeping this information to herself, my mother told me.

When my mom and I were tucking ourselves in for the night back at our dusty motel, I was lulled to sleep by the sound of her raging about my father's blatant disregard for her feelings. How dare he parade that teen girl in front of her while she was dealing with all of this bullshit; he was the most selfish person she had ever met. Some people like sound machines as they drift off, but my mother's anger puts me right to sleep.

After several weeks, I reminded my parents that I had missed a great deal of school and perhaps we should start thinking about heading back to Florida. The doctors said this wasn't possible, as my brother wouldn't be able to fly for months. Months?! Months feel like years when you're thirteen, and years feel like centuries at the hospital. We couldn't afford to stay in that motel room for months, so my mother began looking into cheap housing near the hospital.

Eventually, she found the Ronald McDonald House. It's a building with individual bedrooms and a shared kitchen for low-income people with a loved one in the hospital. And it's completely free. Yay, McDonald's! It turns out my father wasn't just funding Chardonnay's chicken nugget habit; he was also indirectly funding my mom's future housing.

"This whole thing is so fucked up, I bet most of these people are in the hospital *because* of McDonald's," my mom said as she was moving into her new housing. She hated that the standard American diet was putting a roof over her head.

Still not knowing what to do about me and my education, my parents put their heads together and decided . . . to send me back to Florida by myself. Yep, at thirteen I was going to get on a plane and go live in our little house in Clearwater completely alone. I was to feed myself, put myself to bed, and get myself up for school for several months. My mom's new boyfriend was back in Clearwater, so he would drive me to school and give me money for takeout or groceries when I needed it. My mom decided to ignore the fact that her new boyfriend, Joe, was a mute alcoholic and somehow this ended up actually being the official plan. Which I happily agreed to, because anything was better than being stuck in that perfectly delightful, absolutely horrible children's hospital.

Home Alone

I FLEW BACK TO CLEARWATER AND JOE PICKED ME UP FROM THE AIRPORT. He was the quietest person I had ever met in my life. He even looked quiet. He was a balding, gray-haired white man whose face somehow made you think, *I bet that dude is super quiet*. Needless to say, we drove in silence. Here I was back from the greatest tragedy of my life and this man didn't have a single question to ask me. I asked him how work was, to which he replied, "Okay." Then more silence, because I truly could not think of any other questions to ask him.

Finally, mercifully, we arrived at my small, aging house. He gave me some cash for food and then dropped me off. I unlocked the door and stepped into the emptiness. It's not like I hadn't been home alone before. Over the past few years, I was almost always home alone. When my mom was off volunteering and my brother was off with his friends, I would call my mom and beg her to come home because I hated going to sleep alone. Of course, she never could come home because she was always doing something for Scientology that I still don't completely understand. So even though being alone wasn't new, this level of loneliness was. Knowing that no one was going to be home tomorrow or the next day or the next week intensified my already very close relationship with feeling lonely.

At bedtime, I plugged in my mom's alarm clock knowing that, for the first time in my life, she wasn't going to be there to wake me up, and then I went to sleep. Well actually, I washed my face before I went to sleep, which is something you just always do when you have acne. After a night out, my clear-skinned friends would drunkenly pass out with a face full of makeup, but I would stumble to the bathroom and wash my face, so help me God. If I had lost my hands in a tragic accident, I would have used my feet to wash my face.

One of the biggest fears I had about my skin was that people thought I was dirty. They'd take one look at my infected pores and just assume that I didn't bathe. This fear has been made real several times when people have looked at my skin and given me unsolicited advice like "You know, I bet your skin would clear up if you stopped touching your face" or "You should really change your pillowcase more often." I want to scream at them, "I change my pillowcase every day and I haven't touched my face since I was ten!" I think most people with acne are actually much cleaner than people without it. My vanity forced me to step up my hygiene game. I was like a disinfected doctor, all scrubbed in for surgery, twenty-four hours a day.

After diligently washing my face, I went to sleep and slept until that alarm clock woke me up. Then I washed my face again. At the time, I was probably using Proactiv or some other acne cleansing program "guaranteed" to clear up my skin, but really it just bleached all my towels and made my face itchy. Then I got dressed and called my mom's boyfriend to ask him for an incredibly awkward ride to school.

I can't remember what kind of car Joe had because it was as low-key and unassuming as he was. This drive was the first of many drives to school with Joe. Every time I drove with him, he would blow through a stop sign, or swerve into the wrong lane, or drive up on the curb. I would always think *Jeez, this guy is a terrible driver.* Years later, I learned Joe was actually blackout drunk during those drives, and the fact that he didn't kill us both is a miracle.

On my first day back at school, Tori was there protecting me and making sure I was okay. It felt so good to be back with her. My other friends seemed scared to ask me about my brother, so they just acted like I hadn't been gone for weeks. I was a little disappointed. I wanted to feel special. I wanted to feel like I had gone through something. I wanted sympathy and attention. Halfway through the day, Ms. Russo—a young, pretty teacher—pulled me out of class. Ms. Russo was considered the "cool" teacher. She hung out with some of the popular girls outside of school. She would sometimes even have slumber parties with them. She was the teacher everyone wanted to be friends with, so when she called me out of class I felt amazing.

As I walked up to her in the hallway, I knew she was going to comfort me about my sick brother. *I'm gonna cry,* I thought. *Yeah, I'll cry and she'll hold me and tell me she's so sorry about what happened to my brother. Then I'll tell her I'm living alone, and she'll have me come live with her until my mom gets back, and we'll be bonded for life.* But it turns out, she just wanted to inform me that she'd found out I was hanging out in the library instead of being in class a few months before, and because of that, the school decided to kick me off the Student Leadership Council.

At the beginning of the school year, I had campaigned for Student Leadership Council Treasurer and won. I was very proud of that particular election and now, because of something I did months ago, I was being kicked off. I had never been kicked off anything before. I hated it. Did she even know my brother got cancer and was now blind? I felt like a celebrity being arrested by a small-town cop. I wanted to say, "Do you know who I am?!" I don't think she knew about my brother. And if she did, she was a sociopath.

That was the beginning of the end of me giving a crap about school. I had earned straight As on every report card since kindergarten. In fifth grade, I got a President's List letter from Bill Clinton. Even *he* was impressed with my grades. But something in me snapped around the time Ms. Russo kicked me off of the Student Leadership Council.

All the sad circumstances of my life collided perfectly. My parents truly did not care about what I was doing. I was living alone. My brother was going through unimaginable horrors. My face looked like bees had attacked it. I was done. I started asking my mom to call in to school for me so I could stay home. The average student misses less than ten days per year, but I ended up missing fifty-six days of school in eighth grade. Whenever I did go to school, I wore sweatpants with my brother's old T-shirts. I stopped wearing makeup and styling my hair. My grades became Cs and Ds. I just gave up.

One day, out of sheer boredom combined with apathy, I walked to the Chevron by my house, unzipped my backpack, put two forty-ounce bottles of Colt 45 malt liquor inside of it, zipped it back up, and walked out. As I left, I waved to the oblivious cashier who smiled back at the sweet thirteen-year-old girl who was clearly on her way to school.

Tori and I each chugged one of my stolen forties in her back-yard. Then we stumbled to school. I grooved down those middle school hallways feeling incredible. I chatted with kids I'd never met. I popped into a class that wasn't mine just out of curiosity. Tori, however, spent the whole morning in the bathroom barfing and then found me in the hallway giving unsolicited advice to an eleven-year-old who I didn't know.

We decided not to get hammered before school ever again. But I still couldn't bring myself to care about school. When you live alone, there's no one forcing you to do anything, so everything seems point-less. I never touched homework. Forget about school projects. Field trips could go fuck themselves. There was no parent in my house marking important activities on a wall calendar or helping me stay organized. I thankfully just randomly happened to be at school on the most important day of the year, the day they were taking pictures for eighth-grade superlatives. This picture of me would go in the year-book under the heading "Most Popular," that all-important title that had made life worth living a few months back.

During lunchtime, my friend Brian asked if I was excited to get our picture taken. I had absolutely no idea what he was talking about because I was living minute to minute. Brian was voted the "Most Popular" male that year and we were going to be in the pic-ture together. He informed me that it was superlative picture day and our full-body picture was going in the yearbook where it would remain for eternity. I panicked. I was wearing stained sweatpants and my brother's FUBU shirt. I had no makeup covering my skin and no gel restraining my curls. I had two options: leave town and never come back or try to fix this disaster with very few resources.

I called my mom in LA and explained my terrible predicament. I'm sure she was taken aback by my ridiculousness. I'm sure she thought her current predicament, living in McDonald's sponsored housing and nursing her brain-damaged son, was way more terrible than mine. But instead of judging me, she just called the school nurse and lied, telling her to let me go home and get my "medicine."

Tori gave me her house key. She lived right across the street from our school, so I raced there, took a shower, styled my hair, caked makeup on my bloodshot face, and threw on one of Tori's sexiest Wet Seal dresses. I made it back just in time to take that picture. I stood awkwardly next to Brian with his frosted tips, drowning in my heavily gelled curls, staring deeply into the lens, and hoping the photo would come out good, and then maybe I would start to like myself again.

Blind

EVENTUALLY, MY MOM AND MY BROTHER CAME HOME. IN THE FANTASY version of my brother's life, his friends would have all been waiting outside our house with signs that displayed loving messages about his homecoming. We would have been bombarded with food and well wishes, and our community would have buoyed us through this tragedy. But in real life, no one came to welcome him the day he arrived home. Some friends stopped by eventually, but they were so shocked and bummed by the sight of him that those visits tapered off pretty quickly.

At the time, my brother was six feet tall and still very handsome; however, he had a giant scar on his head that evoked images of Frankenstein's creation. His newly blank eyes gazed off in two completely different directions and appeared to bulge out of his head. And he still had trouble finding his words. It took forever for him to share his thoughts. It was quite shocking if you'd known him months earlier, when he was a sarcastic, pot-smoking heartthrob.

It is so cruel when these things happen to the young. Maybe if his friends had been older, they would've known to let go of their own fears and just be there for their friend. But these were sixteen-year-old kids, most of whom came from broken homes, just like we did, with very few role models in sight. No one knew to bring flowers and casseroles and sit by his bedside just so he wasn't lonely. And unfortunately, Scientology is not a flower-bringing, casserole-making type of religion either.

Recently, a friend of mine lost both of her children in a horrific car accident. They were hit by a drunk driver. My friend is Jewish, so they sat shiva for a week after her children passed away. I came to shiva one evening and the house was full of people, bringing love and food. I marveled at the Jewish culture. How quick everyone was to show up. It wasn't even a question. It was an *of course*. Of course, we come over. Of course, we bring food. Of course, we stay afterward to clean everything up, and of course, we do it all again the next day. Scientology is very different. Scientology prides itself on fixing the lives of its members. Therefore, if you're suffering, they don't rally around you with love and hugs. They tell you to come take a self-improvement course, so pesky life tragedies don't keep getting in your way.

To make matters even worse for my poor brother, I was a complete asshole. I was more selfish than his friends and even less sympathetic than Scientology. I got it in my head that I wasn't going to treat him differently because he had cancer. I couldn't bear to act like there was something wrong with him. I decided I would treat him exactly like I had before. I decided nothing would have to change. But this was a terrible decision because everything had changed.

He wasn't the same person he was a few months before. He wasn't the same clever bully who had been picking on me my whole life; he was a very sick kid who was struggling to do something as simple as string a sentence together. And instead of holding him in my arms and telling him I'd always love him, I teased him for speaking too slowly and tried to continue our dynamic of ragging on each other, even though he was no longer able to participate.

I now know I acted that way partly because I didn't want to admit that everything had changed but also because I was mad at him. I know we're not allowed to be mad at people with cancer, but precancer he was just *so* moody and mean that in my young mind the cancer wasn't enough to wipe his moody, mean slate clean. When someone gets sick, they instantly reach sainthood, they turn into a Jesus-like figure who can do no wrong, and I was supposed to just forget the time he burned all my Barbies in a backyard bonfire, or locked me in the garage for hours, or decided I wasn't cool enough to be his friend anymore when I was seven years old. He had kicked me out of his life and labeled me an annoying little brat. For years, I thought my brother's nickname for me was "Get Outta My Room!" I was supposed to forgive him for everything the moment my mom told me he had a brain tumor . . . but I didn't.

After my brother learned how to read and write again, thanks to my mom, he started thinking about what he wanted to do with the rest of his life. He didn't want being blind to stop him from living a full life and my parents were determined to set him up for success. He weighed all of his possible job options considering his new disability and came up with one that made me really wish I didn't share a wall with him. He decided to learn how to be a DJ.

It's kind of an amazing job for a person living with vision impairment—you just have to learn about music and turntables and off you go. My parents bought him two turntables and a bunch of records, and I listened to my brother scratch those records for twelve hours a day. He had no idea what he was doing, and it never crossed anyone's mind to hire someone to teach him. So he just scratched records. Genuinely, all day, just back and forth. "I love it when you call me Big Pop—Big Pop—Big Pop—Big Pop—Big Poppa. I love it when you call me Big Pop—Big Pop—"

He didn't know what else DJs did, so he just did that. He never really got good at it, because I don't think he knew what he was attempting to get good at—making records skip? But he did get really into music. That was one of the many awe-inspiring things about my brother: each time he lost one of his connections with the external world, he learned to connect in a new way. Since he couldn't see, he got very into hearing. He stole music off the internet, burned CDs, and scratched records. He found so much joy in listening. So when Max first informed us that he was losing his hearing, I began to fear maybe there was no higher power overseeing this crazy spinning ball we were all suffering on.

The doctors told us that the cancer was back and it was affecting more parts of his brain. They said over the next few years he would lose his hearing completely if we couldn't figure out how to get rid of the cancer. My father, in classic my father fashion, was reading about a new untraditional kind of chemotherapy that wasn't approved in the USA yet but was being administered in Mexico with decent results, so, naturally, I dropped out of ninth grade to go live with my mom and my brother in Tijuana.

Mexico

WE DROVE FROM FLORIDA TO MEXICO, AND WHEN WE CROSSED THE border of California into Tijuana, I was overwhelmed by loud street vendors selling bright plastic items that I didn't recognize, stray dogs wandering in small packs searching for food, and intimidating metal gates surrounding every house. I felt very privileged to be experiencing a foreign country, and I was taking mental note of every cultural difference and exotic experience to report to my friends upon my return.

I was also a little intimidated by Mexico because the year before, a racist math teacher told my class that if you smile at any man in Mexico, they will take it as an invitation to have sex with you and they will follow you home. My teacher racist-ly explained, "It's a cultural thing."

Because I didn't know this was a wildly incorrect, demented thing to tell children, I didn't smile at any men for the entire three

months that I lived there. It was like I was a newborn baby all over
again, perplexing everyone around me with my lack of smiling. I'm
sure I was known to the locals as that "miserable gringa." But everyone was very kind despite my refusal to smile back at them, or
maybe they were kind because of it, since they might've thought
something was developmentally wrong with me like my parents did
when I was born.

Because we were in Mexico and the dollar went a long way there,
for the first time in my life, I got to stay in a hotel instead of a motel. I couldn't believe I was actually staying in a real hotel. I was
blown away by the luxuries. The room didn't smell like cigarettes,
the bathtub wasn't stained, there were no mysterious wet spots on
the carpet—I felt like a billionaire.

During my few months in Mexico, I took more photos of that
hotel than anything else. When I told people back home where we
were staying, I made sure to hit the "h" really hard so they didn't
think I said motel. Every day, I would wake up next to my mom in
our very basic hotel room, wrap myself in the ratty complimentary
bathrobe, and step out onto the tiny, bird-shit-splattered balcony
feeling like Beyoncé at the Ritz. Then my mom would tell me to
hurry the hell up and get dressed so we could walk my brother to
his experimental chemotherapy sessions, and the dream would all
come crashing down.

During these morning walks, either my mom or I would have
my brother hold on to the back of our elbow, which is how you're
supposed to walk with a person who is visually impaired, so they
can feel if you're going to take a step down or a step up. You're also
supposed to announce when you're going to take a step down or
a step up, but my mom and I could never quite get used to that

and the walking process was always: Walk, walk, walk, trip. "Oops, sorry. That was a curb." Walk, walk, walk, thud. "Oops, sorry. That was a branch." My poor brother. Every time he stumbled, due to our neglect, my mom and I would stifle a laugh, until we saw my brother was laughing too, then we would all crack up, in a sort of *ha ha our lives are very painful and challenging* type of way.

The laughter during those years was wild. It was intense and breathtaking. When the three of us would start laughing, it was almost like we were all screaming *help me!* But that desperate, screaming feeling came out of our bodies in raucous, loud guffaws. And once we started, we couldn't stop. My brother would be struggling through a sentence and then forget what he was trying to say, and instead of crying and ranting about how his brain didn't work anymore, he would laugh, then my mom and I would explode. Like we had been holding in laughter for one thousand years and my brother's slightest chuckle gave us permission to let it out.

We would howl and bend over, clutching our stomachs, with tears streaming out of our eyes, our bodies covered in sweat. We would look at each other and telepathically say, *he's so brain damaged! Our lives are a waking nightmare!* And for some reason this made us laugh uncontrollably. My brother would pick up on our mental messages and telepathically add, *I had my whole life ahead of me and now it's a struggle just to walk through the house!* And we would keep laughing uproariously.

Honestly, nothing has ever made me laugh as much as I did in those days. No comedian or sitcom can come close to the hilarity of real human suffering, the agonizing pain that builds up and can only be released through maniacal laughter. Maybe I'm alone in this, or maybe everyone else is also secretly chuckling at their dying grandma or dog with wheels for legs. I find so much humor in the big and small tragedies of life and that humor has gotten me through all of it.

At the Mexican chemotherapy center, my brother would sit in a leather recliner and crack open a fresh bag of anticancer drugs. My mom and I would sit with him for as long as we could stand it and then tell him we were going to run errands. "Run errands" meant we'd go around the corner to a cheap restaurant and order giant red sangrias. The drinking laws were more lax in Mexico and, at fourteen years old, I was able to drink freely without anyone caring.

We'd drink a few sangrias and then go back to Max's chemo room, which looked like a La-Z-Boy showroom if you didn't know better. Random Americans, who either couldn't afford or didn't believe in American medicine, were plugged into IV bags full of chemo, watching Mexican daytime television. We didn't have health insurance, so my dad was paying for this whole experiment out of pocket. Our lack of health insurance must have had something to do with why, despite having a severe skin condition for three years, I still hadn't been to an actual dermatologist. But since we were in Mexico, and their health care system was more affordable, my mom decided to finally take me to one.

I bet you thought, since we were in Mexico getting chemo for my seriously ill brother, that I had momentarily forgotten about the acne. You're wrong. I never forget about the acne. I think about it constantly. On my deathbed, I won't be thinking about all the people I love, I'll be hoping my skin will look good at my funeral.

I was absolutely thrilled to finally have a medical professional look at my breakouts, but I was also very nervous. What were they going to say? Wash my face more? If I washed it any more, I feared my skin would disintegrate. The doctor was very nice and obviously felt very bad for this ninety-five-pound, frizzy-haired teen girl with cysts on her face and sangria on her breath. First, he showed me how to lance my own zits to keep them from scarring. He jammed a tiny needle in the center of a cyst and then pressed on either side and it exploded with pus. It was incredibly painful, but I greatly disliked myself, so the pain was also incredibly satisfying. It was my version of cutting, and I instantly became obsessed with lancing my face. The doctor also recommended I take a medication called Accutane, a.k.a. isotretinoin.

Accutane is a very strong but very effective acne medication. It has severe side effects like hallucination, depression, and even suicide. The medication is so intense that American dermatologists make you take regular emotional tests to make sure you're not thinking of killing yourself, but remember, in Mexico things were a little more lax. They just gave me a six-month supply of the pills and told me to avoid alcohol because Accutane is very hard on the liver.

But hold on, alcohol was quickly becoming my only reason for living, the only thing that brought me any respite from overwhelming grief and anger. . . . I had to choose: (A) No more alcohol and finally have clear skin? Or (B) keep drinking my relief juice and keep having red-hot cysts all over my face? I chose option C—keep drinking *and* take the medication, because who gives a shit?! But I told my mother and the doctor I would do option A, and they agreed to give me the medicine.

This meant I had to quit drinking in front of my mom, which was probably something I should've done anyway. As soon as I realized I was going to have to live in Tijuana sans sangrias, I brought up that pesky question of my education again and my mom decided it was time for me to go back to Florida by myself to try and finish ninth grade.

Harassment

I GUESS, TECHNICALLY, I WASN'T BY MYSELF. MY MOM'S QUIET BOYFRIEND, Joe, had just moved onto our property, into that tiny studio apartment attached to our garage, but he never left the apartment. Ever. And he only opened the door to give me cash if I asked for it. My mom likes to say, "Oh, gimme a break. You didn't live by yourself twice, Laura." But I definitely did.

Now that I was back, I had to figure out how to get caught up on the last several months of school, rekindle all my friendships, and think about what I wanted to do with the rest of my life. But then I walked by a mirror and saw that the Accutane was working and my skin was clearing up, so I forgot about all that other bullshit and decided it was time to lose my virginity.

I hadn't even thought about having sex, because the idea of having a boy so close to my raw face was too overwhelming to think about, but now that my skin was healing, I suddenly began to consider it. All my friends were already having sex, every single one of them. I was a fourteen-year-old virgin and that was considered weird in my friend group.

One of my friends lost her virginity when she was twelve to her older brother's nineteen-year-old friend. She said he crept into her bedroom in the middle of the night and took her virginity. At the time I thought that sounded *so* cool, but now I can see clearly that she was raped. There was such a fine line between cool and raped in those days. We had no idea that certain behavior was inappropriate because it was all normal to us.

Every day at my public school, boys would grab my vagina while I would yell with a smile, "Stop, Tim! Seriously!" Or a boy would run up, slap my tit, and say, "Breast cancer!" while I would giggle and try to run away. I have giggled and squealed my way through so much sexual harassment, I had no idea that it was harmful and slowly making me think of myself as a valueless object with no feelings. If I had taken a sexual harassment quiz I would've failed miserably.

What is it called when someone grabs your vagina without permission?
Flirting.

What is it called when someone slaps your tit without permission?
Teasing.

What is it called when several boys tell you that you have nice dick-sucking lips?
A compliment.

I have only recently fully absorbed what sexual harassment is and accepted that I have been consistently sexually harassed since I was eleven years old. Because I was so used to this behavior, I never noticed a problem as it continued into adulthood. I once worked with a guy who would massage my shoulders while we were working. I allowed this partly because, at the time, I genuinely didn't know it was inappropriate, and also because I friggin' love massages. Human touch is so relaxing to me that it short-circuits my ability to give a crap about who is touching me. I would happily take a neck massage from the Boston Strangler. Other coworkers eventually told this dude to stop rubbing my shoulders and I was like, *darn*.

A few years after that, a man who was technically my boss asked me if my boobs were real. I casually replied, "Yes," as if he had asked me if my hair color was natural, although I'm not sure if that question would have been appropriate either, but I'm clearly the wrong person to ask about appropriate behavior. A nearby coworker overheard my boss question the authenticity of my breasts and he was horrified. He told our other boss and suddenly everyone had to talk to everyone else about "the incident," and the whole time I was wondering, *did my boss do something wrong?*

I used to serve tables in a family-friendly restaurant, and at least once a shift my manager would whisper all the things he wanted to do to my naked body in his office. I would laugh and say, "Come on, Daniel, stop, I gotta go refill the waters." I used to serve cocktails at a not-so-family-friendly night club in Hollywood, and a group of celebrities came in and sat in the VIP section. One of them would grab my wrist every time I walked by and pull me toward him. "Is your pussy wet?" he asked me, over and over again. "Um, nope!" I said each time with a smile and then ran off to go fetch him more drinks.

When you are raised by a father who believes women should be submissive, and you go to school with boys who repeatedly grab you and demand to know if you stuff your bra, how can you possibly learn that this behavior is not okay? I wasn't going to learn it from movies or music videos, because entertainment feeds this idea that women are sexual objects and not only is it okay to grab them and talk dirty to them without permission, but they *love* it.

Honestly, it never crossed my mind that life could be any other way. I never considered going to school and not having my vagina grabbed. That was as much a part of school as Scantron sheets and lockers. I am so thankful for the recent anti–sexual harassment movements because they're showing creepy people that their behavior will no longer be tolerated, and also, they're showing *me* that a man who asks me about my breasts at work is creepy. He's not funny, he's not playful, he's not flirting, he's creepy.

All the people brave enough to come forward and tell the stories of how they have been abused have shown me how much abuse I have allowed and at times welcomed. When you think very little of yourself, you can't imagine ever having control over what happens to your body or having agency over how you are spoken to. That is something I have had to learn. I'm very grateful to all the brave humans who have stepped into the light to show the rest of us we have been living in the dark.

And back in 2000, we were all very much still living in the dark. A friend of mine—let's call her Xavier so no one will ever find out her real name—was in a car with four boys smoking weed and they told her they wouldn't drive her home unless she had sex with all of them . . . so she did. Xavier had sex with four boys for a ten-minute ride home.

At the time, I actually knew that was closer to raped and further from cool, but Xavier didn't. She wanted a ride home and didn't see the problem with the ultimatum. When I asked her why she didn't just get out of the car and walk home, she said, "I wasn't fully sure if they were gonna let me get outta the car and I didn't wanna turn it into a whole thing." And I thought, *yeah, I get that.* Xavier figured, rather than create drama and upset these four boys, she should just have sex with all of them. I probably don't have to tell you she didn't have a strong parental figure in her life, teaching her about her worth and showing her how to stand up for herself.

Another friend, let's call her Hercules, gave blow jobs to three different dudes in my closet, one right after the other, simply because they asked her to. That story at the time was very salacious, but now that I think about it, *good for her.* Hercules wanted to suck some dicks and she did. She wasn't coerced or threatened. She wasn't drunk or even tipsy. That was actually closer to cool and further from raped. The only real downside about that whole thing was my shameful part in it. Tori found out that Hercules had blown those three dudes and one of the dudes happened to be a boy Tori was in love with. Tori was pissed, and we told several people what sweet Hercules had done in my closet. Eventually, the entire school found out.

Everyone tortured her. If you were a boy, you could grab vaginas, slap tits, and coerce a girl into having sex with you and all of your friends in your car, but if you were a girl, you were *not allowed* to suck dicks because you wanted to. If you did, you were slut-shamed and verbally abused until the next girl decided to explore her sexuality; then they'd finally leave you alone to go torment her.

I was so complicit in this slut-shaming it makes me nauseous. Thankfully, I wasn't cruel enough to ever bully anyone, so I never shouted at her in the halls or wrote on her locker like the other kids, but I never stood up for her. I started the forest fire and then just watched while all the trees burned. I was like, *Don't look at me and my jacked-up face and tragic family! Look at that dick sucker! She probably sucked those dicks because she's craving love and connection just like I am, but who cares?! Destroy her!*

I actually know for a fact that she was craving love and connection because in sixth grade her dad committed suicide and in seventh grade her mobile home and all of her belongings were demolished in a storm. Poor Hercules. I should've been protecting her and caring for her, but my ignorance was impenetrable. Empathy was not getting through.

I honestly believed what society had been teaching me: girls should be chaste and virginal, and if they strayed from that imagery, they deserved to suffer. My school was like 1500s England. When a girl deviated from her godly duties, we dragged her up to stand before a court of her peers and condemned her.

Shame! Shame! the whole student body seemed to moan as Hercules walked down the halls. I barely felt any guilt about the way she was treated. At the time, it was all a big shrug, like, *Yeah, I guess don't suck several dicks if you don't wanna get hung, strung, and quartered, dummy.*

So I obviously had a complicated relationship with sex and sexuality, but I didn't know how long this window of clear skin was going to last. And I wanted to do some exploring in case the pustules returned and I had to go back into hiding. Enter Tom O'Connor. He moved to Clearwater right when I got back from Mexico, and he looked like he had been created in a boy-band factory. He and his little brother, Bobby O'Connor, had blond spikey hair, blue eyes, and pale, scrawny bodies. Justin Timberlake was my masculine ideal, so these boys were perfect. Plus, they only knew me as that clear-skinned girl, who for some reason just got back from Mexico, the fools!

I instantly fell for Tom. Meanwhile, sweet little Bobby, who was my age, fell in love with me. I would ride my bike to their house to hang out with little Bobby and when I was leaving, Tom would walk me out and then finger me in their front yard. I don't think Bobby knew his big brother was fingering me in their front yard because he kept telling me how much he loved me. He actually said, "The moment I met you, I fell in love with you." It might have been because I was a sweet, pretty girl, worthy of love, but I thought the Accutane and my brand-new, very clear, painfully dry skin was bringing all the boys to the yard. Specifically, the front yard.

After Tom fingered me twenty more times in random locations in his neighborhood—under a bridge, on his roof, in a parking lot, on an old tree stump—I started to wonder how to kick things up a notch. I figured maybe if we were indoors, things could go a little further. And it's not like there were any adults at my house. I was a free agent! I just had to figure out how to get him to my house and I couldn't just outright ask him, because somehow that felt even more vulnerable than letting him finger me on a tire swing.

Then a perfect plan came to me while I was making a chicken salad sandwich . . . I opened the fridge and realized I was out of mayonnaise. I decided to kill two birds and call Tom O'Connor to ask if I could borrow some mayo. That way we could hook up *and* I'd get to eat my sandwich. Tom said he would bring the mayo over and I ran around the house trying to straighten it up, but my house was *very* cluttered because fourteen-year-olds should not live alone.

I did the best I could, but our house presented as messy even after it was cleaned. Our kitchen did not have any cupboard doors or drawers, so you could see all of our plates, bowls, cereal, and spices. Everything was out in the open. We only had the husk of a normal kitchen because one day, my mom got very angry about how shitty our kitchen was and unscrewed all the cupboard doors and ripped out all the drawers, yelling about how my father wouldn't give her money for a new kitchen so she was going to "just fuckin' build a new kitchen" herself. But she never did. The husk remains to this day. When I recently asked my mom about finally putting in new cupboard doors she said, "Eh, then I'd have to deal with opening and shutting doors all day."

Instead of fantasizing about having a pony like other little girls, I used to fantasize about having matching dishware. Every dish we owned was purchased piecemeal from thrift stores. All of our glasses were different shapes and sizes. My matching dishware fetish grew even more intense after there were no cupboard doors to hide all of our shamefully eclectic cups and plates. I would go to friends' houses and see their identical glassware sets and long for that level of organized simplicity. When I asked my mom if she would buy us matching dishware, she called me a "princess" and told me I was born into the wrong family. She said it like she was joking, but I could tell she wasn't.

Tom knocked at the door with my mayonnaise, so I just had to pretend like we had a whole kitchen and invite him in. My plan of moving him indoors for further sexual exploration worked perfectly because after he fingered me for an hour on my couch, he went down on me! Hooray! Exploring! I don't think I actually enjoyed it, but I know I enjoyed crossing it off my list. What I didn't realize was his little brother Bobby was outside my house watching us through the window. He watched his big brother eat out the girl he loved, and then he watched us both eat chicken salad sandwiches.

Bobby confessed months later, "I watched my brother go down on you." That was it. Very matter-of-fact. I felt ashamed. A boy could spy on a girl while she went through a very private sexual experience without any shame at all, but the girl, with her grabbed vagina and slapped tits, would feel very ashamed indeed. But thank God it wasn't me watching myself through the window because I would have told the whole school and slut-shamed myself for weeks.

Virgin

I HAD OFFICIALLY EXPLORED FOREPLAY, BUT I STILL HADN'T GIVEN ANYONE A blow job. I was too overwhelmed by the way Hercules was treated at school and just couldn't bear being lumped into the devastating category of slut, so I decided to skip blow jobs and go straight to boning. Somehow girls who had sex weren't treated as badly as girls who gave blow jobs; the rules were confusing and made up by teenagers.

The natural candidate to take my virginity was Tom O'Connor, but he had recently started fingering Tori too, so it felt weird to have him be my first. It is odd that a boy started fingering my best friend in the same month that he and I were hooking up, but Tori and I weirdly weren't jealous of each other's Tom experiences. We shared his mouth and fingers like non–broken home fourteen-year-old girls might share a pair of earrings. Tori and I were very close and treated each other like sisters. Anything I had, she could have. If I had twenty dollars, that meant we each had ten. I would've shared anything with her . . . until we met Donny.

Donny danced into our lives and our friendship changed forever. Letting a boy come between a friendship is not something I am proud of, but you have to understand Donny was beautiful. Not beautiful like the kid you liked in ninth grade, but beautiful like art. He was shadowy and mysterious, with heavily gelled hair, a smile full of crooked teeth, random tattoos, a pierced tongue, and giant silver hoop earrings. I know . . . he sounds disgusting, but he wasn't. He was actually perfect. He danced like a Britney Spears backup dancer, and he was constantly dancing.

I remember his dancing better than I remember anything he ever said. He was from New York . . . maybe? Or he just decided to talk in a vaguely East Coast accent. He said things like, "Word is bond, son." And Tori and I would swoon. We were both in love with him. We talked about him relentlessly and eagerly waited for him to give us some kind of sign that he was interested in one of us.

Since there were no adults in my house, Donny and his eighteen-year-old friend group met my friend group and decided to basically live at my house. They would take acid and ecstasy and dance to techno and wave glow sticks around my bedroom into the wee hours of the morning. I didn't take hard drugs; my parents constantly badgered me about staying away from them. Scientology was vehemently against drugs, and even though I was barely a Scientologist at this point, I thankfully was still too afraid to break that rule.

Although, if there were any adults around at the time, it would have looked like I had suddenly become a full-on MDMA addict. Because right after I met Donny, I went to Spencer Gifts and bought two black lights, six black light posters, one thousand glow-in-the-dark stars, two lava lamps, and a lifetime supply of glow sticks. It was the make-Donny-like-me starter kit and I went all in on it. But no matter how much paraphernalia I bought, Donny seemed taken with Tori. He was always laughing at her jokes and complimenting her dancing. I know it sounds like I grew up in a Broadway musical—*Why was everyone dancing all the time?*—but remember, everyone was pretty much always high out of their minds on party drugs, so the constant dancing made sense.

It pained me to watch Donny give Tori all of his attention. Especially because my skin was finally clear, goddammit! Sure, it was very dry and very flaky, but why did he like her and not me? Well, she did dance amazingly, she also was super clever and funny, she took drugs with reckless abandon, and her body was so lean and tight she looked like an Olympic swimmer at a rave. She was just inherently cooler than me and there was nothing I could do about it.

I was a terrible dancer. I was born without rhythm. It was quite a serious condition and the doctors said there was nothing they could do. I was somehow physically unable to move my body to any beat without causing people to wince. And my condition was especially hard because I spent my developmental years living inside a drug-induced teenage musical. I was always accused of "dancing like a white girl," but I think it was worse than that. I think I danced like a recently animated white mannequin who was hearing music for the first time.

To make matters worse, one ecstasy-fueled night, Donny asked us if we were virgins, to which all my friends replied something like, "No, of course not, what are we, losers?" But one of my friends, who I still have not forgiven, yelled, "Laura is! She's never done *anything*." I wanted to shout, "That's not true! Tom O'Connor borrowed mayonnaise just last week!" But I kept quiet. I was too humiliated. The horror of being fourteen years old and still a virgin.

I now realize losing your virginity so young is not normal or recommended, but I didn't know that at the time. So I heartbreakingly admitted to myself that my chances with Donny were zero. There was no way he was going to pick this rhythmically challenged, elderly virgin whose face was peeling like a banana over Tori. I imagined Donny and Tori having a chic, drug-addicted baby that would dance out of Tori's womb, and I cried myself to sleep that night.

After that, I stopped trying so hard and just started being myself. I wasn't a good dancer and I wasn't cool. I didn't have baggy JNCO jeans that hung sexily over my visible hip bones—I didn't even have visible hip bones. I liked to sit on the couch, with my soft nonathletic body, and drink Zimas, watching everyone else revel in their unselfconscious freedom.

One night, a very high Donny announced that there was a raccoon riding a tricycle in my driveway and ran out the door. He chased his tricycle-riding-raccoon hallucination around the neighborhood for about an hour. Then he ran back inside, sat down next to me on the couch, and kissed me. I was stunned. I could feel Tori's eyes burning into me. I tried to signal her with my mind, *I'm so sorry, I know you love him, but I love him too, I don't want to hurt you*. But my eyes were shut and my hands were wrapped around his body, so it was probably hard for her to get that message.

Donny picked me up, carried me into my bedroom, and went down on me for a literal hour, then he left. I don't know why boys liked going down on me so much back then, maybe it was my wispy blonde pubes. After he left, I was on my back on my bed, looking up at the glow-in-the-dark stars stuck to my ceiling, listening to Ginuwine's "So Anxious," feeling, for the first time in a long time, anything but anxious.

I felt incredible. I felt like I had just won Most Popular all over again. Someone had chosen me. *Me?!* over Tori, who I considered to be the coolest, hottest, most enviable girl on the planet. After months of posturing and pretending to be a girl Donny would like, he finally noticed me after I stopped trying. Or maybe he had noticed me all along. Or maybe he was hallucinating that I was that tricycle-riding raccoon, and he had been chasing it around the neighborhood because he wanted to go down on it. Who cares?! He picked me!

My anxiety kicked back in when I thought about Tori's feelings. When I walked out of my room and told Tori what happened, she covered whatever she was actually feeling and just acted happy for me, but our friendship was different after that. We started to grow apart. And I don't think we ever actually talked about it. We never talked about how much it hurt her feelings or how much it meant to my incredibly low self-esteem that he liked me. I didn't take care of her emotions or support her in any way. I was too scared to admit that I was hurting my friend, and I was unwilling to give him up. So Donny continued to go down on me every time he saw me, and Tori and I continued our new, more distant version of friendship.

For some reason, Donny never seemed to want any sexual favors in return. He also didn't try to finger any of my friends; he was a true gentleman. I loved him with my whole soul. His approval of me made me believe there was something good about me. I didn't know what it was, but I knew it was something.

He never became my official boyfriend and we never had a traditional relationship; we always hung out in groups, only separating from the pack so he could go down on me in private. But after many *many* months of doing that, I asked him to take my virginity.

He said no at first. A serious freakin' gentleman. He said I was too young and that I wasn't really ready to lose my virginity. He was right. But I was clueless and insisted he take my virginity, so finally, he did. It was weird and kind of uneventful. It wasn't pleasurable at all, but at least no one could call me a fourteen-year-old virgin anymore.

Fighting

ODDLY, SOON AFTER HE TOOK MY VIRGINITY, DONNY THE GENTLEMAN made out with one of my friends at a party. I found out at school that Monday and the news shook me. My drug-addicted nonboyfriend, whom I had never actually had a full conversation with, cheated on me?! The worst part was that the girl he kissed had been listening to me talk about Donny for the past year. I was obsessed with him and all I did was talk about him. Probably a mistake, as I was basically advertising him: "There's this kid, Donny, he's gorgeous. He'll go down on you for a year and you never have to do anything in return!" Still, I felt so betrayed. My friend had no right to make out with him.

I found her in school and this brand-new feeling came over me; I think it was courage. I walked up to her and shoved her up against the wall and demanded to know if she had made out with my nonboyfriend. She looked terrified, which only made my courage grow,

81

and she admitted that she had cuckolded me. At that exact moment, I lost all my feelings for Donny.

I had never been "cheated" on before, and there was something so pathetic and icky about it. The thing that made me feel so amazing with Donny is that he had chosen me. He made me feel special. As soon as that special feeling went away, I lost interest in him completely. Basically, I didn't actually love him like I thought I did, and his sole purpose in my life was to validate me.

After I released my scared friend from the wall, I felt like a goddamn badass. I was small for my age and definitely not an intimidating presence, but maybe I was scarier than I thought? I developed not quite a bloodlust but a shove-lust, and I couldn't wait to shove someone up against a wall again. My opportunity presented itself a few weeks later.

Tori found me in the hall and told me that some girl she had never spoken to had decided she wanted to fight Tori at lunch. *Damn, good luck with that.* But before I could abandon my best friend like I normally would have, I remembered my recent badass courage, so I told Tori, "Don't worry, I got your back," and I mentally prepared my shoving stance.

At lunch, I saw a group of kids in a crowd, which always meant there was a fight. I pushed my way to the front and saw an absolutely *giant* girl beating the living shit out of Tori. Oh wow, she was a lot taller and more muscular than my Donny-kissing friend. I couldn't quite shove her as I had imagined, but I was able to awkwardly jump on her back.

I tried to pull the giant off Tori while the giant tried to fling me off of her three-foot-wide back. I felt like David as I tried to restrain Goliath's arms to stop her from pummeling my friend.

Tori eventually got out from under Goliath and the crowd began chanting my name. Not really, but they definitely were on my side, I could feel it.

Goliath eventually shook me off her back, but by then Tori had gained the upper hand. Finally, police officers arrived and tried to pull Tori off Goliath. Tori ended up punching one of the officers in the face, which really escalated matters. Tori and Goliath were both arrested as I sort of slunk into the crowd, feeling like that was enough courage for one day. But it turned out the fight wasn't over.

As soon as Goliath returned to school, she told everyone that she had been pregnant during that fight and that I had killed her baby. Not Tori. *Me.* Somehow, she decided that when I jumped on her back, I must have killed her unborn fetus. I tried to point out the fact that fourteen-year-old Goliath was the one who secretly got pregnant and then decided to pick a fight with someone she didn't know, but no one cared. They all decided I was a baby killer. Several girls wanted to fight me because of this, so I decided to stay home for the three remaining days of the school year, and my newfound courage went to its final resting place.

Years later, Goliath told me she hadn't actually been pregnant at all; she made the whole thing up. I asked her if she could maybe tell some other people that so I would stop being known as the "abortion doctor," but she told me she was too embarrassed to tell anyone else. Sure, I get that, heaven forbid *you* get embarrassed about me accidentally killing the baby that *you* made up. Ugh, teenagers.

Fighting was incredibly common at my school. It was a tough public school and the girls got physical with each other nearly as often as the boys. An emergency medical helicopter once landed on our football field to pick up a girl who had been badly beaten up in the ladies' bathroom. Apparently, that poor girl had wandered into a ladies' room trap set by a group of sisters who we'll call the Scary Sisters. The Scary Sisters were a group of Irish sisters who all had bright red hair, piercing green eyes, and a penchant for pummeling other girls.

There are so many rumors about the Scary Sisters and there is no way of knowing if any of them are true, but I'll repeat them anyway because they're entertaining. One rumor that was probably true: their father beat them up regularly, which made them all very violent and good at fighting. One that probably wasn't true: they all got AIDS from having sex with their father. One that might've been true: there were ten sisters total and they were all one year apart. One that probably wasn't true: the older sisters were actually the moms of the younger sisters because they all had sex with their father.

Either way, Emergency Helicopter Girl secretly blew one of the Scary Sisters' boyfriends and thought the Sisters would never find out . . . but they did. And not only were the Scary Sisters good at fighting, they were also extremely crafty. They pretended not to know Helicopter Girl had blown one of their boyfriends and one of the Sisters innocently asked Helicopter Girl to skip class with her in the ladies' bathroom. Helicopter Girl walked into the bathroom where some other Scary Sisters were waiting.

They turned off all the lights and, in the dark, beat her to the point where only a helicopter could save her, although I don't know if the helicopter actually did save her because after they strapped her to a gurney and flew her away from our school, I never saw Helicopter Girl again. Needless to say, if courage wasn't something you were chock-full of, you did not want to mess with the Scary Sisters. So when, out of nowhere, one of the Scary Sisters purposefully clipped me with her shoulder in the hallway, I considered moving back to Tijuana.

I asked my friends if they knew why one of the Scary Sisters would suddenly have me on their radar, but no one had heard anything. My only option was to ask the youngest Scary Sister if she knew anything. I was a couple of years older than her, but I was still terrified of her. She was probably five feet tall and ninety pounds, but I was *still* terrified of her. As scared as I was, I knew she was the least likely to kill me, so I tracked her down and told her what happened.

"Oh yeah, my sister wants to fight you, 'cause you called Cottie 'baby' and did cocaine with him all night in the bathroom." What the hell was she talking about? Okay fine, I had called Cottie "baby" at a party a week before. But that was because Cottie was my friend, and I remembered exactly what I said to him: "Can I have a cigarette, baby?" But I called everyone "baby" back then. It was my catchphrase; I was like a teenage Terminator. And why did the Scary Sisters care about who did what with Cottie? The littlest Scary Sister informed me that one of her sisters had recently started dating Cottie. Okay fine, I would stop calling him "baby," but I definitely did *not* do cocaine with him; I had never done cocaine in my life. But the preteen I was negotiating with just shrugged her skinny shoulders and looked at me like my fate was already sealed.

When I returned to my friends and reported what I had learned, my friend Charlene sort of laughed, "Oh damn, that was me. I snorted cocaine with Cottie in the bathroom that night." I was baffled. Why was I being confused with Charlene? She was a foot taller than me and had straight black hair and gorgeous skin. . . . I took a moment with that realization. Had the Accutane I was currently taking made the Scary Sisters mistake me, the cystic wonder, with the smooth-skinned Charlene? Wow. That was actually wonderful news! But I still had to figure out how to not be murdered by a group of sisters who may or may not be each other's moms.

Then Charlene did something that to this day is the most heroic thing anyone has ever done for me: she told the Scary Sisters the truth—*she* was the one who snorted cocaine with Cottie in the bathroom. I do not know why she did that for me, but since then, I have looked at Charlene as the bravest, most loyal person from my entire childhood. But instead of respecting Charlene for her honesty, as I did, the Scary Sisters wanted to "stomp her whore ass," and they planned on meeting outside of school to do just that.

Our whole friend group showed up as if to say, *We love you, Charlene*, but we all stood a few feet away from her as if to say, *You're completely on your own with this.* Two of the biggest Scary Sisters approached Charlene, and as they got closer, we realized they were each swinging a padlock on a metal chain. *Someone should stop this*, I thought as they cracked Charlene on the side of the head with a padlock and she fell to the ground. *Damn, someone should really stop this.* But we all just stood there, sending a lot of *we love you* energy to Charlene while not moving one fucking muscle to protect her.

The Scary Sisters and Charlene rolled around in the dirt for a few minutes, taking swings at each other while my friends shouted words of encouragement like, "Get her!" or "Mess that bitch up!" and I yelled, "Better you than me!" Or maybe I was just thinking that. Then suddenly, both sides tired out at the exact same time and they all just got up and walked away. We spent the rest of the day telling Charlene what a freakin' bad bitch she was and assuring her that the new padlock-shaped dent in her skull would go away soon.

It might seem appalling that we didn't jump in for our friend, but we were not a super loyal bunch of ladies. We were not "ride or die" chicks. We were chicks who would ride away immediately and leave you to die. My friends and I were like roughneck alley cats all fighting over the same fish skeleton. We didn't coddle each other, braid each other's hair, and buy each other little gifts. We were all too busy trying to survive.

There was a deep love that ran through the group, but there was also a feeling like if you turned your back for a split second, someone would make out with the drugged-out dancer who just took your virginity; or abandon you at 2 a.m., barfing outside a nightclub in Tampa; or spill liquid makeup all over your brand-new sheet set, promise to buy you new sheets, and never do it. Tori still owes me new sheets. Being a loyal, good, trustworthy, selfless friend felt like a luxury we couldn't afford. But we did the best we could for each other. We all came from broken, angry families, and together we built a new broken, angry family, but our new family was way more fun than our old ones.

Accutane

MY MOM AND BROTHER RETURNED HOME FROM MEXICO IN PRETTY MUCH the same condition they were in when they left. The experimental treatment had not cured my brother, the cancer in his brain was still spreading, and my mom was still an angry divorcée with a speechless, alcoholic boyfriend. But I, however, had completely changed.

The Accutane had not only cleared my face acne but had also cleared the painful welts and whiteheads from the rest of my body. I no longer had neck acne, or chest acne, or bacne. It was a miracle. I began wearing clothes that were low-cut, backless, tube-shaped, or all of the above. I no longer felt like I had to hide any part of myself from the world, so I didn't. Plus, I wasn't a virgin anymore and I wanted my outfits to reflect that.

My nipples and vagina were the only covered parts of me as I strutted through malls, bowling alleys, and house parties in miniskirts and minishirts. Some girls get new fake boobs and show them off in fun and creative ways, but I had new clear skin, thanks to Accutane, and I proudly showcased it wherever I went. Accutane should start its own clothing line of skimpy, barely there wear for the newly not-disfigured. I also started wearing a lot of red, which is something you simply cannot do when you have an inflamed skin condition, lest your red clothes and red skin merge together and become one. My confidence was exploding because my skin finally wasn't, but the universe found new ways to humiliate me.

Joe, who had been quietly drinking himself to death in the tiny apartment on our property, emerged when my mom came back from Mexico. My mom moved him into our main house and suddenly became aware of how much alcohol this man consumed. She decided that she didn't want him to drink anymore and made him promise to stop. He slurred an "I promish" and continued drinking profusely. My mom decided to force him to stop drinking, so she took all of his money and credit cards away so he couldn't buy booze. He, of course, kept buying booze, but she couldn't figure out how.

One sad afternoon, when I was home with Joe, I heard a jingling sound coming from my mom's bedroom. I walked by and saw Joe hiding a cup of loose change in the closet. I called my mom and informed her that Joe had a stash of change. "Well, take it away from him," my mom said, as if telling a teen girl to take change away from a fifty-year-old man was a normal request. So I went into Joe's room and asked him for his cup of change. The worst part was, he handed it over immediately. He didn't even put up a fight. I mean, sure I had successfully held Goliath's arms back for a few minutes and everyone thought I killed her baby, but Joe didn't know that. He could've beaten the crap out of me if he wanted to.

It's actually pretty wild to think about all of the things Joe could've done to me back then if he wanted to. My mom left me alone with a man she vaguely knew and I wasn't raped, molested, beaten, or emotionally abused only because *he didn't want to*. The only thing standing between me and untold horrors was the simple fact that Joe didn't feel like doing anything horrible to me and thank God for that. I look back on those days very thankful that he was just tongue-tied and drunk instead of much worse. If only this world were filled with Joes, it would be much safer and much *much* quieter. Unless of course you were driving near him while he was drunk behind the wheel—then you probably should have watched the fuck out.

So instead of putting up a fight when I asked for his stash of change, Joe just handed me his pathetic cup of quarters and looked at the ground in shame. The whole thing was so embarrassing, I wanted to die. I took his change, ran into my room, popped a fresh Accutane in my mouth, squeezed into a Jessica Rabbit dress, and got the hell outta there.

Finally, my mom realized she was never going to be able to stop Joe's binge drinking, so she decided to marry him and spend the rest of her life failing to stop Joe's binge drinking. After their wedding, Joe momentarily stopped drinking and went back to just being uncommunicative. He would watch the news in silence, eat dinner with us in silence, and leave for work in silence. He was a computer programmer, a job he most assuredly did in silence.

But every few months, he would go back to binge drinking, and that's when my mom would roll up her sleeves and get to work. I don't know whose addiction was stronger, Joe's addiction to drinking or my mom's addiction to trying to stop him. She finally took his car keys, so he couldn't drive to the liquor store, and all of his shoes, so he couldn't walk to the liquor store. If he wanted to drink, he would have to walk a mile barefoot and beg for free booze; she knew he'd finally have to give up. But he didn't.

My friends and I were piled into an SUV driven by someone cooler and older than we were when we passed a bald man stumbling down the street in stolen shoes. My friend, who I have still not forgiven, said, "Laura, isn't that your stepdad?" Everyone in the SUV looked out the window to see Joe, walking to the liquor store, with half of his feet sticking out the back of my mom's lavender ladies' flats. "Um, yeah . . . I guess so," I replied, turning bright red, not full-on acne red, but my face and my red tube top did merge for one humiliating moment.

Meanwhile, upon returning from Mexico, my brother decided he wanted to get a job. He was still practicing to be a DJ, but so far none of our neighbors had overheard him skipping records and rushed over to ask him to DJ their party, and since there was no way for anyone else to discover him, his DJ career wasn't exactly taking off. But he was eighteen and wanted to start bringing in some money of his own, so my mom set out to find a company that would hire a teenager with disabilities.

He really wanted to be a grocery store cashier, so my mom drove to every grocery store in Clearwater and tried to convince them that one did not actually need vision to be able to scan fruits and vegetables, but her attempts were ineffectual. No one would hire him. Until the absolute angels at Firehouse Subs stepped up.

After my mom applied there on my brother's behalf, they hired him to stand outside and pass out fliers. Now, my older, more evolved self looks at this situation and thinks: *Wow, Firehouse Subs is an incredible company. Unlike all those ableist grocery stores, Firehouse Subs knew how capable my brother was. They gave him a job, a uniform, and a new sense of belonging and purpose. And I can't even believe how brave my brother was for putting himself out there like that and being willing to work hard, no matter the task.* But my less evolved, superficial fourteen-year-old self was absolutely horrified.

My older brother, the kid who was always cooler than me and more popular than me and better than me at everything, was going to stand outside on a street that was so busy it was literally called Main Street, where everyone I knew would see him blindly and vulnerably handing out fliers for a fast-food restaurant. It was too much. My vanity and insensitivity kicked in full force. And when my friends and I were piled into an SUV driving down Main Street, one of my friends, who I have recently forgiven, said, "Laura, isn't that your brother?" And she pointed at the incredibly brave kid in the Firehouse Subs polo shirt. I looked where she was pointing and said . . . "No." And with that, I betrayed the person I loved the most in the whole world. The person I looked up to my entire life now humiliated me worse than acne ever had, and there was no pill I could take that would clear up that situation.

Accutane had healed my face, neck, chest, and back; it seemed like a wonder pill until, like with all pills, the side effects kicked in. First it was dry skin, then peeling skin, then every day I would shed my entire face like a snake. My lips were painfully cracked and bloody, so for the third time in my life, I didn't smile for months. Then my vision started to get weird.

At first, I thought I had a brain tumor like my brother and I was going to be a blind DJ, passing out Firehouse Subs fliers in a matter of weeks, but then I learned Accutane actually causes problems with night vision. I had just started learning to drive, and when I was behind the wheel at night everything through the windshield looked pretty blurry. But I didn't want to give up the skin-saving meds, and

I really wanted to get my driver's license, so I kept quiet about it. I think I could've handled all of those side effects, but the depression really started to kick my ass.

A modern version of Accutane called Absorica has this warning on their website: *"Absorica can cause serious mental health problems including depression, psychosis, and suicide. Some patients have had thoughts of hurting themselves or suicide."* I was one of those patients. But I can't be 100 percent certain that it was the Accutane that caused the depression and suicidal ideation. I mean, it wasn't like I was living the perfect life and then I was suddenly depressed for no reason. My life *sucked*. It would have been weirder if Accutane made me *not* depressed. My home life was obviously traumatic and my social life was barely less so, but the severity of the depression still felt like it was connected to the Accutane somehow. Maybe it was the mass quantities of alcohol I was consuming while taking the Accutane after I was specifically directed not to? Either way, I was having a very tough time emotionally.

Tori had just started dating a kid named Ben. Our friendship was already drifting apart after the years of Donny, and now Ben was putting another wedge between us. Tori and Ben grew so close so fast, it was as if my best friend had evaporated into thin air. I never hung out with Tori alone anymore. Ben was always there and they were either whispering in each other's ears and giggling or fighting and crying.

One afternoon, at my house, after they finished screaming at each other about some trivial thing, Tori threatened to break up with Ben. He said, "If you do, I'll kill myself!" He wasn't even on Accutane; he was just naturally suicidal. Then he drove around my neighborhood with a bat, smashing mailboxes. An hour later, he begged her to take him back and she, of course, did. I know that doesn't sound like a love story to envy, but I did. I wanted a boyfriend so badly. I had never had a real boyfriend, and even though Tori and Ben were obviously chaotic, they still had each other to cling to for support and shelter from their stressful families.

I felt agonizingly lonely, and that loneliness began to take over my mind. It seemed like the whole world was in a relationship. And it wasn't just Tori; a lot of my other friends were experiencing their first loves at the same time. I would have short flings with boys, but none of these casual make-outs or hookups ever resulted in anyone wanting to be my *real* boyfriend. I began to feel unlovable and became convinced that there was something inherently wrong with me. Thoughts of ending my life sprouted from the dark corners of my mind like weeds that I could not pull fast enough.

Suicide is something I do not take lightly, even though I do make a lot of jokes about it. The belief that death will suddenly free you from all the problems of your life can take over even the most logical person. Since I was on Mexican Accutane, no dermatologist was monitoring my emotional health like they would have been in America. If someone had been monitoring me, they most certainly would have taken me off the medication because I became obsessed with hanging myself in my backyard. I thought about it every day for months.

I was stuck in a feeling that seemed endless. It was as if there was no way through this feeling. It felt like it was going to be there for the rest of my life, and if it did stay forever, I surely could not keep living. The feeling was miles below shame and several feet below worthlessness. It was a deep hatred of everything that was me. The sound of my voice, the shape of my body, even my clear skin disgusted me. I would get off the phone and hate every word I had just said. I felt like my existence was a mistake and that the world shuddered with embarrassment every time I left the house. I simply did not want to be alive anymore.

It would have been so tragic if I had given in to that feeling. There was so much beauty waiting for me on the other side. There is so much beauty waiting for all of us on the other side of that feeling, so much love, so much healing, and so much hope. Everything, no matter how painful, eventually passes. I did not know that then, but somehow, I got through it. Everything eventually passes and life is a precious gift. I know that now.

When I talk about that suicidal phase, some people nod knowingly and other people seem shocked and say things like, "You *actually* thought about killing yourself?" And my reply is an even more shocked, "You've *never* thought about killing yourself?!" Those suicidal thoughts were so loud and lasted for so long that I can't even imagine a world where they had never crossed my mind.

I guarantee those people who are so shocked by even the thought of suicide have never had cystic acne. Thankfully, I eventually ran out of Accutane and my depression lightened up a lot. There is supposed to be a specific length of time that you stay on Accutane and it's supposed to be sensitively handled by a dermatologist, but I just ran out of pills and that was that. The good news is my will to live and my night vision came back; the bad news is my acne came back too, almost instantly.

Florida

I WANTED TO TELL MY MOM THAT MY SKIN WAS STARTING TO BREAK OUT again, but it wasn't the best time to ask her for help, since Tori had just fucked our bathroom sink off the wall. Tori and Ben were very on-again, off-again. During an off-again, Tori hooked up with a guy named Tito in our tiny bathroom. Tito picked her up and placed her on top of our cheap, fragile sink. They had sex on it until it ripped off the wall and shattered on the ground. My mom was not thrilled. She didn't love how Tori's dramatic life was perpetually spilling all over our house.

She was especially pissed when Tori's boyfriend, Ben, had taken that bat and smashed every mailbox in our neighborhood a few months earlier. My mom could handle the chaos inside our doors, but letting it get out into the neighborhood was too humiliating. I tried to remind her that our neighborhood was so insane that a heartbroken teenager smashing mailboxes was barely an incident.

I mean, the dude down the street had just sent his kids to go stay with their mother so he could shoot himself in the face on Halloween night. Tori and I got woken up early in the morning on November first by the sound of a woman screaming as she discovered our neighbor on his living room floor missing most of his face. Part of me wondered if, at first, the woman mistook the scene for a Halloween prank. Did she shake him a few times, chuckling to herself, before she realized all that blood wasn't fake?

Around the corner, a man who had recently returned from war (I didn't know which war, but I knew a war was involved) used to beat his children so loudly that we could hear their pained yells from around the block. A few houses down, a five-year-old girl testified against her grandfather in court because he had forced her to give him a blow job.

A few doors down from that tragedy, a man was murdered, shot in the chest on his front porch while his wife was working out in the backyard. It turned out the wife wasn't actually working out in the backyard; she was standing on the front porch with a gun, shooting her husband in the chest. But we didn't discover that until months later, when she burned down her own house to try and collect insurance money.

The insurance company began investigating her and discovered she had taken out a sizable life insurance policy on her husband, right before he was randomly shot in the chest. She ended up going to jail for life, leaving behind a blackened, empty lot in our already less than gorgeous neighborhood. The point is, let Ben smash a few mailboxes. No one gives a shit.

There are intense stories behind every door in my neighborhood, and the rest of Clearwater is no different. There is something about Florida. The whole state feels like it is sitting on top of a sacred, ancient burial ground and the gods are pissed about it. Almost every Floridian I know has a tragic yet colorful backstory. It's like the gods want to punish Floridians, but not in some lame-ass, boring way; they want to punish us with style and flourish.

My friend Zoe's father died when she was nine years old, but he didn't die in a mundane way, he died in a colorful way: trying to buy heroin in the middle of the night. After he paid his dealer, he complained because he thought his dealer was trying to sell him fake heroin. His dealer responded, like any good dealer should, by stabbing my friend's father in the stomach.

Incredibly, her father got back in his car and drove down the street. As soon as he turned the corner, he must have realized he had been stabbed, because he drove directly into a wall and died moments later. And the night this all went down? Christmas Eve. Yep, my nine-year-old friend had just eaten a cozy chicken dinner with her dad before he decided to go buy fake heroin and complain about it. Every time Zoe and I drive past that spot, she points to where his car hit the wall and says, "That's where my dad crashed his car after he was stabbed in the stomach, buying heroin." As if I could ever forget.

Another friend inherited a bunch of life insurance money after his mother died. That's not particularly unusual or Floridian. It's the fact that his father murdered his mother and then went to jail, leaving my freshly eighteen-year-old friend with no parents and a small fortune, that makes it perfectly Floridian. But the orange on top is that my friend spent that small fortune on a new house, covered all the windows with aluminum foil, and began growing weed inside of it.

A very dear friend lost her father in a motorcycle accident. The night he died, he had three loose pennies in his jacket pocket. My friend's mom had those three pennies attached to tiny gold chains and gave one to each of her three children. A beautiful token of their late father that they could wear on their neck forever. Until a meth addict broke into their house and stole their TV, their stereo, and the three tiny gold chains with pennies dangling from them.

The thief must have thought, *What the hell are these? Whatever, I'll get a couple bucks for 'em.* Florida isn't just sad, it's entertainingly sad, which is why we are always in the news. It's easy to read Florida headlines and forget that we are actual human beings and not just ridiculous cartoon criminals. Floridians don't just commit crimes. We commit flamboyant crimes. We don't just hold up a liquor store with a gun, we hold up a liquor store with a small alligator we found in a nearby swamp. We're Floridians goddammit. We're out of our freaking minds and we *really* want everyone to know it.

Color

MOVING TO A PLACE LIKE FLORIDA FROM A PLACE LIKE CALIFORNIA CAN be a major culture shock, especially if you're nine years old and your parents never told you that you were mixed race. Growing up in a household where every single person had a different skin color resulted in me being genuinely color blind. Not in the offensive "post-racial" way that certain white people claim they are color blind and don't see race, when of course they do and are full of shit. I was actually color blind.

No one ever explained to me that because so many people on our planet are too simpleminded to tolerate differences in each other, and because our governments have exploited this fact to aggressively turn people against each other so they're more easily controlled, skin color is actually a very big deal. I never questioned why my dad's skin was brown, why my brother's skin was light brown, or why my mom's skin was pale. My friend Shanice had very dark brown skin and my other friend Samantha had fair skin with freckles, and I never thought about it.

I must've just assumed people came in different colors like cats or dogs, or birds, or fish. Are we the only species that hates and judges based on color? Are we the dumbest animals on the planet? My parents were extremely open and tolerant of all people; I never heard them say a discouraging word about another race or even acknowledge there was any difference between us and any other human being. In my small mountain neighborhood in Los Angeles, I was able to live nine blissful years without anyone ever telling me what a naïve dummy I was. But my first day of fourth grade at my new public elementary school in Florida woke me right up.

I made it through a public school lunch line for the first time in my life without incident. I paid for my processed food-like meal with my dollar and twenty-five cents and carried my little Styrofoam tray to an empty table. Then a white kid, Mitchell Crawford, only nine years old and already a terrible person, approached me and said, "You can't sit here, this is where the n*****s sit." I had never heard the N-word in my life. I had no idea what he was talking about. But he seemed serious. I got scared and stood up and moved to another table. I looked over at Mitchell Crawford to see if the new table I was now standing near was okay for me to sit at and he sort of nodded. I sat down and waited for whatever he was talking about to happen at my former table.

Eventually, Erica and a group of girls who were in my class sat at that table. *Erica?* I didn't understand. Erica was the only person who had been nice to me that morning. Our desks were next to each other. She smiled at me and asked me my name. She told me what they had been reading and even tried to catch me up to speed on the parts of the book I had missed. I felt immediately welcomed by her. She'd gone out of her way to make me more comfortable on my terrifying first day.

I looked at Erica and her friends laughing and eating their lunch. I looked at Mitchell Crawford. I tried to make sense of why he told me I couldn't sit there and why he had called them that word. I decided maybe Erica and her friends were part of some club and, even though it didn't seem like Erica to be unwelcoming, maybe they really didn't want anyone else sitting with them.

When I got home, I told my mom what happened in school. She looked at me like, *Oops, we probably should have told you about this before we moved to the South.* Then she explained the whole damn thing to me. First, she explained that she was white and my father was Black and that Max and I were biracial. She told me that because I was so fair-skinned, Mitchell Crawford didn't know I was half Black and that's why he said those offensive things to me.

Then she told me all about slavery. Somehow, with my thorough Scientology education, I knew the dictionary definition of the word "the" but I had missed out on basic American history. Slavery was so hard for nine-year-old me to understand. But the hatred of someone else based on their skin color was even harder to grasp. My mom explained that people like Mitchell Crawford were, of course, wrong, but she tried to get me to accept that people really did feel this way.

But I still couldn't accept that. I knew my father. I knew he was an eccentric genius (he was one of only ten Black students in his class at Boston Latin School, an incredibly prestigious high school that accepted only honor roll students). I knew he was creative and talented; he got into Berklee College of Music to study saxophone after high school.

I knew he really loved jazz, and every year at Christmastime, predivorce, I would lay my head in his lap and we would sit in front of our lit-up tree while he would pet my head and tell me about the musicians we were listening to. I knew he was hardworking and resilient and taught himself how to program computers, giving himself a whole career. I knew he was silly and fun, even when he was tired. He would get on his hands and knees and crawl around on the ground offering "horsey rides" to my brother and me after he had just spent ten hours writing computer programs.

I knew I could call him anytime night or day and he would drop everything and be there for me if I needed him to. I knew he was an extremely loving father, and I knew in my core, in my nine-year-old heart, that nothing about his skin color could diminish him as a human being in any way. And then I sort of decided my mom was wrong. Because there was just no way that someone could hate someone else based on skin color, a detail that I didn't even really notice until someone forced me to.

In the coming years, I learned my mom was, of course, not wrong at all. I quickly discovered that almost every person on the planet is intolerant or prejudiced against some other skin color, gender, sexuality, culture, or religion, but I do not believe that behavior is human nature. I believe that behavior is learned and my nine-year-old self is proof of that.

I do think if you raised a child exclusively around one skin color for years and years, the first time they saw a person with a different skin color they might think, *What the fuck happened to their skin?* But I don't think they would hate them for being lighter or darker. And maybe if children were exposed to all different types of people early on and not programmed with hateful messages from their parents, then all skin colors would be seen as equally beautiful and powerful and the whole concept of racism would disappear forever.

That first experience with Mitchell Crawford's racism started my lifelong career as a spy for Black people. Since I appear white, I am privy to the most vile behavior from certain white people, the kind of white people who claim to be racially tolerant and know how to act appropriately in front of people of color but then say the N-word as soon as they're solely in the company of other white people. It's like they speed home from their diverse school or multicultural job and, as soon as they shut their door, say the N-word a bunch of times to anyone that will listen.

As disturbing as it was to discover how intolerant some white people were of other races, I eventually got used to being a low-key Black spy. I would quietly listen to a white person I had just met say horrible things about every nonwhite race. My friends would look at me, knowing I was just waiting for my moment, and then after this white person had really dug a giant racist hole for themselves, I would relish informing them that I was part Black. The look on their face became the sweetest revenge. Their eyes would go wide, their mouths would dry up, and they would croak out a "You're half Black?" I would nod slowly like, *Gotcha, bitch.*

Then they would stammer about how much they actually loved Black people and how their best friend Earl was Black. They would explain, it's really that they didn't like *some* Black people but most Black people were super cool. Then they would list all the amazing traits of their imaginary Black best friend, Earl. And finally, they would come up with an extremely creative excuse for having just used the N-word a bunch of times, and it went something like this:

"Not all Black people are n*****s. To me, a n***** is just another word for a criminal or a bad person. White people can be n*****s too; my Aunt Irene is a n*****, and she's white. And my cousin Mike, he's a n***** too!"

I would sit quietly and listen to them call every member of their family the N-word as they tried desperately to climb out of their racist hole. I would tell them that word was decidedly not just another word for a criminal or a bad person. It was historically specifically used to degrade Black people and that perhaps they should try another word to describe their Aunt Irene and other undesirables. But I was a child, so I probably said something more like, "No, you really shouldn't use that word. It hurts people's feelings." They would nod and act interested, like I was shedding light on something they didn't already know. And they would always leave me with something like, "Just so you know, I'm not like, racist or anything."

That was the weirdest part about those people, they all wanted to say racist things and act super racist, but they couldn't *stand* to be called racist. I have never met a proud racist in my entire life. They have all been sneaky racists who act deeply ashamed as soon as I inform them of my background. They all know it is wrong to be racist, but they just aren't capable of not being racist. The desire to degrade and demean a group of people is too strong. The feeling of superiority they made up in their heads is too addictive.

My appearing white but being half Black regularly exposed how truly moronic racism is. Several times in my life, I would meet a guy and he would want to date me, and then I would tell him I was half Black and he'd quietly be like, *never mind*. He was attracted to my face, my body, and my personality, but the blood that ran through my veins was somehow something he couldn't deal with. Cats don't care if they're about to mate with an orange cat or a calico cat; they're smart enough to know a cat is a cat. When are we going to learn that a person is a person? When are we going to be as smart as cats?

Other

AS DELIGHTFUL AS IT WAS WATCHING IGNORANT PEOPLE STAMMER AND insult their entire families, being mixed really did come with weird identity issues. I know I'm not Black because I could never begin to understand what it is like to go through astronomical suffering because of the color of my skin. And I know I'm not white because . . . I'm literally not. I'm British, Irish, Nigerian, and Ghanaian. But there's no word for that, so I'm just other. I always check the "other" box when I'm filling out medical forms and I've always felt "other" in life. I have never belonged to a group or a race or a culture.

I have always felt like I was on an island. But I couldn't exist on an island because my town was deeply segregated and you had to pick a side. White people stuck together and Black people stuck together; very rarely did the two groups intermingle. I had close Black friends in my classes, but at lunchtime, I'd sit at a long table staring at all white faces, and the table next to ours would be filled with all Black students. I don't remember actively picking a side, it was somehow picked for me.

I was generally accepted by the white community of Clearwater because I appeared white, but I never felt white and certainly never claimed to be white. I didn't feel Black either. I just felt other. I used to wish I had darker skin, like my brother, then everyone would immediately know I was mixed with something and at least I would feel more firmly rooted in the mixed group. This new form of self-hatred gave me yet another reason to loathe my skin.

My Black cousins on my dad's side had a very close relationship with my grandmother Evelyn, my dad's mom. They all called her "auntie" and they always seemed like a tight-knit group. I longed to be a part of that group but I didn't know how. My grandmother was, justifiably, wary of white people. I'm sure she wasn't thrilled when my dad brought home a white wife and somehow they created a stark white, blonde daughter. My grandmother never outwardly complained about me looking white, but she sure as shit outwardly complained about white people, and she had every right to.

She told me stories of growing up in rural Alabama in the thirties. And let's just hold on for one second, can you even imagine being a Black girl in Alabama in the 1930s? Can you even imagine how much strength, courage, and resilience my grandmother had? And what she had to overcome every single day? She said little white girls would throw rocks at her head as she walked to school, for no reason other than the color of her skin. She said she went to a school that was only for Black children, and it was in much worse condition than the nearby school for white children. She said she had to swim in different swimming pools than white people and drink out of different water fountains.

Her father drove a Black taxicab. When she told me this, I asked, "Why was it black and not yellow?" She took a pause, probably thinking, *this dumb ass white bitch*, but instead she said, in her comforting Southern accent, "I mean, it was a cab only for Black people, dear." *Oh, right.* Jesus, I was dumb, and she was incredibly patient. I can only imagine what she thought of me. She was always very kind to my brother and me, but we never got extremely close. It must have been such a strange experience: *My son gave me a granddaughter who looks like the girls who threw rocks at me in my childhood, and she asks the stupidest fucking questions. But I love her anyway, goddammit.*

That feeling of not belonging was so painful. I was longing to find a group, but there was no gang of half-Black, half-white, closeted Scientologists with Asian-sounding last names that I could hide in. It was just me. My last name, Chinn, really confused people. When I first moved to Florida, kids would try to make fun of me about it. Mitchell Crawford, that nine-year-old piece of shit, used to say, "Chinn? What are you *Chinese*?" He would say "Chinese" like he was saying some horrible insult, but again, I didn't understand racism, so I wasn't insulted. I would just very earnestly say, "No, I'm actually half Black and half white." Then he would look confused as to why I wasn't hurt by his taunting.

Now that I'm an adult, the Mitchell Crawfords of the world have, thankfully, stopped trying to make fun of my last name, but it still does confuse people. Whenever I show up to a meeting, I can always tell when the person I'm meeting with was expecting an Asian woman. On a few occasions, I have sat in a waiting room and watched someone poke their head out several times, look at me, and then leave. Eventually, I have to be like, "Are you looking for me? I'm Laura Chinn." And they give me a flustered, "Right, yes, of course, you are. I knew that! I definitely wasn't expecting anyone who looks completely different than you." As if, by assuming that Laura Chinn was an Asian woman, they have somehow committed a racist act.

Chinn is actually an Old English last name. Apparently, it was an English nickname for someone with a prominent chin, and over time it became a surname. My ancestors inherited the last name Chinn after being enslaved on the Chinn plantation in Virginia. There are several Black Americans with the last name Chinn who have done some amazing things, and I pretend I'm related to all of them.

My grandma told me Dr. May Edward Chinn, a prominent Black female doctor in the 1920s, when such a thing was almost unheard of, is a distant cousin of ours, and I've been repeating that ever since, but I don't actually know if it's true. However, Alva Chinn, an eighties supermodel and former Halstonette; Henry Chinn, an LGBTQ+ activist; and Aklia Chinn, the longtime owner of a popular Hollywood boutique called Aklia's, are definitely my actual, 100 percent confirmed relatives. And of that, I am very proud.

It is so hard for people to understand that I am half Black. Even when I tell nonracist people that my dad is Black, the first thing most people say is "No, he isn't!" Which is weird. I don't really know what to say after that. "Um, yeah, he is?" I don't blame them though. I have always wondered if my dad also suspected that I wasn't his kid. When I slipped out of my mom, pale as the driven snow, covered in hair so blonde it was almost white, did he for one second think, *Who fucked my wife?*

He very confidently tells me, "I always knew you were mine." And now it is an undeniable fact. I have my father's exact same face. If my father ever wondered what he would look like as a dirty-blonde white woman, he now has the answer. Recently, I was out to dinner with my cousin, Aklia, and I happened to know our waiter. I introduced our waiter to my cousin and our waiter said, "Shut the fuck up! *This* is your cousin? Are you part Black?" Aklia's jaw dropped. She had never seen this kind of interaction, but I had grown quite used to it.

I explained to our waiter that my dad was Black. "Holy crap! You can't tell at all. I thought you were like Swedish or something!" Aklia could not believe someone would act that way. Race is a very personal issue and this waiter was displaying zero couth. I told my cousin it happened to me constantly. People are so shocked my appearance doesn't match my DNA that they just have to react, and apparently, they have no control over their reaction. My cousin was like, "People need to get out more. There's a whole world of mixed people out here and everyone looks different." I agreed. *What the hell is wrong with those people?* Then a few months later, I became those people.

I was hanging out with an acquaintance I didn't know that well. She looked like a white girl with straight brown hair. Somehow it came up that my dad was Black and this girl said, "My dad's Black too."

To which I said, "No, he isn't!"

She replied, "Um, yeah, he is?"

And despite living my entire life as me, I doubled down. "But your hair is so straight!"

She came back quickly with "Well, your skin is so white."

Damn, she had me there. But her skin was so white too! How was this possible? There was just no way her dad was—*Oh my god, I just did it to her.* I denied her identity and negated her ancestry. I did exactly what everyone else always does to me and I didn't realize it until it was over. Then I thought maybe this was human nature. Maybe we're all just so conditioned to think certain people have to look a certain way, and when we find out we're wrong, our brains short circuit and we just have to say something about it. Either that or some people are just dumb and obnoxious and I'm one of them.

I've always envied people who fit neatly into a specific cultural or ethnic group. I observe groups of Mexican Americans or Indian Americans, and in my fantasy, everyone is completely comfortable in their own skin and feels right at home around their own ethnicity. I know that isn't true, but since I can't check a box, that's what I've always fantasized about. I've wondered what it would be like to walk down the street and see a person who came from the same exact culture I did. I would nod hello and they would nod back and our nods would contain *I see you, I understand you, I know what it's like to have your skin color and your hair texture, I know what holidays you celebrated growing up, I know all about your culture.*

Maybe that's what it would feel like if I were to nod at someone with a skin condition. My red-hot face would nod at their red-hot face and that nod would contain *I see you, I understand you, I know what it's like to have eternal chickenpox, I know how many painful medicated creams you have tried, I know all about your self-hatred.* If Indian Americans share passed-down recipes for paneer tikka or swap saris to wear on Diwali, then acned Americans share home remedies that can make a zit disappear overnight and swap clay masks to soothe the burning. God, my group is so uncool.

The hardest part about being in my group is that no one ever talks about being in my group. Or maybe that was just me. I have spent most of my life covered in zits, but I have *never* talked about them. Only my closest friends and my mom have seen me sob

openly about the breakouts. I was never one of those girls who complained about their zits in front of other people.

If five girls are doing their makeup in the mirror, one of them always says, "Oh my God, look at this freakin' zit," and then points to
a lone zit on a perfectly clear landscape. Then the other girls have to
say, "Dude, it's so tiny," or "You can barely even see it." But my face
was drowning in zits. I would have said, "Oh my God, look at these
seventy zits." And the other girls would have said, "Dude, it looks
more like forty zits, I swear," or "Yeah . . . maybe don't leave the
house?" I knew there were no real words of comfort anyone could
give me, so I just never said anything about it.

It's interesting to not talk about something that is right out there
for everyone to see. It was like I had a live raccoon on my face and
I just slathered makeup all over it and acted like it wasn't there.
I would go to parties and this live raccoon would be on my face,
growling and hissing at everyone, and I would be like, "Great party!
I love your house!" And the people around me would have to ignore
the raccoon too. That feral raccoon was staring at them with beady
eyes, daring them to comment, but they would have to fight the
urge and instead say, "I love your hair!" And that's how my life went
most of the time. Me and my makeup covered face-raccoon moving
through the world completely exposed, but somehow also a secret.

Burbank

AFTER SHE FINALLY FORGAVE TORI FOR FUCKING OUR SINK OFF THE WALL, I asked my mom to help me with my new breakouts. She found a quaint little spa in downtown Clearwater and dropped me off for my first facial appointment. As I walked in, the aesthetician's eyes said, *Oh boy, her skin is jacked, I can't help her.* But her mouth said, "Don't worry, sweetie. We're gonna get this under control." It turned out her eyes were right and after a dozen extraordinarily painful facials, which included sadistic blackhead extractions and what felt like an epidermal power sander, my skin was still jacked.

My dad tried to comfort me by continuing to promise I would grow out of it same as he did. I wanted to just go to sleep and wake up in a few years, after I'd grown out of it. My dad was still in Los Angeles, living in the suburb of Burbank, in a two-bedroom apartment with his roommate, Mark Kowalski. Why did my fifty-something-year-old father have a roommate? To save money, of course.

My father would splurge on things like Mustang convertibles with chameleon paint jobs (a kind of paint that changes color as the sun hits it), but he would save money in other ways, like roommates and furniture. My father's apartment in Burbank was very sparsely furnished. In the living room was a couch and a stereo (a two-hundred-disc CD changer to be exact) and that was it. In his bedroom, there was a queen-size bed (a Sleep Number adjustable bed to be exact) and a dresser.

I don't know what was in Mark Kowalski's room because I thankfully never went in there, but that was pretty much all the furniture my dad owned. No art on the walls, no decorations, no rugs. My dad considered that "women's stuff." To care about the aesthetics of a living space was apparently a triviality only women concerned themselves with.

My father used to speak for all men a lot. Because my father didn't like decorating and didn't care about art, he would say, "Men don't care about that stuff." Because my father didn't like cleaning, he would say, "Men don't like cleaning, that's a woman's job." He assumed that his unique and specific personality was true for all men. He told me men are not capable of being monogamous more times than I can count. Instead of infidelity being his issue, it was a man issue. He was, therefore, not responsible for his actions, because infidelity was in his gender makeup.

He also seemed to think that all the tasks he didn't enjoy, such as cleaning and cooking and caring for a house, were like crack cocaine to a woman. In his mind, newborn baby girls shot out of the womb and raced to put on dishwashing gloves; they couldn't wait to get their mitts on some dirty pots and pans. Being female meant that you lived for the sweet rumbling sound of a vacuum or the gentle thud of a carrot being chopped. He must have thought I was jonesing for a fix anytime I wasn't wiping a mirror or sautéing a vegetable.

One day, when my father and I were having one of our classic arguments about women, he said, "Modern women are miserable. They just *had* to go and join the workforce and now they don't get to stay home with their kids and take care of the household." I asked him why he thought all modern women were miserable and he said, "Because they complain all the time. You never heard a woman complain back in the fifties." He looked very satisfied with that indisputable point he had just made. "That's because they weren't *allowed* to complain in the fifties!" I said back, exasperated and ready to fight but also trying to keep a respectful tone in my voice, because my domineering dad, quite frankly, scared the crap out of me.

"Okay, well, we don't have to talk about that anymore." That's what my dad always said whenever he lost an argument.

My dad subscribed to the fallacy that women historically have always stayed home and taken care of children while men went out and provided for their family. This is of course completely incorrect. Pre-agriculture, a.k.a. most of human history, men and women brought in equal amounts of calories, a.k.a. money, to the household. The hunter-gatherer way of life meant that the sexes were of equal value.

Women didn't have to stay home alone watching daytime talk shows, developing a pill and pinot grigio addiction, while their bored, useless children complained that they didn't have enough toys, because everyone, including the children, went out and provided for the family together. Some research shows that it might have actually been early humans' gender equality that helped us evolve beyond the chimpanzees with their aggressive, male-dominated hierarchies. When tribes of early humans allowed *everyone* to do *everything*, it broadened the social network and new technology was created faster and more easily. Take note, Silicon Valley!

Of course, some evolutionary psychologists claim that men are naturally more aggressive than women and have a strong urge toward promiscuity so they can spread their seed around. Okay so, maybe men evolved this way, but that doesn't mean they have to stay this way. The argument "chimpanzees live like this therefore I have to" is a weak one. Chimpanzees also pretty much only eat raw fruit, so if you have evolved enough to eat pepperoni pizza, maybe you've evolved enough not to cheat on your wife? That being said, marriage is a construct that came about so men could feel complete ownership over their wives and ensure that their offspring were legitimate, so maybe we need to *keep* evolving to a whole new form of equality and freedom-based romantic partnerships.

Oddly enough, even though my dad honestly did think women were much better off "barefoot and pregnant," a phrase he used in a semi-joking but fully problematic manner, he was always encouraging me to follow my dreams and go after whatever I wanted in life. He was so proud of me for wanting to write and perform. He told me every time we spoke that I was capable of anything.

"The sky is the limit for you" is something he has said hundreds of times and still does to this day.

I once asked him, "Why do you think it's okay for me to pursue a career, but you think other women shouldn't?"

He said, "Honey, you're my daughter, it's different."

"But every woman is someone's daughter!" I said, trying to keep a respectful tone.

"Okay, well, we don't have to talk about that anymore."

In an attempt to keep encouraging me to follow my dreams, my father called me one day, saying he wanted to do something special for me, and offered me one of two options. Option A: he would take me to New York City so I could see a Broadway play, something I'd been talking about for years. In my mind, New York City was the absolute most glamorous place on earth, and theater was my first love. Before the acne, I performed in every theater program in Clearwater. I was obsessed with acting. But after the acne, I thought it best to not stand under bright stage lights in front of strangers. I couldn't believe my father was offering me this opportunity. My parents did not spoil us; my brother and I had to earn almost everything we got, so this no-strings-attached Broadway offer was huge.

Then my father offered me Option B: instead of me going to Los Angeles to visit him by myself, like I had every year, I could bring my best friend Tori with me that year. He offered to pay for Tori's whole trip. Now in hindsight, that was a much bigger gift to Tori than me, but at the time it was a really tough decision. I could see New York for the first time and watch a dazzling Broadway show, I could be exposed to art and culture and discover a whole new, life-changing world, or I could bring my drug-addled friend who I saw every single day to a place I had already been to many times. I chose Option B because I was a true dumbass and should not have been allowed to make that decision on my own. But Tori was thrilled that I made that decision on my own, as she had always had her sights set on visiting LA, and now she was going all expenses paid.

We arrived at my dad's apartment in Burbank with a long list of places we wanted to visit. Tori wanted to see the stars on Hollywood

Boulevard, Venice Beach, and a movie studio, to name a few, and I was excited to show her all of those things. But on day one, we walked by the pool in my dad's small apartment complex and saw two hot older men laying out and decided not to leave the apartment complex for the rest of the trip.

We stayed by the pool for three days, trying to get the attention of these dudes. We learned they were twenty-five years old. We lied and told them we were sixteen. We learned they were actors from Oklahoma, which meant they were waiters from Oklahoma, but we didn't realize that back then. Tori became convinced that the guy she was interested in was going to become a famous actor and she just had to hook up with him before that happened. I'm sure my dad was surprised when every morning he would ask, "Do you guys wanna go check out Malibu or something?" And we'd be like, "That's okay, we're going to the pool again, bye."

At the end of day three, we began to wear these two adult men down and they finally asked if we wanted some tequila. Before they could finish the word "tequila," Tori and I slammed four shots and were hammered and slurring our words, asking to see the inside of the studio apartment they shared. The sun was setting and the four of us were inside their studio now with the door shut, ripping through tequila shots and playing card games. Somehow the rules of the card game involved everyone kissing each other and Tori and I took turns making out with each twenty-five-year-old.

Then Tori grabbed the one she liked the most and pulled him over to one of the two twin beds in the living room / only room. Tori and this grown man started having sex and I didn't know what to do. I definitely wasn't going to have sex with the other guy. I had only known him for three days, I didn't have a firm grasp on what his first name was, and he had a soul patch, and even back then I knew that wasn't cool. So I decided to, you guessed it, let him go down on me for a while. After he stopped, I just sat up and got dressed. I still hadn't given anyone a blow job and my first time wasn't going to be Soul Patch. But Tori and the other guy were still going at it.

I looked over at Tori sitting on top of this guy, riding him, as the light from the window turned her barely pubescent body into a skinny silhouette. Then, just past Tori, outside the window, I saw my father storming up to the apartment and I froze. Earlier that day, before the tequila had loosened up my judgment, my dad told me it was okay for us to hang out with those dudes by the pool, but we were not allowed to go into their apartment. I had broken one of my father's rules. This was entirely new territory to me. My father was never around. I put myself in all kinds of rebellious situations back home and my mom didn't even notice.

My mom once walked in on Donny and me having sex and she just closed the door and never said anything about it. What does a daughter do when her father catches her doing something bad? I had no idea. I had to improvise. My father banged on the door and Tori jumped off that statutory rapist's struggling-actor penis and ran around naked in drunken, frantic circles. I finally grabbed her and pulled her into a closet. There were no other bedrooms, so the closet was my only option.

We could hear the two dudes open the door for my father. My six-foot-tall, looks-like-he-works-out father screamed, "Where the fuck are they?! They're fourteen years old!" I wish I could've seen the look on those dudes' faces. I heard them say, "Sir, we didn't know that. Sir, sir—we did not know that." How could they not have known we were fourteen? We looked like we were ten. Tori had a concave chest, and I was masked with zits. At the time, I actually felt bad for lying to them about my age, but they obviously shouldn't have been hooking up with fourteen-year-olds or sixteen-year-olds, so that's on them.

I could hear my father storming around, and I suddenly became aware that Tori was completely naked. I found a random T-shirt on the ground and threw it at her. She pulled it on just as my father ripped open the closet door and told us to get the hell out of there. He was so enraged and worried that he never noticed Tori didn't have any pants on or that we were standing in a closet.

Tori and I ran ahead of my father back to his apartment. His roommate, Mark Kowalski, had just moved out, so Tori and I were sleeping on twin air mattresses in Mark's old, empty bedroom. We ran into that room and shut the door. Tori sat on her air mattress and then instantly slumped over and fell asleep. . . . Okay, I guess I was on my own. I hadn't lived with my dad for five years and I had no idea how to handle a dad. I lay on my mattress thinking about what girls on TV who had dads did when they got in trouble? What did they say? What did the dads say? Was my dad going to kill me? Was he going to ignore it like my mom?

I remembered when I lived with my dad when I was small, he was always the disciplinarian. I was terrified of him. All he had to do was look at me with anger and I would cower. My dad knocked on the door. *Shit*. He asked me to come out and talk to him. He sounded so pissed. I followed him out to the living room. He looked at me, revved up for a speech, but something savage came over me. Maybe it was the tequila or maybe it was a desperate defense mechanism, but before my father could talk, I blurted out, "No! You don't get to talk to me. You don't get to say anything. I've lived by myself for months and I've taken care of myself for years! I raised myself and you don't get to scold me and be my dad now! I don't wanna hear *anything* from you!" I had never spoken to him that way in my entire life. My dad was stunned silent.

I turned around, walked away, and slammed Mark Kowalski's door. I lay on my air-filled bed, breathless. I was in shock. It was as if a spirit had commandeered my body. A brave, outspoken, ballsy ghost stepped into my body and told my dad to *fuck off.* I felt like a god. If I could stand up to my intimidating dad, what else could I do? Anything! Everything! I *was* a god! Plus, I finally got to tell my dad how abandoned and angry I felt. I won! But a few minutes later, that brave ghost politely exited my body and I became nervous Laura again, by herself in the dark, analyzing what had just occurred from every angle and guessing at all the ways in which I would meet my demise the next day.

When Tori and I woke up, my dad was already at work. He left a full laundry basket on the table with a note that said, *You are not allowed to go anywhere and I want all this laundry done by the time I get home.* Okay, so maybe I didn't fully win. Especially because the laundry room in the apartment complex was right next to Soul Patch and Pedophile's apartment. If we did this laundry, we would surely run into the two men we had just lied to about our age. We couldn't face them—my father had screamed at them. It was all too humiliating, so we decided to hang all the laundry on the balcony in the sun so it would smell cleaner, then we folded everything and put it back in the basket like fresh laundry. Take that, Dad!

For the next two days, Tori and I just sulked around the apartment; our only joy came from watching my dad unknowingly walk around in dirty clothes. My dad was never around to protect me, and the one time he was, I was furious at him for it. Being a parent seems fun. Our fancy five-day tour of Los Angeles became five days in a Burbank apartment complex, but Tori was walking around acting like she had just fucked a movie star and wasn't the least bit disappointed. I, however, had visions of New York City and Broadway lights and a dad that didn't think I was a bacchanalian Lolita and wished I could've gone back in time and chosen Option A.

Shively

WHEN WE GOT BACK TO FLORIDA, TORI TOLD ALL OF OUR FRIENDS, "I met this actor in LA who's, like, on his way to becoming a major movie star and we had the most magical five days together. Oh, and Laura let some dude with a soul patch go down on her." Our friends were very jealous of Tori's trip and made me promise I'd ask my dad about flying each of them out to LA in the future. But I knew he would absolutely never do that again and I didn't want him to. I decided what normally happens in Florida should stay in Florida. And I learned a lot had happened in Florida while I was gone.

My stepfather, Joe, was drinking again. No one told me this, but I figured it out on my own when I pulled up to my house and saw a takeout salad strewn all over the lawn and a pizza, cheese down, on our front porch. I opened the front door and my stepfather was passed out on the living room floor. I keenly assessed that he must have consumed a bunch of liquor and then driven to pick up a pizza and salad. He probably took a few shots of whiskey at the pizza place and then drove home. Judging by the odd angle his truck was parked at in the driveway, he was definitely blacked out the whole time. Somehow, he got the pizza and salad out of the car, but of course he dropped it all over the place on his way to the front door and then face planted in the living room, where he was now resting.

My mom heard me walk in and entered the living room, casually stepping over her husband to give me a welcome-home hug. This became the norm. Stepping over my stepfather passed out on the ground became as nonchalant as stepping over an old family dog. *Is this why they're called stepfathers?* I wondered as I stepped over him in the kitchen, or the garage, or the back porch.

But my brother, being visually impaired and all, could never quite get used to it, and I would often hear him exclaim, "Dammit, Joe!" as he tripped over our stepfather on the way to the bathroom. My mom encouraged my brother to use his probing cane inside the house, to avoid tripping over Joe, but Max hated the probing cane. He used to jokingly call it his "pimp cane," but calling it that wasn't enough to make him feel cool using it.

The cane made him feel vulnerable, as if his disability was on display. He used to make jokes about being blind to cover his vulnerability. His favorite joke was, "What did the blind man say when he walked past the fish market? Hello, ladies!" Although, that joke is more of a dig on women and their filthy vaginas than it is a dig on people with vision impairment.

Since he refused to use a probing cane, my mom thought maybe he should get a guide dog. Max loved this idea. Rather than being a vulnerable blind kid, always rolling a cane back and forth in front of him, he would be a cool blind kid with a badass black

Labrador guiding him along. He became obsessed with the idea of having a black Lab. We didn't know why it had to be black. He couldn't see, what did it matter what color the dog was? But to him, black was the raddest color a dog could be and he was determined to have one.

My mom did all the research and found a guide dog school a few hours away. She applied and my brother got in. He was going to get a highly trained guide dog, completely free of charge, and we were all very excited. Well actually, *they* were very excited. The day I found out, I was probably laying out in the sun topless, on our roof, with Tori, smoking a blunt and listening to Trick Daddy, and didn't really give a shit at all.

My brother had to go stay at this guide dog school for twenty days to train with his new dog. He was going to live on their campus, in a dormitory-style room, and every day he was going to wake up and spend hours working with his two-year-old guide dog. When he got there, he found out that his Labrador, unfortunately, wasn't going to be black, and it also wasn't going to be a Labrador. They presented him with a calico-colored collie and Max was justifiably bummed. The collie was the exact opposite of the sleek black Lab he had been yearning for, but they began to bond and Max stopped worrying about how cool or uncool he looked walking around with her.

The training was intense. He had to learn how to walk with a guide dog, how to let her lead, and how to trust her. When she refused to move forward, that meant there was danger ahead and he should never force her to move. He also learned a bunch of impressive commands that she understood, such as "find the door" or "find the stairs." My brother could tap someone on the shoulder and say "follow" and the dog would follow the person he just tapped.

This dog was going to offer my brother an incredible amount of independence and freedom. Her name was Shively. And before my brother even brought Shively home, my mom was already complaining about her fur getting all over our house.

My mother is an extremely clean person. It might seem like, with all the chaos that swirled around us and our household, she might be one of those moms who lets stuff pile up or attracts clutter, but my mom always had a messy life and a spotless house. My stepfather was passing out on a floor that was so clean you could eat pizza and salad off of it. The only mess in the whole house was him.

Maybe that's where my father got the idea that women loved cleaning. Maybe he thought he represented all men and my mother represented all women because she really did seem to always be vacuuming or washing dishes. But she didn't seem to love it and was always complaining that no one helped her, and she was right. We never helped her. Ever. My brother had the excuse of being visually impaired, but I had no excuse, I was just an asshole. So when my mom heard that a long-haired collie was coming to stay with us forever, she mostly thought of all the future vacuuming.

Max arrived home with Shively and he was all business. He informed us that no one was allowed to pet her while she was "working." When her harness was on, she was to solely focus on guiding my brother around. Guide dogs have to adhere to strict rules or they will forget all of their training. The guide dog school drilled this into my brother's head because it is very, very serious. We absolutely could not feed her from the table, or distract her while she was working, or treat her like a family pet in any way. She was not allowed on the furniture and my brother was the only person allowed to give her commands.

None of this should've been that big of a deal really. It's a privilege to have a guide dog and one should respect all the rules that come with it, but my mom is not exactly a rule follower. She would be more accurately described as a deliberate rule breaker. She is a person who has no desire to go swimming until she sees a "NO SWIMMING" sign, then she's forcing us all to get in our bathing suits. If a sign says, "DO NOT BACK UP," she is throwing her car in reverse. If a sign says, "DANGER HIGH VOLTAGE," her first thought is, *It's probably not that high.* "Oh, come on, what's the worst that could happen?" will be her epitaph.

When I was a toddler, we were driving through a neighborhood and my mom yelled, "Prickly pears!" Max and I looked out the window at a long driveway. At the end of the driveway, right next to a complete stranger's house, was a giant cactus. My mom pointed to this stranger's cactus, "Oh, prickly pears! I've always wanted to try prickly pears!" Even as a toddler I thought, *This isn't going to go well.* My midforties mom only used her whiny, teenage girl voice when she was really excited. And she only got really excited when she was doing something naughty, something frowned upon, or something downright illegal, and we were about to do all three.

My mom got us out of the car and we walked up the long driveway, toward a cactus that didn't belong to us. She told us to quickly grab as many prickly pears as we could carry and we did. When we made it back to the car, I felt relieved that no one caught us. *We got away with it*, I thought as my mom drove away, but I was wrong.

After a few minutes, I started to notice little, almost invisible, splinters embedded in my right hand. I tried to pull them out with my left hand but that just made them spread to my left hand. I tried to pull them out with my teeth, but that just made them spread to the inside of my mouth. My brother must have been having the same experience, because we began to cry at the exact same time.

"Hmmm, maybe we should've used gloves," my mom pondered as she realized painful microscopic splinters were thoroughly embedded in both of her children. And maybe we shouldn't have trespassed and stolen private property? And maybe rules exist for a reason? No, it was probably just the gloves thing. Those splinters stuck around forever; I'm still not convinced I've gotten them all out. Whenever I feel a pain in my mouth, I think about those fucking prickly pears. My mom's penchant for rule breaking trickled down and eventually we all became pretty mischievous people. So obviously, this dog, with all of her new rules, was pretty much doomed from the beginning.

It started with feeding Shively at the table. I'm not sure who started it, my mom or my brother or my stepdad, but someone did, and it all unraveled from there. We'd be eating and Shively would just be sitting right by my brother's chair, and she was a dog after all. Who could resist? Someone would quietly give her a few little harmless pieces of meat. Then my brother got serious about the rules again and reminded everyone, including himself, that no one could feed her from the table. "Oh, come on, what's the worst that could happen?" my mother said, quoting her future tombstone.

After a few days, my brother started feeding her from the table again. What the hell? He'd just gone through all that work, training her and living at a guide dog school, but I guess he figured, *What's the worst that could happen?* Then Shively started begging at the dinner table, which was very un–guide dog of her. Once she started begging, nudging everyone with her nose and softly whining, they all just started openly feeding her. *A few bites for me, a few bites for Shively, what's the worst that could happen, bing bang boom.*

I, however, was vehemently against it. As a way to rebel against my mom's rebellious ways, I liked to follow the rules from time to time and this was one of those times. I also didn't like spoiling children or dogs. My strict father had drilled into my head that giving in to bratty behavior could create a monster, and it turned out he was right. I saw how much worse her behavior was getting and I told them that breaking the rules was clearly the problem, but no one gave a crap about what I had to say.

After a few weeks of them treating Shively to a handfed buffet every night, my mom made a roast for dinner and invited my aunt and uncle over. My mom placed the roast on the center of the table and then went back into the kitchen. We were all in the kitchen—Max; Stepdad Joe, who was upright for a change; my aunt; my uncle; and me. While we were chatting, we noticed Shively casually walk by with the entire roast in her mouth. My mom screamed. My brother asked, "What happened?!" and everyone shouted that Shively had just stolen the roast off the table. Then Shively slipped out the doggie door and I chased after her, running outside in the pouring rain.

She tore around the wet backyard until I finally caught up with her and tried to rip the roast out of her mouth. Everyone was outside now, standing in the downpour, watching me furiously wrestle with Shively. When I finally got the roast, I held it up to the sky; lightning flashed and thunder roared as I turned to the group and yelled, "Thy way and thy doings have procured these things unto thee! This is thy wickedness!"

Okay, so things had gone a little too far. We had to regroup. Obviously feeding her from the table was a bad idea and now everyone knew, so we just needed to start over. Unfortunately, it doesn't work that way.

There is something so smug and wonderful about having a guide dog. You can bring it anywhere in the world *legally*. Shively wasn't a questionable emotional support dog like so many people bring on airplanes. Shively was the real deal and no one could tell us we couldn't bring her somewhere. No one. We could bring Shively to a water park if we wanted to, we could bring her to a cooking class, we could bring her to any establishment no matter how stuffy or pet unfriendly it was. I loved bringing her to restaurants. The hostess would see Shively and be like, "Excuse me, you can't—" and then she'd notice my brother's blindness and be like, "Oh my god, I'm so sorry, you can do anything you want. I'm gonna go fire myself for my insensitivity!" But after the roast incident, bringing Shively to restaurants became tricky.

At Ruby Tuesday, a nice family smiled at my brother and Shively, right before Shively put her paws up on their table and started eating their Ruby's Classic Trio. We would all gasp and feign shock, saying things like "I'm so sorry, wow, that's never happened before." And what were these people going to do? Get mad at the blind kid? They would say, "No, it's our fault for ordering a dish your dog liked!" After a dozen more of these incidents, we started to grow tired of Shively.

We also became aware of the dangers of an unruly house pet, who was probably just searching for food at that point, guiding my brother around. My mom called the guide dog school and asked them if they would take Shively back: "I think you gave us a lemon." They happily agreed to take her back. I'm sure they knew it was our fault and they wanted to save her before we ruined her for good.

My brother, it turned out, was extremely happy to be rid of her. He confessed it was too hard to take care of her with all of his disabilities. After Shively was gone, my mom went into my brother's room to do a deep clean. She discovered Max had broken another guide dog golden rule and let Shively lay on all the furniture in his bedroom. She vacuumed about a foot of dog fur off of every surface and made us all promise we would never get a dog again. Then my brother went back to his probing cane. It might not have been as "cool" as a guide dog, but at least it didn't come with a bunch of pesky rules just begging to be broken.

Uncle Dog

Shively moved out right around the time Uncle Dog moved in. Unlike Shively, and contrary to his name, Uncle Dog was a human. More specifically, he was an Argentinian man in his forties who moved into our garage. His real name was Gonzolo, but my brother gave him the nickname Uncle Dog.

My brother was still using the word "dog" as a slang term, as in "What's up, dog?" or "Yo, dog, can I get a cigarette?" The word was already out of fashion at this point, but my brother had been blind for two years and was slowly going deaf, so he wasn't able to keep up with the latest trends. And why did Gonzolo move into our non-insulated garage during a particularly merciless Florida summer? I have no idea. I know he was married to my mom's twin sister. Yes, my mom has a twin sister, and they look alike, and sound alike, and make similarly interesting life decisions.

My mom's twin sister was living near Los Angeles and teaching English as a second language, and Gonzolo was one of her students. After he graduated, they started dating and got married. And for some reason, during that period, Gonzolo moved to Florida to live in our garage. When I recently asked my mom why he lived with us, she said, "I think he had a job in Clearwater or something." And she was right, Gonzolo did have a job in Clearwater. He worked as a cashier at our local Walmart. But I have to believe he could've worked at a Walmart near Los Angeles. So I may never know the real reason why he lived with us, but I do know having an adult male stranger sleeping on a mattress on the floor while you're doing laundry in your sweltering garage is super weird. He was as reticent as my stepdad and drank as much as my stepdad, which tells you that the twins had similar taste in men.

Gonzolo almost never spoke to me during the six months he lived with us, but I loved him with my whole heart because he was very kind to my brother. By this point, all of Max's friends had disappeared and he had no one to hang out with. And as much as my mom tried to guilt me into bringing Max to nightclubs with my fifteen-year-old-girl posse, I absolutely would not do it. I tried to explain to my mom that I was having a hard enough time trying to get into the twenty-one-and-over nightclubs in Tampa with my janky fake ID, surely bringing a six-foot-two visually impaired kid who, by the way, was also not twenty-one, would have made entry into those nightclubs impossible.

She eventually stopped asking me to take him to nightclubs, but one night when I was heading out to a keg party, she seized the opportunity.

"Why don't you take your brother? You don't need a fake ID for a keg party." We stared at each other. *Dammit.* She had a point and she knew she had a point.

"Well, no, I can't, 'cause . . ." She looked at me expectantly, wondering what bullshit I was going to come up with, but I just told her the truth, "it's too embarrassing."

We stared at each other again. A middle-aged mother who desperately wanted to insert just a tiny bit of joy into her son's hard life and an ableist teenage girl who couldn't fathom caring more about someone else than herself. My mom's eyes said, *I'm ashamed of you.* My eyes said, *I hate you for loving him more than you love me.* Then we went our separate ways.

But when Gonzolo moved in, he started hanging out with my extremely lonely brother and my mother stopped guilt-tripping me, and for that I loved Gonzolo. Gonzolo would take Max to play pool a lot. If you have never played pool with a person who can't see, I'm just warning you, it can take quite a while. Max would walk around the table, gently feeling the felt to locate each ball. He was careful not to move the balls when he touched them, but he had to touch them in order to "see" where they were on the table.

After he touched every . . . single . . . ball, someone had to walk him over to the cue ball and sort of line him up with his pool stick. I greatly disliked taking Max to play pool, not only because it took fourteen hours to finish a game, but also because he beat me every . . . single . . . time. My brother, without sight and a fully working brain, absolutely destroyed me at the pool hall. I wish I could say I was letting him win out of kindness, but I tried really hard and he always crushed me. The worst part was, he couldn't see the balls go in, so he'd hear a clink and cockily ask, "What happened?" Then I'd have to say, "You got one in," and "You got another one in," and

"You got two in," and finally "You won." Describing to someone the ways in which they are beating the living shit out of your pool game is way worse than just plain old losing.

Gonzolo used to take Max to the pool hall all the time, and he didn't mind growing old watching Max touch every ball because he was drinking his weight in cheap red wine and he would've happily stayed there all day. Gonzolo was what you might call a wino. Actually, I just looked up the definition of "wino" and *a person who drinks excessive amounts of cheap wine, especially one who is homeless*, describes Gonzolo exactly. Those hours at the pool hall patiently and drunkenly waiting for Max to take his turn are how Gonzolo earned the affectionate moniker "Uncle Dog."

Max only gave someone a nickname if he really liked them. He called our mom "Mommy Mom." He called our dad "Papa Pops." And he called our stepdad "Joe," because that was Joe's name and Joe just wasn't the sort of person Max would give a nickname to. Max's name for me was "Late." But he didn't call me Late because I was late a lot; my name morphed organically over the years. First, he called me "Little Laura," then "Lattle Laura," then "Lattle Late," then I was just simply Late. Max is, obviously, the only person who has ever called me Late, because it is an odd and unique nickname, given to me by my odd and unique brother, and it means more to me than any other nickname I have ever had or ever will have.

Since Gonzolo was spending so much quality time with Max, he could do no wrong in my eyes. When my friends and I pulled up to our local Walmart so Vic, my friend's twenty-one-year-old boyfriend, could steal a new CD player for his Acura, we saw Gonzolo, wearing a blue vest and gathering blue shopping carts in the parking lot. One of my friends, who I immediately forgave, said, "Isn't that the drunk dude who lives in your garage?" and I didn't even get embarrassed. I just smiled and said, "Yes. Yes, it is." That's how much I loved Gonzolo. Okay, I got a little embarrassed, and I might've said, "No. No, it isn't." But the point is, I loved Gonzolo. Not only because he spent so much time with my brother, but also because . . . he had really intense cystic acne. His face was so incredibly inflamed and so vividly red that it made my face look slightly less so, and that meant a lot to me.

We humans love to compare ourselves to others. Most of us will grasp at anything to make ourselves feel superior. I used to volunteer for visually impaired children, and one day we told them we were all going to make stuffed animals and then drop them off at the Burbank Center for the Retarded and the blind children immediately laughed (that is what it was called back then, before that word was abused and became a slur. It is now called BCR "A Place to Grow").

Those visually impaired kids started snickering and making jokes about the intellectually disabled kids. You would think those children, because of their own challenges, would have had so much empathy for anyone who was challenged in any way, but those blind kids didn't give a shit about those intellectually disabled kids. They were belittling them and looking down on them. They continued to make fun of them even after the other volunteers and I tried to chastise them. They didn't give one shit.

So Gonzolo's skin condition was more challenging than my skin condition, and instead of having empathy for him, I just used his suffering to make myself feel better. And I desperately needed to feel better because my skin was in really rough shape. The Accutane had left my system and my whole face and neck were covered in large, white bumps. My brother would slowly move through the house, using his probing cane and struggling to hear what everyone was saying, and I would think, "Goddammit, his skin is beyond gorgeous. It's so unfair!" Narcissism was high and empathy was low.

I was learning about leper colonies in school and I felt jealous of the colony residents. *Those lucky people got to hide from society*, I thought, *meanwhile, I have to bring this face to the mall, nightclubs, keg parties, and the beach.* Plus, they were all together going through the same thing. For some reason, I always felt like a pustule-covered island surrounded by a vast ocean of clear-skinned people. I was a leper with no colony, besides Gonzolo, and I pitied myself.

My father could tell I was in a terrible emotional place and he suggested maybe I needed a change of scenery. My grades had gotten really bad and my only hobby was drinking Bud Light. My dad asked if maybe I wanted to move back to Los Angeles to live with my half sister.

My half sister is my father's daughter from a previous marriage. Despite her being thirteen years older than me and having a different mom, we were always very tight. No matter how much time we spent apart, when we saw each other, we always fell into being sisters. My sister got pregnant when she was seventeen years old. And she lived with us when she gave birth to her daughter, Jasmine. All six of us lived crammed into our 827-square-foot house in our Los Angeles suburb. Her daughter Jasmine was only four years younger than me, so it felt weird calling her my niece. She was more like my little sister.

So I took stock of my life and had to decide between living with my slowly disintegrating brother, my angry mom who was regularly stepping over my unconscious stepdad, and Uncle Dog who was drinking and sweating excessively in our garage, or my big sister, my eleven-year-old niece, and Hollywood. I picked the latter. I was going back to Los Angeles. This time minus Tori and hopefully minus all the drama. I really wanted to get my life together.

Much like my brother, years earlier, I hoped living in a house with more structure would help me do better in school and start working toward some kind of a future plan. Plus, despite all my self-hatred and insecurity, I still really wanted to be an actress. . . . Or maybe I wanted to be an actress because of all my self-hatred and insecurity? Either way, Los Angeles was the place to be if I wanted to actually figure out how to have an acting career. So I packed all of my stuff and flew to California.

Los Angeles

MY SISTER WAS LIVING IN WOODLAND HILLS, A TRANQUIL SUBURB ABOUT thirty minutes outside of Los Angeles. She was renting the bottom half of a two-story duplex on a sleepy little street. The duplex had two bedrooms; one for my sister and her boyfriend, Eli, and one for my niece, Jasmine. Jasmine was what we called back in those days a "tomboy," but nowadays she would probably be called gender nonconforming. She started cutting her own hair very short when she was three years old. She refused to ever wear it long.

At the beach, she wouldn't wear a bikini. She wore board shorts with no shirt until she started sprouting breasts, then she covered them with an oversized T-shirt, but she did not want to be called a boy. Whenever waiters would assume, based on her short hair, backward hat, and baggy shorts, that she was a boy and call her "young man" or "sir," she would say, "I'm not a boy." It wasn't like she was shocked or offended, but she would always correct people.

At the time I thought, *Why do you dress like that if you don't want people to call you a boy?* But Jasmine was just ahead of her time.

The younger generation was born into this stuffy conservative world and they're taking all of the old rules and gender norms and saying, *Eh, no thanks, I think I'll just do whatever feels right and not be stuffed in a box.* But I grew up at a time when people thought you very much needed to check a box and pick a side. Identity was a huge deal. Not just your gender, but your sexuality, your hobbies, your clothing, everything needed to be neatly labeled so everyone could understand very clearly "what" you were.

When I first arrived in Woodland Hills, I called my old friend, Samantha, from when I had lived in LA years before, and the first thing she asked me was, "So, what are you?" I didn't understand the question.

She explained, "Are you a prep, or a goth, or a jock, or like, artsy?" I felt like I was suddenly in a high school movie. I had never labeled myself in that way. I wasn't wealthy enough to be preppy, I wasn't bold enough to be a goth, I wasn't strong enough to be a jock, and I wasn't exactly sure what artsy meant. In Florida, I had sort of just existed as a half-Black, half-white girl who wore nonspecific clothes and had very curly hair, but apparently in Los Angeles I had to pick a category and a subcategory.

I finally replied, "I don't know, I'm just me, I guess." My friend seemed bored with that answer and we never spoke again.

Was something wrong with me? Why couldn't I label myself? What was I? Did I need to know? Would labeling myself make me happier? I spent the rest of the day trying to slap some kind of label on myself, but my niece Jasmine seemed to have no desire to label herself, fit into a box, or make her appearance match traditional gender norms. She just was who she was and she didn't care what anyone else thought. She was far more evolved than everyone around her.

She preferred to appear masculine. She wanted people to call her Jaz—she liked the neutrality of that name—but she didn't identify as a boy and she called herself a girl, though she said it casually as if she was completely unattached to the idea, like, "Uh, yeah, I guess, I'm a girl. Who cares?" She was staggeringly cooler than I was in every way. In 2002, I was unironically rocking out to Nickelback while Jaz was listening to Tegan and Sara, before anyone else had ever even heard of them. She skateboarded and played basketball, while my only physical activity for the day was dialing the phone. She graciously allowed me to share her bedroom, and I started sleeping in the trundle bed that pulled out from under Jaz's twin bed.

My sister's boyfriend, Eli, was dreamy. He was very handsome, and I think he was in Mensa or something because he had the energy of someone who had been officially told by an outside entity that he was a genius. He looked very Nordic, with soft features and light blonde hair. When he stood next to my mixed-race sister, with her olive skin and dark blonde Afro, they made a stunning couple.

They both smoked American Spirit lights in the yellow box, and they took pity on my well-established addiction, and lack of ability to satiate it, and gave me the occasional cigarette. We would sit outside at night, by the ice-cold duplex pool, and blow all-natural tobacco smoke into the desert air, and I'd hear about Eli's work, although I can't remember what he did, and my sister's work, she was teaching at a private Scientology school, and I'd tell them about my wild life back home.

One day Eli said to me, "You know, you should take an IQ test. I bet you have a really high IQ." And those words lodged into my brain forever. I can't remember what the guy did for a living, but I remember those exact words. They meant so much to me. His kindness meant so much to me. Their normal, quiet life meant *so* much to me.

They bought a used bright red BMW—it was fifteen years old, but in mint condition—and Eli used to take me driving. I had my learner's permit and I got to drive that beautiful car around the winding, hilly roads of Los Angeles with someone who thought I had a really high IQ. New feelings were arising in me. Happiness? Solidity? Whatever it was, I liked it.

My sister enrolled me temporarily in the private Scientology school where she was teaching. Jaz was a student there and we figured I should check it out and see if that might be my long-term school. On my first day, I woke up early with my sister. She was giving herself a hot oil treatment, sitting in the early morning light with a heating cap on her extremely tight 4A curls. She explained that we curly-haired girls need to make sure we moisturize and she gave me my first hot oil treatment.

Then Eli and Jaz woke up and we made breakfast. We ate eggs at a table. No one had cancer, no one was drunk, no one was angry. Then we all made sandwiches to pack in our lunch boxes. I hadn't packed a lunch box in years. When I was little, my mom lovingly made us the most amazingly healthy lunches, but she hadn't done that in forever. My sister, Jaz, and I piled into their other car, an old Isuzu, and we headed off toward school. My sister rolled all the windows down and the wind wrapped itself around us. She turned on the radio and Alanis Morrisette was passionately screaming "Uninvited." My sister cranked the volume and the lyrics pumped into my ears. I knew every word and I joined in with Alanis, screaming about being an uncharted territory and a hot-blooded woman.

Suddenly I wanted to explode. All the emotions I had kept inside for so long began to pour out of me. I finally felt safe enough and in a calm enough environment to feel my feelings and they came rushing to the surface. Rage at my parents, rage at my brother, rage at myself, overwhelming survivor's guilt, and I started to hyperventilate. I didn't want to cry in front of my sister and Jaz. They seemed so happy and so normal. Instead, I kept scream-singing so loudly that I broke into a sweat and ruptured a couple vocal cords.

My sister must've thought I *really* loved Alanis Morrisette. I still hadn't cried about my parents' divorce. Five years before, when my mom threw the phone across the house and yelled, "Ask your fucking father! He's divorcing me!" my brother went outside and kicked the fence, and he said he actually hurt his foot pretty badly, but I just went into my room, closed the door, and sat on my bed.

At least my brother got to kick something. I kicked nothing and said nothing. I just kept going on every day with whatever the new normal was. *Your father is never going to live with us again. Okay. Your brother has cancer. Okay. Your brother is going to be blind forever. Okay. Joe lives with us now. Okay. Joe is blackout drunk. Okay. Joe is never drinking again. Okay. Joe is drinking again. Okay.*

After the divorce, I flew by myself to LA to visit my father. He sat down with me and said he was so sorry this was happening. He started crying and said he was sorry over and over again. I didn't cry. I just sat with him. Watching him with my ten-year-old eyes, guarding my ten-year-old heart. *You'll have to navigate life without me from now on. Okay. I won't be there to make sure you brush your teeth. Okay. I won't kiss you goodnight ever again. Okay.* I did not cry. But now in my sister's car, after getting my first hot oil treatment, after eating eggs with a nice man who thought I was smart, after packing my lunch for the day, I wanted to cry so badly. But I didn't. Instead, I screamed with Alanis, and Alanis is an amazing screaming partner.

High School

THE SCIENTOLOGY PRIVATE SCHOOL I WAS GOING TO ATTEND, LEWIS CAR-
roll Academy, had a very clean, well-kept campus with a sparse
population of all white, mostly very wealthy students. It was the
exact opposite of my public high school in Florida. Dunedin High
School was diverse and densely populated, and upper middle class
was as wealthy as it got. Dunedin High was also undergoing massive construction while I was a student there. They were essentially
rebuilding the entire school, and they definitely should not have
allowed children to be educated in a hazardous construction site for
four years.

The bathroom pipes exploded daily, flooding the hallways with
toilet water and fecal matter. The air smelled like deep-fried tater
tots and recently digested deep-fried tater tots. The outdoor walk-
ways were caged on either side by metal fences to keep kids from
wandering into dangerous construction areas. The construction

workers were always cutting metal, so sparks flew everywhere. Everyone swore they saw sparks fly into a freshman girl's hair. They swore she screamed as her hair caught fire, and she couldn't put it out so eventually her head looked like a deep-fried tater tot, but I wasn't there that day so I can't confirm.

Buildings would randomly close for demolition midway through the semester, and your classroom would be moved to a temporary trailer. Every day felt like a chaotic scientific experiment was taking place. *What happens when you take a group of stressed-out, highly emotional teenage mice and stuff them in a perilous cage being rebuilt from the ground up?* The results were predictable: we became more stressed and more emotional.

But there were some advantages; all of that construction created a lot of blind spots. In the middle of the school day, we could stand behind half-demolished, abandoned buildings and smoke cigarettes and weed to medicate our anxieties. And whenever my friends and I didn't want to be at school anymore, we could just leave. There were at least ten easy ways to sneak off our haphazard campus unseen.

My days of being "Most Popular" were over. I had completely given up on wearing cute clothes or covering my flawed skin. I came to school every day in sweatpants. My old friends from middle school were still very popular, but I didn't have anything in common with them anymore. They all had disciplinarians and curfews and participated in a thing called extracurricular activities. I didn't understand those kids at all.

When I was in ninth grade, one of my friends from middle school astutely pointed out, "Isn't it crazy how everyone who was voted most popular or most talented or whatever in middle school is, like, a total nobody now?" *Ouch.* Yeah, wow, that *is* crazy, *Amber.* But maybe those people reached the mountaintop years ago and realized it didn't mean anything. Maybe they felt like there's no point in getting a part-time job just to afford Abercrombie & Fitch and hair bleach when life was just going to keep cutting your legs out from under you over and over again. But I probably just said, "Uh, yeah, I guess." I had never thought of myself as "like, a total nobody now." But after hearing it, I knew she was right.

If I absolutely had to slap a label on myself at Dunedin High School, I was probably considered one of the bad girls. When my LA friend had asked me what I was, I guess I could've said, "Low-Income, Stoner Bad Girl with a splash of Alcoholic?" I looked down on all the straight-haired, white, upper-middle-class girls who wore Aéropostale T-shirts tucked into white shorts. The girls who drove brand-new Jeep Grand Cherokees, with names like Jenny, and Gabby, and Haley. Jenny's parents gave her a white Jeep Wrangler for her sixteenth birthday with CLUELESS printed in huge letters on the front window. The exact same car Cher Horowitz drove in the movie. I looked down on Jenny the most. I feared those girls looked down on me so I decided, *Actually, no, I look down on you first.*

I wore my broken family like a badge of honor. Anyone who had never seen their stepfather stumble to the liquor store in their mother's shoes wasn't interesting to me. Those girls were boring. In my mind, they didn't understand real problems. Every day, after her waitressing shift, my friend's mom would sit down on the couch, slap a fresh morphine patch on her back, light a cigarette, and then pass out. Their living room carpet was covered with long, cigarette-shaped burn marks. She played Russian roulette with her family's lives every evening. Those were my kind of people. The reckless ones. The ones who always had terrible news to share. The ones whose lives were bad and careening toward worse. Those people I understood and respected.

But at Lewis Carroll Academy, I had a chance to majorly re-brand myself. I was starting fresh. I could be anyone I wanted: A good girl? A smart girl? A prude? But I was overwhelmed by the vast differences between me and these Scientologist private school girls. They seemed so pure, so wholesome, and so sheltered that they made Haley and the other good girls back in Florida look like dam-aged goods. These girls were like fresh peaches and I felt like a rot-ten apple that fell off the tree and got chewed on by a rat.

I went to school with the voice of Bart Simpson's daughter and Elvis Presley's granddaughter. These girls were sweet and soft-spoken. Mind you I have no idea what their homelife was like, but in my jealous fantasy, it was all mansions and father-daughter dances. It didn't seem like anyone drank, smoked cigarettes, or hooked up with twenty-five-year-old, soul-patched, struggling ac-tors from Oklahoma. I felt uncomfortable and bad about myself. I didn't know who to talk to or who to relate to.

It turns out I wasn't ready for a major rebrand. It's hard to be-come pure and innocent on the outside when you feel broken and corrupted on the inside. I started to feel very lonely. I missed my wild girls. I missed hearing about who was getting an abortion or who was in a gang bang. I wanted to know if Tori and Ben were back together for the thousandth time. Did Tiffany's boyfriend start selling crack outside the Betty Lane store again? Did the guy Kayla was having sex with ever kiss her on the mouth? (It turns out, no, he didn't. My friend Kayla had sex with a dude like ten times and he never kissed her on the friggin' mouth. But I didn't know that because I was in Los Angeles going to private school and bored out of my mind.)

I couldn't glom on to my niece's social life because Jaz only hung out with eleven-year-old skater boys. I did enjoy watching them skateboard though. It reminded me of Max. The sound of skateboards scraping and cracking on the cement touched my soul like the sound of rain or ocean waves.

After a couple of weeks, I told my sister I wanted to check out the nearby public school. Maybe there I could slide into a group of slightly alcoholic, stoner bad girls. I still wanted to make smarter choices and get my life together . . . but not if it was going to be quite this boring or make me feel quite this bad about myself.

El Camino Real, a public high school in Woodland Hills, housed over ten thousand students. That's what someone told me on my first day. I was overwhelmed by the number of teens covering every square inch of the campus like hormonal, swarming ants. I asked a nearby girl how many students I was looking at and she said, "over ten thousand," very casually. It turns out she was wrong; there were only three thousand students. But it felt like a million. The massive population was very intimidating, and since this was tenth grade, everyone knew everyone already.

Some girls took pity on me and talked to me in geometry class. They asked where I was from, and after I said Florida they asked, "So, what are you?" *Dammit*. That question again. I wanted to give them the answer they wanted, so I took in their clothes and style. I tried to figure out what they were and then maybe I'd just say I was that. But their clothes looked kind of average and nonspecific. *Preppy? Casual? Was casual a category?* I couldn't remember.

Finally, I said, "What do you mean?"

"Well, we all kind of stick to our own groups here. There's a lot of Persians, and Armenians, and Mexicans . . ." I had never heard the words Persian or Armenian before, but after she said Mexicans, I caught on to what she meant. The girls explained that they were Mexican and that all the Mexican kids stuck together. I told them

I was half white and half Black, but they didn't know what to do with that answer, so we never spoke again.

It's remarkable how many similarities public schools have to prisons. Public schools mirror the prison aesthetic perfectly with their fenced-in, intimidating concrete structures. Some even going as far as using barbed wire to cage in the children. Like prisoners, the students group off into racial categories for safety. Both institutions have cafeterias, and exercise yards, and police officers. No one actually wants to be there, but some outside authority is forcing you to stay inside the building. I know I'm not the first person to make this observation, but that makes it even worse. The comparison shouldn't be so obvious.

I did not want to remain a student at El Camino Real High School. My longing for home grew stronger. I used to sit in class and draw pictures of myself in an airplane flying back to Florida. After a couple of weeks, I was done. I hadn't made a single friend. I was desperate to get home. I now know it takes longer than two weeks to feel comfortable in a new place, but I didn't know that then and no one forced me to be patient. I told my dad I wanted to go back to Florida and he understood. But I could feel that he and my sister were frustrated with me. They went to a lot of trouble to try and put me in a better life situation, but I just couldn't do it. I craved the drama of my Florida social life.

Also, my sister and Eli were great surrogate parents, and they did live a much more stable life than my mother's, but I wasn't completely comfortable being myself around them. I deeply missed my mom. My mom was my closest friend and living so far away from her left me without a true confidant.

A few years earlier, my mom had tried to be more than a friend. Since we had just lost our disciplinarian father, she tried to fill that role. But she was very well established in our minds as the soft one, the kind one, the one you would go to after Daddy yelled. When she would raise her voice to try and get us to behave, we would just stare at her. It wasn't scary, like with our dad; it was just weird.

She would scream at us, slamming drawers and doors, and we would just say, "Jesus, Mom, calm down." Before my brother got sick, he and my mom would throw down in some epic fights. She would try to be a real mom and make him stay home for dinner, but he would refuse. All he wanted to do was eat fast food and smoke weed with his friends. He hated being home. He hated her. He hated himself.

My mom knew he wasn't afraid of her and she couldn't control him like my father could, but she tried anyway. She would yell, "If you walk out that door then don't fucking come back here!" He'd say, "Fine." Then he'd leave and not come back. He'd stay out all night at fourteen and fifteen years old. I was eleven and still sleeping in bed with my mom every night. After the divorce, I clung to sleeping in her bed like a baby to a security blanket. There's nothing like polishing off a pack of cigarettes and then climbing in bed with your mommy.

My mom would stare at our cracked ceiling for hours, waiting to hear my brother come home. But he wouldn't come home. She'd call the police and try to report it, but they would tell her the same thing every time: he needs to be gone for forty-eight hours in order to be considered a missing person. I'd try to comfort her. I always knew he'd come back eventually and he always did. He was never gone for more than two days. He was never legally a missing person. After a couple years of this, my mom quit trying. She stopped asking him to come home for dinner. She stopped fighting with him. She stopped disciplining him at all.

When it was my turn to be a teenager, there was no curfew, no dinner to fight about, and nothing to rebel against. My mom had already completely given up on being a mom. But she was my friend. My best friend. I told her everything. I was my genuine self around her because I knew she would never judge me or punish me. She was the person I could come to with anything, no matter how shameful, and she would listen and show me compassion and love. She was my unconditional friend. For those few months at my sister's, it felt like I had real parents. They offered structure, guidance, and boundaries, but I ached for my friend.

Zoe

WHEN I MOVED BACK TO CLEARWATER, I DECIDED TO DROP OUT OF high school. Maybe if my mother had been more than a friend, she would have forbidden it, but she gave me her blessing. She understood that I had already missed so much of tenth grade, the thought of catching up was excruciating. Made more excruciating by the thought of going back to that half-built high school. Also, after getting back from Tijuana the year before, it had taken me forever to catch up in ninth grade, so I finally cried uncle. Tori had already dropped out, along with most of our other friends. It really was not a hard decision to make.

My friend Zoe decided to drop out with me. She and I were growing closer as Tori and I were growing apart. When Zoe and I were investigating how to get our GEDs, we stumbled upon a "high school" that sold bona fide diplomas for $400. After you mailed them a check, they would mail you a stack of open-book tests. If you passed those tests, and remember they were open-book tests so failure was almost impossible, they would send you an actual diploma. Zoe asked her mom and I asked my dad for the cash and a month later, we were "high school graduates."

Zoe was one year older than me. She was one of the most popular girls in her eighth-grade class but, like me, she was "like, a total nobody now." She didn't take hard drugs, but she was a bit of a bad girl; she was having sex, drinking, and smoking cigarettes at a young age, so obviously we became great friends.

She was Greek. Her skin was dark olive. She had thick eyebrows that kids used to call "railroad tracks" back in elementary school, before plucking, because they grew together in one dark line across her forehead. After plucking, she got her revenge and created two of the most gorgeous eyebrows you have ever seen.

She was very pretty and she knew it. She called herself pretty more than anyone I had ever heard. She had a magnetic personality that drew people to her and, like moths, everyone wanted to hang out near her light as long as possible. But her reputation took a bit of a beating toward the end of middle school.

Zoe did not blow three dudes in a closet or have sex with four boys in a car. Zoe's reputation took a hit simply because she had a Black boyfriend in middle school. This was 1999, even though it sounds like 1949. Sadly, not too long ago, if a white girl dated a Black boy at my middle school, she would be ostracized by the white male community. They hurled racial slurs at her and called her a slut. Somehow being in a monogamous relationship with one boy meant you were a slut if that boy happened to have dark skin; the rules were confusing and made up by racist teenagers. They shoved Zoe into the bad-girl category, where I was waiting with open arms.

Zoe's Black boyfriend, whom all those white boys were so upset about, was the most handsome kid in our whole town. No hyperbole. He was beautiful, very popular, and a star athlete, but none of that mattered because his skin color didn't match hers. As a mixed-race person, it is extremely painful to watch racist people shun interracial relationships. Most of the white students who attended my middle school agreed that Black people and white people should not be dating. . . . Therefore, I should not have been born.

Zoe and I loved each other pretty immediately. Since she was my only friend who didn't take hard drugs, I finally had someone to drink Bud Light with while everyone else was high out of their minds on pills and acid. Our friends were quickly turning into drug addicts, while Zoe and I were sitting outside Starbucks, smoking Marlboro Lights and sipping lattes.

Zoe's mom had cancer, so she could relate to my brother's health issues better than anyone. Zoe's father was dead—he was the one who died on Christmas Eve when he drove his car into a wall after he was stabbed in the stomach buying heroin, as if you could ever forget. So Zoe had to raise herself just like I did.

She was my first friend who I could really talk to besides my mom, and we would talk endlessly. We would judge all of our friends for their drug use, gossip about the sex lives of everyone in town, and complain about our families, but mostly we would talk about boys. We were always hung up on some boy who wasn't worthy of our time and devotion, and when we weren't out following that boy around, we were at home wishing we were.

Our hormonally charged Sunday night ritual consisted of listening to JoMama Johnson's *Quiet Storm*, a sexy weekly radio program featuring such horny hits as "T-Shirt & Panties" and "I'll Make Love to You." Then, after we were all revved up from those seductive lyrics, we would watch *Sex and the City*. We lived for *Sex and the City*. We felt exactly like Carrie and company, just less New York, less money, less fashion, less old . . . okay, we were very different from those women, but they were boy crazy and so were we, and somehow that was enough.

Zoe was especially boy crazy. If Zoe had feelings for a boy, nothing else in the world existed for her. If one of your parents is taken from you forever randomly on Christmas Eve, you might end up with some issues later in life. And all of Zoe's issues came to the surface when she met Beckett.

Beckett was white but he wasn't obsessed with Zoe's Black ex-boyfriend like so many of the other white dudes. Beckett took one look at her swarthy beauty and knew he had to be with her. Beckett was raised by his grandmother and she ran a successful business. They lived in an $800,000 house, which seemed like a castle to us. Beckett drove his grandmother's brand-new Mercedes to pick Zoe up for their first date; I felt like my friend was being picked up in a private plane. Zoe got to be upper middle class for an evening and I longed for an above-average-income prince to sweep me off my below-average-income feet.

Beckett was funny and charming. He had the confidence of a dude who was more attractive than he was, but his confidence made him more attractive, so it all balanced out. Beckett and Zoe fell hard in love. I spent so much time with them, I felt like I was in their relationship. They were funny together, silly and playful. Then things would turn dark and they would scream at each other.

Beckett would say unforgiveable things to her. He'd call her a bitch and a fucking whore. She'd come back with even worse insults. He'd say horrible things about her body. She'd say worse things about his. Time would pass and they'd be fine again. Silly and playful. Hateful and screaming. Up and down. Back and forth.

One night, I tried to get in the middle of one of their vicious brawls and Beckett picked me up and tossed me into a nearby ditch. I sprained my ankle and we called the police. Beckett was hand-cuffed and taken away. A few days later, Beckett and Zoe were back together. I still didn't have an actual boyfriend and I was feeling more and more like maybe I didn't want one.

Jobs

Since I no longer had high school clogging up my schedule, I decided to get a full-time job. I was currently working part-time as a telemarketer, cold-calling people, asking if they wanted to buy gas from a different gas company than their current provider. I made ten dollars an hour. I had been doing this job since middle school. From 5 p.m. to 9 p.m. on weeknights and from 9 a.m. to 5 p.m. on Saturdays. It definitely was not legal for me to be working twenty-eight hours a week, but no one told me that.

I worked in a dirty cubicle in a shabby room filled with other teenagers. We each wore a headset and sat in front of a computer screen. I would call people in Ohio, interrupting their evening, and they would say, "How old are you? You sound like you're thirteen." And I would deepen my thirteen-year-old voice to try and sound older. But now that I was sixteen, I could get a better job and maybe even a legal one.

I began working at Ur Name Here, a small kiosk in the middle of Countryside Mall. The kiosk sold gold wire bent into the shape of first names. You could attach your golden first name to a necklace or earrings or a bracelet. Part of my training was learning how to bend gold wire into the shape of any name with small circular pliers, so if a passerby named Nicole, but with an obnoxious yet silent "K" in front of her name like "knock" or "knowledge," asked for a personalized necklace, I could whip up a "*Knicole*" necklace in thirty minutes or less. Sometimes people wanted something more intense than a name, like "*Baby-Girl*" or "*Bomb-Bitch*." And I would make them. I would silently judge their choice, but I would make them. The only other employee was the owner of the kiosk. She was a frizzy-haired blonde who had recently recovered from a brain tumor. I felt like brain tumors were following me around.

She trained me three times before she informed me that she had short-term memory loss from her brain tumor. I was so glad she told me because I felt like I was going insane. She repeated "Always make sure you tighten the loops on the '*Ls*' with the extra small pliers" so many times, I was starting to hear it in my dreams. I worked there for a year. She trained me pretty much every week for a year. So I got *very* good at making those names. I would make them for my friends, which I guess is stealing, but I considered it a reward for allowing this forgetful woman to train me so many times. I made a "*Zoe*" necklace and a "*Tori*" necklace and they wore them proudly. It was a rewarding job and the first creative thing I had done in years.

I was with my mom at a Scientology church when I saw a flier for mineral body wraps. I didn't know what that meant, but it claimed to take inches off your waist, smooth out your cellulite, and clear up your skin. I ripped the flier off the wall and brought it to my mother. We hadn't tried this yet, and I was still very much willing to try anything to clear up my face. A few days later, my mom brought me to a run-down spa. There were posters and fliers everywhere touting the wonders of the mineral body wrap.

A woman who smelled like cigarettes brought me to a back dressing room and told me to strip down to my underwear. She left me alone for a few minutes and then rejoined me, smelling even more like cigarettes, and started measuring my fat with a ratty measuring tape. She wrote down the thickness of my arms, legs, and belly and then began pulling ace bandages out of a hot metal box plugged into the wall.

The ace bandages were floating in a warm mineral solution that was supposed to be the answer to all health problems. She wrapped me head to toe in wet ace bandages. I made her put extra bandages on my face. Then she told me to get on the elliptical. Supposedly, working out while wearing the ace bandages was also the answer to all health problems. I looked like an Egyptian mummy at an LA Fitness. I worked out for twenty minutes and then was guided into a sauna.

After my sauna time was up, the woman, who somehow smelled even more like cigarettes, removed my bandages, measured me again, and insisted that I had lost a bunch of inches. I ignored her and examined my face in the smudged mirror. My skin looked slightly less red! I didn't know if it was the workout, or the sweat, or the minerals, but I wanted to do another wrap right away. I thought maybe if I did one every day, in a few months my face would be completely nonred.

On my way out, I asked the receptionist about pricing and learned that I could never afford to do one every day. But the receptionist informed me that they were currently training body wrap technicians and if I worked there, I could give myself free wraps. I had no other career prospects, so Body Wrap Technician seemed like a decent option.

I spent a weekend at that spa with three other trainees, learning all the tips and tricks for how to wrap someone in ace bandages and how to get them on an elliptical. Part of our training was wrapping each other. I got three wraps that weekend. After each wrap, I ran to the mirror. Was my skin less red? Sort of? Good enough for me! I threw myself into body wraps. They called me the most passionate trainee they had seen in a long time, mostly because I kept volunteering to be wrapped. "We need someone to get wrapped again, so we can show you guys the most common ways people slip and fall." My hand shot up. *I'll do it! I'll do anything for the team!*

After my training weekend, I learned that these body wraps might not have been quite as popular as they had led us to believe. Most of the days were spent sitting around waiting for customers to show up. But the owners had a way of making the technicians feel like the slowness was our responsibility, so they sent us out on the street to hand out fliers. I stood on busy streets handing out fliers, not unlike my brother was doing for Firehouse Subs, except my brother didn't have to deal with all the verbal abuse.

"What the fuck is that supposed to mean?!" A woman snapped at me after I handed out my first flier. She crumpled it up and threw it on the ground. I was confused. I looked at the fliers again and realized what was happening. I was handing out little pieces of paper with "Wrap Yourself Skinny" printed across them. The name of the company was offending people and I was the spokesperson.

Somehow, my job became fat shaming female strangers on the streets of Clearwater. Also, the enticing idea of getting free wraps wasn't actually true. Every time I tried to give myself one, I got guilted about wasting expensive products. So my face was still red and my future was still bleak.

Kay Jewelers

WHILE I WAS FAT SHAMING INNOCENT WOMEN AND BENDING GOLD WIRE into names, Zoe was working as a hostess at Ruby Tuesday, also in Countryside Mall. The same Ruby Tuesday my brother's seeing eye dog had turned into her own personal buffet months earlier. This was back when they still had smoking sections in restaurants; I would visit Zoe during her shift, fill my plate at the salad bar, eat endless salad, and suck down a pack of cigarettes while Zoe sat customers.

Zoe and I worked really hard, what felt like all the time, but we never had any money. Whenever we did have a little cash, we'd quickly spend it at T.J. Maxx. We'd buy Marc by Marc Jacobs sweaters, last season's Kate Spade purses, and pretty much any other item that made us feel a little less poor. One winter we spent quite a bit of money on white, puffy winter jackets. We loved those jackets. They made us feel fancy and rich. I felt like a woman who spent her winters in Aspen, although I didn't know if Aspen was a country or a resort, but I knew it was where rich people traveled.

Zoe would come over to my house and we would sit outside on my mom's front yard couch, drinking beer and smoking cigarettes. If you don't know what a front yard couch is then you've never been in a low-income neighborhood. It was a particularly cold winter; we were in the middle of a Florida freeze. So when we sat on my mom's front yard couch, we could feel ice cracking underneath our bodies.

My mom put one of those big orange Home Depot buckets filled with sand in front of the couch so we would put our cigarette butts in there instead of on the dying lawn. But we refused to put our cigarette butts in the bucket; flicking them on the lawn was too enticing. Zoe and I were sitting there when Zoe told me she thought she might be pregnant. We were wearing our white, puffy jackets when we drove to Eckerd drug store to get Zoe a pregnancy test. I was fifteen and she had just turned seventeen when we saw those two terrifying lines appear on that pregnancy test. One line means your life stays the same. Two lines mean your life changes forever.

Zoe didn't know what to do. All of our friends had been having abortions for years. No one had ever kept a baby. She called Beckett to tell him while he was at work in the shoe department at JCPenney, also at Countryside Mall. Beckett told her to have an abortion. Zoe's mom told her to have an abortion. Beckett's grandmother told her to have an abortion. She and I drove to the beach. We sat under a bridge and smoked and talked about how exciting it would be if she had a baby. I had no fucking clue what a baby meant, but it sounded so adorable and romantic.

We talked about Beckett and their toxic relationship. What had started as a small harmless relationship cyst had quickly grown into a cancerous relationship tumor. She didn't know what to do.

She said she wanted something of her own. She wanted a family. Her own family was so painfully broken. She wanted something that could be hers. Something that wouldn't leave her. I told her I'd be there for her no matter what she decided. Part of me really wanted her to keep it. I was so young and so naïve. We both were. We had no idea how impossibly challenging being a teen mom was going to be. Days later, she got an ultrasound and decided to stay pregnant.

The pregnancy was very hard on Zoe, but I had a blast. I helped her build the baby's furniture and figure out what to name it. We decorated the baby's room at Zoe's mom's house. Zoe's mom's house only had two bedrooms, so Zoe and the baby were going to have to share, but we made it really adorable with wallpaper and sweet little curtains.

Beckett was starting to get into heavier and heavier drugs and he would frequently disappear for weeks at a time. I would step in and take on the role of teen dad. I would rub Zoe's swollen feet and buy her bags of lemons—she craved lemons. She ate lemons covered in salt all day long, which is why her feet were so swollen. They looked like wide paddles. Zoe could've gone scuba diving with no flippers, her giant feet could've easily propelled her around the ocean. Her whole body was swollen, she gained seventy pounds and for some reason cut all of her hair off. Instead of an accidental teen mom, she looked like a late-in-life IVF mom.

Her self-esteem took a hit and she stopped constantly calling herself pretty. She was openly jealous of me, my empty womb, my nonswollen feet, my tan from hanging out with other nonpregnant teen girls at the beach, while she was at home trying to keep her paddle feet elevated. It was slowly dawning on her how massively life-changing this having a baby thing was.

Whenever she got depressed and tired of being pregnant, she would talk about how excited she was to meet her sweet baby. She couldn't wait for their new life to start. She was, however, more and more concerned with Beckett's drug use. She was also convinced he was cheating on her, but I would talk her down. "Beckett loves you," I would say. *But he's definitely cheating on you*, I would think.

One night, Zoe called me very worried. She told me she had a really bad feeling about Beckett. He hadn't answered his phone in days. Zoe was four days away from her due date. She was worried she would go into labor and Beckett wouldn't be around. It was moments like these that would make me remember, *Oh right, I'm not the dad, Beckett is and he'll probably want to be there for the birth.* She became determined to find Beckett. She asked me to come with her to do a drive-by.

There are two kinds of drive-bys: The first is when a gang member slowly drives by a house or a person, pulls out a gun and shoots at that house or person, and then drives away. The second is when sad, codependent teen girls, usually raised without fathers, slowly drive by the house of the person they're in love with to sneakily find out what they're up to. Zoe wanted to do the latter type of drive-by and she didn't want to do it alone.

Zoe picked me up and told me she had a strong suspicion Beckett was at his friend Kevin's house. Pretty much all of Beckett's friends hung out at Kevin's house. Kevin was kind, mild mannered, and the only person we knew who didn't live with his parents. So his house quickly became party central. I told Zoe we had to keep this drive-by very low-profile because I was going to a keg party at Kevin's that weekend and I didn't want everyone seeing me sneakily driving back and forth all night.

We drove by Kevin's and for the first time in the history of drive-bys, there was something vaguely interesting going on. Usually a drive-by consisted of looking at the house, confirming that your love's car was parked outside, and then driving away, but this time seven boys were standing outside. No one had ever been standing outside during a drive-by—things were heating up!

We ducked low in Zoe's car and they didn't notice us passing through. We parked a few houses down so we could spy from a safe distance. We quietly got out of Zoe's car and watched them drinking and talking shit to each other, spitting and flicking cigarettes on the lawn. A car pulled up and parked near us. A random boy got out of the car and started walking up behind us toward Kevin's house. When we noticed him walking toward us, we quickly dropped to the ground. Zoe was crouching down with her huge belly, trying not to crush her baby, while also trying not to be seen. I was lying on the street on my stomach. I looked under the car at Zoe, who was on her hands and knees. We locked eyes and held in a giggle at our ridiculous situation. After the random boy was far enough away from us, we slowly got back up on our feet to continue spying.

The scene was pretty boring. We could see that Beckett was among them and they were all laughing about something and clearly razzing each other. After ten minutes of watching this, I started thinking about how to convince Zoe to take me home. I was about to state my case when suddenly everything changed. Zoe gasped and I followed her gaze to one skinny blonde girl stepping outside of Kevin's house. One girl? Very odd. These weren't the type of boys that had girlfriends or even girl *friends*. They usually just hung out with other dudes, a pack of sausages, he-man woman haters club. Beckett had Zoe but he rarely brought her around his friends. Beckett and most of these boys treated women as other, and by other, I mean lesser.

Beckett often referred to women as "ribs." The part of the bible where God used one of Adam's ribs to make Adam a companion, thus creating womankind, was apparently the only part Beckett had read. So who was this pretty blonde "rib" hanging out alone with all of these "Adams?" As we were squinting trying to make out who this mystery girl was, Beckett walked over to his car and got something out of his trunk. The object was hanging from a strap; he slung it over his shoulder and started heading back to the group.

"What'd he just get outta his car?" I whispered to Zoe. She looked at me with a new level of anxiety in her eyes.

"His grandma's video camera . . ." *Oh shit.* In my town, boys only recorded themselves doing things that they would *not* want to come back and haunt them later in life. It was like they waited until they were about to do something deplorable, like getting a blow job from an underage girl or robbing a friend's weed plants, and then they'd hit record. All of their decent moments were lost forever. All of their shameful moments were caught on film.

The evidence against Beckett was mounting; Zoe and I had to get a closer look. We crept behind some bushes, a much better vantage point, but the group was starting to head inside Kevin's house. *Dammit.* Zoe looked panicked. She said she had a really bad feeling about all of this. She wanted to look inside the windows and find out who that girl was. I didn't want to be caught spying on these intimidating boys with my nine-months-pregnant friend, but I agreed to look in the windows with her.

Behind every window was an innocent scene: Kevin rolling a joint in the kitchen, a few boys playing video games in the living room—where was Beckett? When we reached the one remaining window we had yet to spy in, we heard moaning. Sex moaning. I got nauseous. Zoe couldn't move. She pushed me ahead to look in the window. There was Beckett, naked, with another boy, and that blonde girl. They were both having sex with her. It was a lot to take in.

"They're having sex." I mouthed to Zoe.

"What?!" she mouthed back.

"THEY! ARE! HAVING! SEX!" I mouthed back, still silent, but somehow louder.

"What do I do? What do I do?!" she mouthed to me.

Having no fucking clue what to do, I pressed my face up against the window and said loudly, "Hi, Beckett!" Beckett let out an animal sound, like a wolf who had just stepped on a trap. He opened the closet door and hid inside the closet. Zoe and I burst in the front door. The other boys who were innocently rolling joints and playing video games looked stunned; they knew Zoe, they knew she was pregnant, they knew Beckett was in the middle of a threesome. Zoe marched past them and opened the threesome door to find the other boy and the blonde girl weirdly pretending to have sex. The other boy said, "Get out! It's just two of us in here!" Which was a very funny, bad lie, but at least he tried.

Zoe opened the closet door to find Beckett naked and cowering. Zoe cussed him out, Jerry Springer style, while all the boys and the naked blonde girl watched. I noticed Beckett's grandmother's video camera blinking on the dresser. For some reason, I grabbed it. Zoe was now cussing at the blonde girl, who we knew from back when we were high school students. The blonde girl was trying to put her underwear on while Zoe was screaming at her. I was afraid Zoe was going to get in a fist fight and I didn't want this blonde girl to become a baby killer—I knew how hard that label was to shake—so I grabbed Zoe and forced her to leave with me. *Bye, y'all, see you at the keg party this weekend!*

We drove home in opposite states. Zoe was silent and deep in thought; I was hyperventilating and dramatic. I felt sick to my stomach. I made Zoe pull over and I dry heaved while my very pregnant friend, the one who was actually going through something, just sat there calmly. We huddled together on my washing machine in my garage and watched the amateur porn footage of the threesome we had just interrupted.

On the tape, Beckett mentioned all the recent times he'd had sex with that blonde girl. Last week. The week before. Zoe was quietly fuming. The next day, Zoe gave the video camera back to Beckett's grandmother; she didn't know what else to do with it. Zoe told Beckett's grandmother what was on the tape, but his grandmother never said another word about it.

Four days later, Zoe gave birth. When Beckett showed up at the hospital to be the loving baby daddy by Zoe's side, again I remembered, *Oh right, I'm not the dad, this guy is.* As much as I felt like a teen dad, I wasn't. I was Zoe's friend, not her boyfriend. And whenever Beckett came back into the picture, I was pushed to the side.

After the doctor told Zoe that she had to have an emergency C-section and she could only have two people in the operating room with her, I was genuinely hurt that she picked her mother and Beckett. I know that is insane. Beckett was the baby's father for Christ's sake, but I was the one who built all the baby's furniture. I was the one who brought Zoe whole milk and chocolate ice cream whenever she was craving the former poured over the latter in a tall glass cup. I felt like that baby was our baby. I knew it was Beckett's, but wasn't it also mine? I sat in the waiting room while Beckett put on scrubs and went into the operating room to record the birth of our baby with his *grandmother's video camera*.

I am very thankful that I was exposed to motherhood at such a young age; it was the best kind of birth control. Watching Zoe give up her whole teenage world to take care of this extremely needy, loud creature made me never want sperm anywhere near me. Her every move became a whole production. She couldn't leave her house without a thousand diapers, a million wipes, and enough snacks and juice boxes for a Little League team. There was nothing adorable or romantic about it.

It would take Zoe two hours just to get ready to go to the mall. To escape the oppressive Florida heat, we walked around the mall with her tiny newborn every day. People would stare at us, but we didn't care. We looked like unsupervised children pushing a baby around in a stroller and we knew it. For lunch, we went to Ruby Tuesday to take advantage of the cheap bottomless salad bar. We would park her infant in the nonsmoking section like responsible parents and then we would sit over in the smoking section and rip through a pack of cigarettes. I guess we weighed the options and decided that letting a baby get kidnapped was better than giving a baby lung cancer.

Eventually, Zoe and Beckett decided to move in together. Shortly after, Beckett proposed to Zoe. He gave her a small diamond ring from Kay Jewelers. He couldn't afford to buy the ring outright, so he put it on a payment plan. Months later, our local radio station had a contest: *Did you have a crush or were you crushed?* They asked the listeners to call in and tell their most heartwarming love story or their most heartbreaking betrayal story. They offered a prize to the teller of the best story. Zoe called in and told the whole story of her pregnancy, Beckett, and the threesome. Our local DJ was horrified. He said it was the worst story he had ever heard and he announced Zoe the winner. The prize? A one-hundred-dollar gift certificate to Kay Jewelers. She gave it to Beckett to help pay off her engagement ring.

J-E-L-L-O

M Y CRAVING FOR DRAMA WAS NOW SATIATED AND I WAS CRAVING STABIL- ity again. My mom helped me enroll in our local community college and I began acing my college level classes. *Maybe my sister's boyfriend was right about my IQ,* I thought as I, at sixteen years old, excelled beyond my older peers. It had been at least five years since I had received a good grade and I had started to see myself as dumb. College was giving me a much-needed self-image boost. My mom decided to enroll with me, since she never finished college, and we began taking courses together. I enjoyed studying with her; it felt like I had my mom all to myself whenever we were discussing our ethics course or cramming for an English exam.

My father, always looking for an opportunity to motivate me to better my life, told me he'd start paying me for my grades if I kept them up. He offered me one hundred dollars for every A and seventy-five dollars for every B. He knew I desperately wanted a car and he was never one to give me anything for free.

Back then, I used to fantasize about having a dad who would surprise me with a car. Every holiday season, I'd see those commercials where the teen girl steps outside to find a brand-new car with a red ribbon on it sitting in the driveway and I'd daydream about my dad surprising me with a car, or surprising me with any gift at all really. But I did not have that kind of dad. There were no surprises.

If I wanted something, I had to ask for it, and then he would present me with the longest, hardest possible way of attaining it. Back then, I hated that. Now, I'm eternally grateful. I have the work ethic of a pyramid-building Egyptian because I learned very early that doing the work is the only method of achieving anything . . . unless your life is like Jenny's, or Gabby's, or Haley's—then you just have to step outside your front door and that thing you wanted will be wrapped in a red ribbon on your driveway. And you know what? *Good for you.* And putting my bitterness and jealousy aside for a second, honestly, good for you. Life is long and filled with curveballs; receive those ribbon-wrapped surprise gifts with open arms. Accept your blessings.

Between the money my dad was giving me for my grades and the money I was earning wrapping women in wet ace bandages and making jewelry, I eventually had $3,000 saved to buy a car. I bought a 1993 Honda Civic with 123,000 miles on it and loved it like a daughter. It was bright red and reminded me of my sister's BMW that I had passionately driven the year before. I hung a polyester floral lei from the rearview mirror and installed loud, bass-thumping speakers in the trunk.

I felt like an unstoppable force. I was a high-performing college student and I had a car. Things were looking up. I was studying so much there was no time to drink or party. I had a real opportunity to get out of my own way and make something of myself, but then a nightclub called Greenbacks opened up in downtown Clearwater and I decided to go back to full-time partying instead.

Greenbacks was a bare-bones bar seven minutes from my mom's house. It was way more conveniently located than all the faraway Tampa nightclubs, but no one knew Greenbacks existed. I don't remember how my friends and I ended up there on a sleepy Thursday night, but I know we were very unimpressed. The club was sparsely populated and the owner kept hassling my friends and me, asking us if we wanted to Jell-O wrestle. *Do what now?* He gestured to a kiddie pool in the middle of the bar filled with chunks of clear Jell-O. *Oh, no, thank you.* He told us he had a vision of Greenbacks becoming a super hot nightclub. We laughed. Clearwater was known for its beaches, not its nightclubs. And looking around that lame bar, it was very obvious his vision was not going to come true.

Then he offered us a free bar tab in exchange for Jell-O wrestling. *I'm listening* . . . Then he offered us a free bar tab and one hundred dollars cash in exchange for Jell-O wrestling. *Go on* . . . Then he offered us a free bar tab, one hundred dollars, and one hundred extra dollars to the winner of the Jell-O wrestling match. *Sold.*

My two very tall friends, Charlene and Bridget, agreed to throw down in the pool of Jell-O with me. The owner led us to the Employees Only kitchen to change into oversized liquor-branded T-shirts and men's boxer shorts. Then he got on the bar microphone and introduced us to the crowd. "Hey fellas, you wanna see some bitches wrestle?!" The small, vaguely interested crowd gathered around the pool. The three of us stepped in. The Jell-O under our feet was slick and gooey and we walked carefully so as not to face plant.

Okay, now what? I wasn't exactly sure how to "wrestle" and I thought Charlene and Bridget were in the same boat, but they instantly body slammed each other and dragged me down with them. They were both freakishly strong and somehow, without speaking, they simultaneously decided the objective of the wrestling match was to rip each other's oversized T-shirts off. They tossed me around like a rag doll, quickly tore my shirt off, then kicked me to the other end of the pool, where I stayed, legs akimbo, mildly concussed, with my tits out. Through my blurred vision, I saw two men videotaping me, and the thought of those tapes existing somewhere in the world has haunted me ever since.

The small crowd was now keenly interested and they started to grunt their approval of the six Jell-O covered, underage breasts that were now a part of their evening. The owner was emceeing the match on the microphone. "It's hard to tell who the winner is here! Who gets the hundred dollars?!" I coughed up some clear gelatin and shakily pushed myself up to my knees. Charlene and Bridget were still womanhandling each other. Bridget had her vicelike hands on Charlene's boxer shorts and was pulling with all her might to expose Charlene's vagina to the engaged crowd.

The owner continued, "I guess I'll just throw the cash in the middle of the pool and whoever gets it first wins!" He tossed the cash in the center of the pool, but Bridget and Charlene were too busy trying to undress each other to notice. I weakly army crawled through the Jell-O to get to the money. I grabbed it and got out of the pool before either girl knew what happened.

"I guess . . . that girl won!" The owner said as I made my escape. The men surrounding the pool cheered; everyone loves an underdog story.

The next morning, I woke up feeling hungover from tequila and shame. I had never let strangers see my boobs before. Every year on Mardi Gras, we would drive to Tampa and walk along the parade route. Girls our age would flash their tits for cheap beads that they could've easily bought in a store for a few dollars with their shirts on. I looked down on those girls. Even though my vantage point was from the basement, I still managed to look down on a lot of people. I promised myself I would never show my boobs to strangers. During my first Mardi Gras, when I was thirteen, a drunk male reveler shouted at me, while waving enticing beads, "Hey! Show me your tits!"

"No, I have too much respect for myself," I replied, and he looked lucid for a second, like he briefly recognized that I was a human being and not just a bead-thirsty pair of heaving fat sacks that couldn't wait to get out in the fresh night air.

"Aw, man, I love that," he said approvingly. Then he gave me a thick handful of beads. I ended that evening with more beads than some of the flashing girls around me and "I have too much respect for myself" became my Mardi Gras catchphrase.

Our local radio station, 97X, threw a concert every year in a big open grassy field near the ocean. One year, Everclear was set to perform at the 97X concert and I absolutely had to go see them. Their song "Father of Mine," about a kid who missed his absentee father, really resonated with me. There is one lyric about being a scared white boy in a Black neighborhood that is offensive and perpetuates a stereotype, but all the longing for a father stuff felt like someone wrote an essay about my daddy issues and sang it to me.

At the concert, I begged my friend to squeeze up close to the stage so I could sit on his shoulders. When we made it toward the front

and I climbed up on his shoulders, I was blown away by my prox-
imity to Art Alexakis (the lead singer of Everclear—don't act like
you didn't know that). I was dancing and waving my arms, singing
along with Art as he lamented about his father's neglect. I noticed
all the girls around me who were sitting on someone's shoulders
were flashing their breasts at the band, and the stagehands, to thank
those girls for flashing their breasts, were spraying them down with
powerful water hoses.

Eventually, the nearby crowd noticed I had the audacity to sit
on shoulders and not show my breasts and they started chanting at
me, "Show your tits! Show your tits!" I laughed and politely waved
them away. Which was my usual defense against sexual harassment.
After a few minutes of the chanting, a camera man stopped filming
the band and started filming me. Now I was projected on the giant
screens that were supposed to be projecting Art Alexakis's angsty
face to the entire venue. More and more people chanted, "Show
your tits!" until the entire seventeen-thousand-person crowd was
chanting, "Show your tits!"

I felt uncomfortable on account of the mass harassment, but
also thrilled on account of the mass attention. I kept shaking my
head "no" and this riled the people up even more. The stagehands
started spraying me with all the water hoses. Their thought process
seemed to be, if her shirt gets *really* wet, maybe she'll want to take
it off. But I managed to stay strong. Art Alexakis was screaming
about the bottomless hole of abandonment that he fell into after
his father left while the crowd was screaming, "Show your tits!"

My sweet friend, let's call him Shoulders, finally looked up at
me and yelled, "Are you okay? Do you wanna get down?" That option had not crossed my mind before that point. I gratefully got
down and a nearby security guard grabbed Shoulders and me and

asked if we wanted to go backstage. I didn't know if this was just a nice gesture or an attempt to prevent the crowd from rioting over my selfishness with my own body. Either way, Shoulders and I slid backstage. We didn't get to meet Everclear, but we did smoke a joint with Unwritten Law (look them up, it's a cool brag, trust me).

A few weeks later, I was at a party when an older male stranger approached me with wide eyes and asked if I was "the 97X girl." After I confirmed his assumption, he said, "Man, that was so nuts. I felt really bad for you. I can't wait to tell my friends that I met you . . . and that you're okay." I was stoked! I was famous for not showing my breasts! And apparently, some people I didn't know felt really bad for me, which I guess is also cool!

Anyway, the point is, I had survived the pressure of seventeen-thousand people demanding that I expose myself, but somehow one Jell-O wrestling match later and there I was, a girl who let strangers see her tits, accidentally, but still. *I bet Julia Roberts has never Jell-O wrestled with her shirt ripped off*, I thought, *I guess I can kiss my acting career goodbye.* I vowed never to return to Greenbacks.

But later that day, my extremely skilled Jell-O wrestling partner Bridget excitedly informed me that Bubba the Love Sponge, a problematic shock jock on one of our local radio stations, was talking about our Greenbacks Jell-O wrestling match *on the friggin' radio*. She said Bubba the Love Sponge heard about it from some dude who happened to be there. He said the girls were unhinged and the wrestling was lawless, and he encouraged his listeners to check out Greenbacks in quiet downtown Clearwater.

After that, Greenbacks exploded. Every high school girl within a twenty-mile radius, with any excuse for a fake ID, would line up to Jell-O wrestle at Greenbacks. The bar was packed every single night. The owner remembered my friends and me and gave us special treatment, but I never Jell-O wrestled again.

That's a lie. I Jell-O wrestled one more time, but only because I *really* needed the prize money. Plus, I had learned to keep my shirt tightly pulled down, so the second time no one saw my breasts. I eventually started emceeing the wrestling matches because the owner liked me and I would sarcastically announce the play-by-plays over the microphone in exchange for a free bar tab.

I remember standing at the microphone making all sorts of sexist, antifeminist announcements, but mercifully I have blocked out exactly what filth I spewed. "Look at these dumb ass bitches!" feels familiar, but I don't want to think about it too much. The whole thing is a blemish on my record and I'd very much like to banish it back to the far-reaching corners of my mind. The owner kept upgrading the place and even hired professional cameramen to film the wrestling matches. The footage was displayed live on TV screens throughout the bar, so patrons could see gelatinous breasts and vaginas from any seat in the house.

During Greenbacks's successful run, Liquid Blue opened their doors. Liquid Blue was also located in downtown Clearwater. It was an upscale version of Greenbacks. The lighting was swankier, the walls were mirrored, the dress code for men was greasy-douchebag-business-casual, the dress code for women was attention-starved-call-girl. They even had a classier take on the Jell-O filled kiddie pool: Fight Night.

Every Friday night, Liquid Blue installed a full-on boxing ring in the middle of the club and encouraged drunk, fancily dressed clubgoers to beat the living shit out of each other. They would supply boxing gloves and anyone could fight anyone who was willing. Dudes would use it as a chance to display their masculinity. Girls who hated each other would finally have a chance to exchange blows. Two best friends would glove up, get in the ring, and during the course of the boxing match, become lifelong enemies. I managed to avoid having to box anyone in my high heels and miniskirts, but I did watch a lot of people get their noses broken in an establishment meant for suggestive dancing and shouting meaningless conversations over loud music.

Between Greenbacks and Liquid Blue, I was getting blackout drunk at least four nights a week. I weighed one hundred pounds and I could drink nine beers and four shots and still walk around. But who was taking my friends and me to these bars? How were we getting there? Well, I was driving us, of course. My sweet little red Civic that I loved so much became the most dangerous car on the road.

I was drinking copious amounts of alcohol, getting behind the wheel, and then waking up in my bed with no memory of driving all the way home or of dropping all my friends off. I got away with this despicable behavior for a few months and then one horrific night, I almost killed one of my best friends and myself.

I was driving away from an evening of getting absolutely shitcanned and my precious friend was in the front seat next to me—BLACKOUT.

I was back at my mom's and she was dunking my head in our bathtub filled with water and slapping me in the face while I was sobbing—BLACKOUT.

I woke up in bed the next morning with a sore arm. I had such a heavy feeling of dread but no memory of what happened. I vaguely remembered we were in some kind of accident and I thought about my friend. Was she okay? I sat up and realized she was sleeping next to me.

After she woke up, she explained that we were driving out of a gated community and the gate was closing, but I drove through it and clipped the gate. My car spun off the road and I was weaving in and out of trees, crashing into some, missing others. The car in front of us stopped and the people got out to make sure we were okay, but I was belligerent. They got my friend and me out and then drove my totaled car, on its sparking rims, to an empty parking lot. They left my car there and drove us home.

I was so hammered and sobbing so loudly that my mom woke up and dunked my head under cold bathtub water and slapped the shit out of me repeatedly, maybe to sober me up or maybe because she was furious. All the other scenarios that could have taken place ran through my mind. My friend could be dead. I could be dead. I could have killed some innocent stranger. I could have killed a child. Or, way less severe but also terrible, I could've gotten a much-deserved DUI, gone to jail, lost my license, and had to pay more money in fines then I had ever earned in my entire life. I threw up all morning and avoided talking to my mom, or even worse, my dad. The shame was strangling me. I wanted to be a good, responsible person so badly, but I kept making the choices of a bad, grossly irresponsible one.

My mom could not believe I was adding myself to her already overwhelming list of problems. There wasn't enough room in our house for two drunk-driving alcoholics trying to do themselves in. After my mom told my dad everything, he called and told me I was on my own. He would not help me buy a new car or pay to fix the old one. Ever since I was ten years old, my parents had let me do whatever I wanted—no curfew, no rules, no boundaries—and whenever that unique parenting plan went wrong, they were very disappointed in me for not raising myself right.

I had to figure out how to get to the community college and to my two jobs without a car. I slowly earned the money to fix my old car. My insurance wouldn't cover it because I had the cheapest policy possible. So I had to pay the $1,500 myself. That was over half the cost of the car and an astronomical sum to me at the time. By the time my car was fixed, my parents had forgiven me, but I was at least fifteen years away from forgiving myself. To this day, every time I hear about some devastatingly tragic loss of innocent life due to drunk driving my heart stops. *That could've been me. I could've taken that life.* And I feel the guilt all over again.

Because I had been partying so much, I had gradually decreased the number of college classes I was taking each semester and was down to just one. At that rate, I would graduate in ten years with a two-year degree. I knew I needed a change. A big one. I wasn't strong enough to turn my life around on my own, so you're not going to believe this but . . . I decided to move back to Los Angeles.

Los Angeles Again

I WAS NOW SEVENTEEN YEARS OLD AND I DECIDED THAT, THIS TIME, MY MOVE to Los Angeles would be permanent. To prove to myself that I was never coming back to Florida, I packed up every single thing I owned and stuffed it into my freshly refurbished Honda Civic. No need to leave anything behind. I was never coming back. Never ever. I was moving to LA to live with my dad and clean up my life . . . again. I was going to start my acting career and, as long as those Jell-O wrestling videos didn't surface, nothing was going to stop me. I needed a friend to drive with me—thirty-six hours was too long for one person—and for some reason, everyone I knew was busy except Charlene.

Charlene and I had never been super close, like I was with Zoe or Tori, but she was a very good, trustworthy friend, who had gotten her ass kicked for me by the Scary Sisters a few years earlier. She was the calmest person I had ever met—absolutely nothing could rile her up. She never got angry and I never heard her say a negative word about anyone. She smoked a lot of weed and spoke very slowly in a deep voice that didn't match her delicate features. Like Zoe, she was white and had a Black boyfriend and was thrown into our bad girl group because of that. I cannot stress enough how deplorably racist these kids were.

Charlene was almost a foot taller than me. She was thick and muscular; if I was a twig, she was an oak tree. She drove a white Ford Taurus, an old cop car she bought at a police auction. That solid, dependable car suited her perfectly. Her astrological sign was also a Taurus and that symbol of the sturdy bull lined up with her energy exactly.

When it was time for me to leave, I said goodbye to Max. My brother's hearing was completely gone by then and we'd all had to learn sign language so we could communicate. Since he still couldn't see, he would feel our hands, Helen Keller–style, as we spelled out words and certain phrases. We weren't fluent in sign language by any stretch, but we knew enough words to get by.

We also carried a small magnetic white board with a bag of multicolored plastic letter magnets, the kind normally used to stick on refrigerators. If we couldn't explain something to Max with sign language, we would spell the word out on the white board and he would slowly feel each magnetized letter to try and work out the message. He had undergone at least three different brain surgeries by this point, so grasping these messages became harder and harder.

I was trying to explain to him that I was moving back to Los Angeles, but I didn't know if he understood me. Finally, I just hugged him for a really long time and eventually he said, "Are you leaving for a while or something?" I nodded "yes" against his shoulder so he could feel it. I was sobbing, but he didn't know that. He just put his arm around me and said, "Okay, well, I'll see you soon, Late." He maintained a generally cheerful disposition throughout his entire battle with cancer. Everyone around him was a heartbroken mess and he would just chat about his day or whatever thoughts he was having with a smile on his face. I finally drove away and cried all the way to Charlene's mom's house to pick up Charlene.

Charlene's mom was a very pretty, young, single mother. All of my friends' moms were single mothers; that was the one thing we all had in common. Charlene's mom had that *if you're going to drink and smoke weed, I'd rather you do it here in the safety of our home* mentality and would frequently drink and smoke pot with us. She was not an overly protective mother, but the thought of Charlene driving across the country without her made her maniacal with worry.

When I left my house earlier, with the intention of never coming back, my mom looked up from signing a word into my brother's hand, while ripping a bottle of vodka out of her husband's, and said, "Bye! Good luck out there!" But Charlene was only leaving for two weeks and her mom was trying not to cry while she put pieces of blue tape next to each lock in my car to remind us to always lock our doors.

She videotaped us as we were leaving so she would have "something to show the police" if anything happened to us. And she made us solemnly swear that if a cop tried to pull us over, we would drive to the nearest exit and pull over at a gas station near witnesses (because she had seen a news story where a rapist stole a cop car and used it to pull over an unsuspecting young woman in the middle of the night). She really nailed this home with all kinds of gory descriptions of the young woman's mangled body until we promised not to get pulled over by an undercover rapist.

And sure enough, in the middle of the night, as Charlene was driving through a desolate Texas landscape on the 10 West, a cop car appeared behind us flashing its lights. We were very stoned and Charlene's mom's words of warning filled our paranoid minds.

"What do I do?" Charlene asked slowly in her deep, vaguely Southern drawl.

"Slow down, move to the right lane, and put on your hazards," I said quickly. We didn't want to pull over because the chance that the cop was a rapist wasn't one we were willing to take. I kept looking back at the cop car. The siren turned on. Somehow the car itself seemed to be getting angrier and angrier.

"Pull. The. Car. Over." A frustrated voice blared out of the loudspeaker behind us.

"Does that sound like a rapist?" Charlene asked.

"I don't know what a rapist sounds like!" I said anxiously.

"Yeah-huh, you remember Braydon who used to always hang out at Frenchie's? He raped a girl."

"What?!"

"I'm just saying, you've heard him talk," she said matter-of-factly.

We debated writing WE ARE AFRAID YOU ARE A RAPIST on a piece of paper and pressing it to the back window. But the only paper we had was rolling papers. We saw a sign that claimed an exit with a gas station was ten miles away.

"Okay, ten miles," I said, trying to keep calm, "and we're going sixty miles an hour. So we'll be there in . . . an hour?" College math was working wonders for me.

". . . Ten minutes," Charlene corrected me, after way too long of a pause.

We sighed, feeling relieved, ten minutes was doable. But it turns out that ten minutes, when you're in a slow-speed chase with a

Texas cop, who might be a Texas rapist, feels like a very long time. That voice on the loudspeaker kept urging us to pull over. We kept ignoring it.

Finally, we reached our exit and smoothly left the freeway with that furious unidentified person in a cop car still following us. The gas station was luckily right by the exit. We approached it, ready to put this whole thing behind us, and were genuinely surprised to find six cop cars, all with their lights flashing, parked at the gas station, where twelve cops, all with their guns drawn, were waiting for us.

"Oh shit, I guess it was a real cop," Charlene said as I quickly stuffed our remaining bag of weed into my underwear.

The cops, who simply were not fucking around at this point, demanded that we get out of the car with our hands up. We complied. They kept their guns on us as a few officers rushed toward us and patted us down, narrowly missing the bag of weed nestled in front of my pubic bone. They handcuffed us, separated us, and questioned us individually about why the hell we didn't pull over. I told them the same story Charlene did. We told them the truth. But they didn't believe us. They said it was too stupid. We just shrugged; *I don't know what to tell ya.*

They searched my entire car, filled to the brim with all of my belongings, looking for something incriminating that would explain why we didn't pull over. One cop, thankfully, thought to call Charlene's mom to ask her about the story and when she proved that she was also very stupid, they relaxed. Then they started laughing at us.

They told us we were lucky we pulled over when we did because they put spikes in the road just past the exit to deflate our tires. They gave Charlene a speeding ticket, which is why they were pulling us over in the first place, and they slapped her with a misdemeanor resisting arrest charge. She was eighteen and I was seventeen so she got the harsher punishment. Then they let us go.

I shudder to think what would've happened if we had been dark-skinned people rather than light-skinned people—we got off *very* easy. An officer even asked us if we needed an escort into town to find lodging for the night. I think he assumed we had extremely low IQs and didn't want to leave us alone. We drove behind him to a motel. After he drove away, when we were safely tucked inside our motel, I removed the weed from my underwear and we smoked it immediately.

Three speeding tickets later, all of which we quickly pulled over to the side of the road to receive, we arrived in Los Angeles. We drove to Burbank to stay at my dad's, on the same old air mattresses, but in a new apartment complex. Since there were no child-molesting, struggling actors to flirt with at my dad's new place, Charlene really wanted to go party in Hollywood, but I was trying to turn over a new leaf. She argued that she was flying back to Florida in one week and, after she left, I could enjoy my boring new leaf for the rest of my lame life. *Damn*, she made a good point.

That evening, we made our way to Sunset Boulevard to check out the famed Sunset Strip in West Hollywood, but I wasn't going to get drunk. Drinking and driving was no longer an option in my mind. We went to a western-themed bar called Saddle Ranch and I rode a mechanical bull. By "rode" I mean that the bull flung me off and across the room a millisecond after it began to move. After I confirmed none of my limbs were broken, we met a group of firemen and they started plying Charlene with drinks. They invited us to come with them to the Body Shop, a famous strip club down the street. I had never been to a strip club and was intrigued by the prospect.

After we skirted past the Body Shop doorman with our fake Florida IDs and found a seat near the stage, I noticed how absolutely hammered Charlene was. She was slurring her words and began heckling the strippers. I tried to silence her, but the firemen were getting a kick out of it.

One of them leaned into Charlene and said jokingly, "Why are you talking shit? You couldn't do better."

"Yeah-huh," Charlene said and before I could do anything about it, she climbed up on the stage. She was taller and more zaftig than all the other strippers and quickly caught the attention of the entire club. She was taking her pants off as I was trying to pull her back down to her seat. She strutted around in her platform shoes, thong underwear, and halter top, with one hand on her beer and the other on a stripper pole.

The crowd started to cheer because they knew she was a civilian and it was apparent this kind of thing didn't happen often. Charlene tried to get her halter top off, but the knot was stuck around her neck. She struggled with it for a very awkward length of time while the crowd cheered her on.

She finally gave up on taking her shirt off and just kept strutting around the stage, "Donald Ducking" in a shirt with no pants, until a manager came over and said, "Get your fucking friend out of here." I was trying to collect Charlene while she was trying to collect all the one-dollar bills people had tossed at her during her brief tenure as a stripper. Finally, she climbed down and I got us out of there. But not before we received a lifetime ban from the Body Shop.

"I made forty-two bucks," she said proudly as we walked to my car. "Would'a made more if I had got my damn shirt off."

After a few more romps around the Los Angeles touristy night scene, Charlene left. I cried after I dropped her off at the airport.

My loyal, funny, beautiful friend was gone. My father was going to take me to the Burbank Ikea to buy me some real bedroom furniture. I really was never going back to Florida. I'll tell you what happened next only if you promise not to judge me. . . . Less than a year later, I was rollerblading in Venice beach and fell, broke my wrist, and quickly moved back to Florida.

In my defense, I felt like I had no choice. I had been waitressing at Coral Cafe in Burbank and Wokcano in West Hollywood and I couldn't very well keep waitressing with a broken wrist. And my father, always looking for an opportunity to teach me responsibility, was making me pay for things like soap, toilet paper, and paper towels.

A few months before I broke my wrist, he had asked me to bring the rent check to the front office and I forgot. When we were slapped with a $300 late fee, he made me pay it. No daughter of his was going to grow up to be a lazy, forgetful, ne'er-do-well. The point is, I needed all my jobs and I couldn't keep any of my jobs with a broken wrist. I also couldn't keep cleaning the toilet and kitchen, my mandatory chores at my dad's apartment, although, I'm sure he would've given me a few months off toilet duty if I had asked.

Also, back in Florida, my brother's health was careening downhill and it began to slowly dawn on me that he might not live very long. A fact that almost every doctor knew, but one I simply could not absorb. Also, when baby falls down and breaks her wrist, baby wants mommy. All of these excuses felt like enough to warrant me flying back home to Florida with my right forearm in a hard cast and my tail firmly planted between my legs.

Another reason I kept returning over and over again to the place and living situation that felt so chaotic and unstable I didn't learn until recently. In a book called *The Body Keeps the Score*, I read about an experiment done on mice who had essentially been traumatized by scientists throughout their mouse childhoods. The scientists played random, really loud noises and periodically withheld food from the baby mice, creating the feeling of a stressful, turbulent upbringing.

When the mice were adults, the scientists introduced them to a stable, calm nest with a steady food supply, but anytime the mice were disturbed or scared, they scurried home to their former loud, unstable nest—no matter what. They did similar experiments with other animals and finally concluded that "scared animals return home, regardless of whether home is safe or frightening." When I read that, it turned on so many lightbulbs.

Suddenly, I understood all the people I knew who had gone back to terrifying relationships that mirrored their parent's terrifying relationship, and all the times I had put myself in stressful situations that mirrored my own stressful childhood. It was a real eye-opener, but when I was seventeen my eyes were still shut tight, so I packed my stuff and flew back to my former loud, unstable nest.

Purif

I WAS NERVOUS ABOUT SEEING ALL MY OLD FLORIDA FRIENDS. I WISHED I had more to show for my time in Los Angeles. I wished I had at least something, truly anything, to brag about, but I really had not accomplished a single thing in the entire ten months I had been gone. I had not become a famous actress and I still had really brutal acne. My dad tried to help me on both counts.

To help my acting career, he paid for me to get some headshots that, even after severe airbrushing, were still really bad headshots. Airbrushing helped erase the acne, the rosacea, the acne scars, and the plastic Invisalign brackets glued to my front teeth, but the airbrushing did not make me look less deathly pale. I think my depression was keeping me away from the sun, and rather than a vibrant, golden-skinned mixed-race girl, I looked like an icy Victorian bride who was about to get married against her will.

Also, the woman I paid to style my hair for the photo shoot took one look at my tight curls and said, "Um . . . looks good to me! I don't think you even need me to do anything." Which is code for "I have no fuckin' clue how to style your ethnic hair. I went to White Hair School not All Hair School, so you are on your own." The photographer snapped away while my lifeless hair just hung thickly over my shoulders like a poodle's overgrown pelt. Somehow, in those headshots, I look both very hot from the weight of my unstyled hair and very cold from the chilling tone of my skin. My depressed eyes stare hauntingly into the lens, full of hope that these photos will make me a very famous actress someday and full of knowing that they definitely will not.

I recently showed those headshots to my dad. "Do you remember these headshots you got me? They're pretty terrible, huh?" I said, baiting him into telling me that they are of course gorgeous and I am insane.

Instead, he looked at them for a long time and said, "Well, honey, we were all going through a really rough time back then."

Jesus, can you please just lie to me? Anyway, the headshots were undeniably bad and they did not lead to Hollywood banging down my door. My father also wanted to help me with my skin and suggested I do a Scientology Purification Rundown to see if that would help clear up my face.

According to scientology.org, "The Purification Rundown is a tightly supervised regimen of exercise, sauna and nutrition. It is conducted in a properly ordered schedule to include sufficient rest. In combination, it results in the elimination of drug residues and other toxins from the body's fatty tissues." My dad thought maybe toxins were the cause of my breakouts. That word "toxins" had been following me around since I was ten years old, since that first little pimple. But when I was ten, there were no real toxins in my body. Now there was a very long list: countless cigarettes, thousands of fast-food meals, hundreds of gallons of alcohol, and radiation from tanning in the sun every day back in Florida. I was very eager to rid my body of all of those toxins, so my dad paid $3,000 for me to do the Purification Rundown, or "Purif," as real Scientologists call it. At this point in my life, I did not consider myself a Scientologist, but I was truly willing to try anything.

I did my Purif at the Celebrity Centre in Hollywood, which is the actual name of a Scientology church. Before Scientology bought and poorly renamed the Celebrity Centre, it was a Hollywood hotel that housed impressive guests like Cary Grant and Katharine Hepburn. Grandiosity and opulence compete with a haunted dustiness to create that genuine old Hollywood feeling in the hallways of the Château Élysée, as the hotel was formerly known. The Purif took place in the basement of the historical hotel and the Purif program worked like this: I would show up, run on a treadmill for thirty minutes, then sit in the sauna for four hours. Yes, four hours is a very long time.

The good news is I was allowed to leave the sauna as often as I wanted to cool down, and there were board games, and books, and cards, and all sorts of damp, sweat-covered activities taking place inside the sauna that made the time go by faster. There were about fifteen other people doing the Purif with me. And we were all directed to drink half a cup of vegetable oil every day to "replace the toxic fat we were losing" and take a cocktail of many different vitamins, including thousands of milligrams of niacin. Yes, that is a lot of niacin.

The niacin would cause an intense flush reaction that felt like severe hives. We were told that the reaction was toxins leaving the body. The average person does the Purif for about fourteen days, the exception being people who have done a lot of heavy drugs—they usually do it for a bit longer. But I, at seventeen years old and with no serious drug use in my past, was on the Purif for sixty days. Yes, that is a lot of days.

I was there longer than anyone else. People riddled with so-called toxins were coming and going quickly, but I was there for two solid months. This happened because there is only one way to end your Purif; you need to have a mind-blowingly incredible experience. This experience was referred to as an "End Phenomenon" and I couldn't wait to have one. Apparently, I would know this indescribably wonderful feeling as soon as I felt it, but several weeks in, I still hadn't felt it.

Finally, I went to my course supervisor and asked, "Hey, I've been here longer than anyone else. So . . . am I done?" She responded meaningfully, "I don't know, *are you?*" Since I still hadn't had my orgasmic "End Phenomenon," I really just wanted her to tell me I was done. But she refused, so I just kept showing up week after week and asking her if I was done, then she would turn around and ask *me* if I was done, but I still hadn't had my amazing feeling, so this went on and on. Meanwhile, everyone around me was sweating for two weeks, announcing an eruption of overwhelming joy and clarity, and whistling out the door.

Midway through, I was approached by a young man in a blue uniform. He was in his early twenties and a member of the Sea Org, a group of Scientologists who volunteer full-time for the church, sort of like nuns or priests. He was very warm and amiable and he started walking me to my car every day and talking to me about my long-term goals. I told him I wanted to be an actress and we talked a lot about that. I showed him my awful new headshots and he winced, but lied to me and said they were great. Take note, Dad!

After a few weeks of this, he asked me to meet him in a nearby office when I was done sweating for the day. Later that day, I entered the office to find my new friend and a few other adult men I didn't know. They were all wearing uniforms—some even had medals pinned to their chests like military officers. They were all smiling and extremely friendly and they gently asked me if I wanted to help them save the planet. "Um, what do you mean?" I said, feeling self-conscious in my workout clothes, with my matted hair caked to my sweaty, pimple-dusted forehead.

"Well, we think you would be a really great fit for the Sea Org." They handed me a Sea Org contract. I glanced at it and quickly read that signing it would commit me to joining the Sea Org for one billion years.

"One billion years? That sounds crazy long," I said, glancing at the door.

"It's just a symbol, to show your commitment to the church. In reality, it would just be for the rest of this lifetime, but people do sometimes return to the Sea Org in their next lifetime," one of the men said, smiling.

"Okay, but I really wanna be an actress and—"

"So you don't want to help mankind?"

"Um . . . I guess not?"

"What are you hoping to gain from Scientology? What made you want to do your Purif?" he asked, hoping that maybe my answer would reveal my deeper side.

"I, um . . . wanted to clear up my skin." They all just stared at me, still smiling, but I could feel their disappointment with me. I felt disappointed with myself. My mom already thought I was the most selfish person on the whole planet, and now these nicely dressed men did too. Plus, I felt a little woozy from all the niacin and sweating. I really just wanted to get the hell outta there. I hastily made my exit.

As I walked down the hall, away from that contract, I felt such a strong pang of guilt. I wished so much that I was the kind of person who wanted to volunteer for the rest of her life, and maybe even future lifetimes, to help save the planet, but that just wasn't me.

It turns out, a couple of years later, the young man who tried to get me to join him for one billion years broke his multilifetime contract and quit the Sea Org to become a fashion photographer. I guess he didn't really want to save the planet either.

Putting my guilt aside, I still had to figure out how to eventually stop doing the Purif. I was starting to give up on my dream of experiencing my miraculous End Phenomenon. In my dream, I would be sitting in the sauna and then I would suddenly be overcome with a feeling of weightlessness and pure ecstasy. I would finally understand myself and everyone else, then my face would heal, and I would go out into the world with clear skin and boundless energy. But it was seeming more and more like that dream would never come true and I really just wanted to get back to my nonsweaty life.

I talked it over with my fellow sauna mates. Everyone listened to my plight as we were wrapping up a salty, damp game of gin rummy. I had become the Purif veteran and I knew everyone really well. I was a fixture there, like the soggy board games and the nausea-inducing vegetable oil. I had been there at least a month longer than all the red-faced, sweat-drenched people I was complaining to.

Finally, a heroin-addicted girl in her twenties, who was there because her parents were strongly encouraging her to be, wiped the heavy beads of moisture off of her face and said, "You just gotta lie. Tell your course supervisor that you feel amazing, like you could fly right out the fuckin' window. Tell them that you know you are one hundred percent done and then, voilà!" I thought she was pranking me. There's no way it was that easy. Then the girl told me this was her third Purif and she guaranteed me it would work.

I went upstairs and told my supervisor exactly what that girl had said and she was right. I was done. I got all of my belongings and headed out the door forever, finally free! I felt amazing! *Maybe <u>this</u> is an End Phenomenon?* I thought as I happily floated to my car. Thank God for that heroin-addicted girl. If not for her, I might've remained in that sauna for the rest of this lifetime. When I got in my car, I flipped down the sun visor, opened the mirror flap, and saw that my acne looked . . . exactly the same as it had sixty days ago, which was a bummer, but at least I had gotten really good at playing gin rummy.

But my new gin rummy skills were not going to impress my Florida friends so I kept all that Purif stuff to myself. When I arrived back in Clearwater, I just told everyone, "I'm probably, most likely, almost certainly very close to becoming a famous actress; I just had to come home on account of my broken wrist and because my brother's getting sicker, but in a few years, I'm gonna go back to LA to finish up the whole becoming a famous actress thing." I don't know if I actually believed I would ever go back to LA, but that was my official homecoming story.

L-O-V-E

WHEN I ARRIVED HOME, I WAS SHOCKED BY MY BROTHER'S APPEARance. He had just undergone another brain surgery and the swelling was so intense that the surgeons could not put his head back together afterward. They said they had to let the swelling go down before they could put his skull back on, so for a few months, a quarter of his head was just soft exposed brain matter with only skin to protect it. This caused his head to look misshapen, bulging in some parts and shrunken in others.

We had to be very cautious around him and he had to be extremely careful not to bump his head. But he couldn't see, so bumping his head was the norm. There is no scenario more tense than a visually impaired kid with his brain exposed to the elements walking through the house. My mom and I became human shields, clearing a path in front of him and moving anything that could even come close to bumping his soft head.

Then, in case that wasn't challenging enough for him, another one of his faculties began to deteriorate. He was becoming less and less able to walk and he would have to sit and take breaks for long periods. He began using the furniture to sort of carry himself through the house. It took us a little while to realize that, eventually, he wasn't using his legs at all.

He would push himself up off the couch with his arms and then use the couch as a grab bar until he could feel around for a coffee table or something that he could put all of his weight on, then he would move on to the next piece of furniture, all through the house. When a doctor suggested he start using a wheelchair, it was a big relief for everyone. I think we needed someone outside the family to suggest it because the thought of my highly athletic, agile brother needing a wheelchair was impossible for us to fathom, no matter how obvious it was.

The wheelchair brought immense relief to the household. My brother could get around much more easily and he was less likely to bump his brain. As my brother's legs got weaker and weaker, my mom's upper body strength became more and more superhuman from lifting her six-foot-two son in and out of his wheelchair all day. At first, she asked me to help her, but she quickly realized my musculature was so useless that me helping her was the same as her doing it by herself.

Max loved when one of us would push him around the neighborhood in his new wheelchair. He couldn't see or hear, but he drank in the fresh air and relished the thought that someone was spending time with him, just him, with no other distractions. The most common words we would sign into his hand were "walk" and "wait." We signed "walk" when we were ready to take him for a walk and "wait" when he was asking over and over to go on a walk and couldn't see or hear that my mom was in the middle of doing the dishes or I was in the middle of doing my makeup, or painting my nails, or some other important thing.

Finally, my mom or I would take him for a walk around the neighborhood and he would chatter on cheerfully about memories of skateboarding with his friends or what he ate for breakfast that day. He couldn't hear our responses so he would just plow through and fill in both sides of the conversation.

A friend of mine lost her mother suddenly and afterward she told me, "I wish I would've told her I loved her more often. Now that she's gone, that's all I can think about. Did she know how much I loved her? Did I tell her enough?" This terrified me. We didn't know if Max was about to die or about to live, blind, deaf, and in a wheelchair, for sixty more years, but I didn't want to take the chance of not telling him that I loved him often enough. One day, I sat in front of his wheelchair, determined to make sure he knew how much I loved him. I used sign language. I spelled out "L" and "O" into his hand.

He guessed, "L-O? Lo? Lu? Lunch? Lunch is ready?"

I signed the word "no" into his hand. And then started over. "L" and "O" and "V—"

He said, "Lowv? Um, Lor? Laura? I know I'm talking to Laura. You're Laura. I know that."

Again, I signed "no" into his hand. I was fiercely determined to get this message across. At this point in his brain damage, it was really hard for him to hold letters in his mind for very long, so spelling out words was almost impossible. I tried again. "L" and "O . . ."

He said, "Um . . . You wanna go for a walk?"

I quickly signed "wait" and then tried again. I felt like a desperate Anne Sullivan signing "water" over and over into Hellen Keller's confused hand. After ten more attempts, I spelled out "L" and "O" and "V" and "E" and he finally said, "Love?"

I screamed with delight and ferociously signed "yes." Then I slammed his hand into his body and screamed, "YOU! I love you, Max! I love you so much." I let down all my walls to allow the force of my love for him to cross the barriers created by his lack of senses. I shoved all the intense love energy I could summon into his body with my mind.

He pondered on the force of me pressing his hand onto his body and guessed, "You love me? Oh, I love you too, Late . . . Duh. Wanna go for a walk?" It was the opposite of a monumental moment for him, but for me it was everything.

This is right around the time my mother was nominated for the Caregiver of the Year Award . . . if such a thing existed. Our society has an award for Outstanding Guest Actor in a Comedy Series, but no awards for the caregivers of the sick. If there was an award for such a thing, I assure you my mom would have won.

She installed a pull-up bar midway up the doorframe to our bathroom so my brother could reach up from his wheelchair, pull himself up, and my mom could pull his pants down. Then he would wheel, with his pants down, to the toilet and my mom would lift him onto the toilet so he could pee. After he was done peeing, the same routine was reversed. And people pee a lot, so this happened many times a day for many months. He was self-conscious about me helping with this ordeal and I was not clamoring to do so.

My mother is an American hero—she schlepped this tall, heavy boy around all day and night all by herself. She was his nurse, his cook, his cleaning lady, his giver of sponge baths, his cutter of hair, clipper of nails, and brusher of teeth. When I asked how she did all of that, and how she never gave up or walked away, she looked baffled as to how I could even ask that and said, "Oh, Laura, I'm his mother, any mother would have done that." But that's actually not true at all. There are countless facilities one could park their sick child in and never look back.

From the very first diagnosis, my mom worked and fought for him to have a better life. She gave up her life to try and give him one. She found him friends who were going through similar challenges and got him involved in activities he was capable of doing. She lived in different Ronald McDonald Houses all over the country so he could receive treatment at cutting-edge hospitals. She drove all over Florida so he could attend schools that trained him how to live without sight. She did all of that and so much more, more than could ever be captured in words.

She was his fiercest protector and loudest coach. She was his advocate and his medical translator. She befriended hundreds of doctors and nurses and educated herself in that sanitized and stainless-steel world that hitherto she had known nothing about and frankly avoided at all costs.

Did she complain? Yes! Did she scream and yell? Of course! Did she try to give him a pill one evening that he refused to take because he thought she was trying to poison him, so she had to stuff the pill down his throat and they ended up in a wrestling match that she won, and their fight didn't resolve until after he had digested the pill and felt confident it wasn't cyanide and she hadn't actually been trying to murder him? Sure! But she was truly an amazing mother to a boy who desperately needed one and I am intensely proud to be her daughter.

Did I hate her back then? Yes! Did I wish she gave *me* all that attention instead of my brother? Of course! Did I rebel against her in every way because I wanted to punish her for abandoning me, like when I pierced my belly button against her wishes when I was thirteen because I subconsciously wanted to mutilate the umbilical cord, the original point of contact between mother and child? Sure! But things get very real when you're in the shit.

Freedom Village

M AX WAS TWENTY-ONE YEARS OLD, AND LIKE ALL TWENTY-ONE-YEAR-
olds—whether blind, deaf, and in a wheelchair or not—he
was craving independence. Before he lost his hearing, he would
lament about still living at home and fantasize about one day getting his own place. My mom did hours of research and found a
nearby low-income apartment complex for people living with disabilities called Freedom Village.

She read Max the entire website, which described private apart-
ments outfitted with accessible showers and grab bars in the bath-
rooms, emergency responders on staff who could be beckoned
anytime day or night with pull cords, a pool, and a community
room where residents could gather and socialize. It was the Four
Seasons of subsidized accessible housing. Or at least the Best Western. My brother said he wanted in, so my mom put him on the

waitlist. The waitlist was years long, but Max was happy to wait because the reward was so sweet.

A few years later, Max was still patiently longing for a Freedom Village apartment to open up when a doctor informed us that after trying every possible thing to get his cancer under control, it had spread to the point of no return and Max only had a few months left to live. He was never going to get a chance to live in Freedom Village. My big brother was dying. When my mom relayed this news to me, I was both completely expecting it and also wildly shocked. No matter how prepared I thought I was to hear it, I was not prepared at all. It somehow didn't make sense, even though he had essentially been dying right in front of my eyes for six years.

From the day I was born, my brother was my life, like air, food, and water. My brother was the stuff of my life. How would I live without my life? What would happen to my world without this essential element that had always been there? I was suddenly even more consumed with myself than usual, obsessing about what would happen to me without him.

What would happen to my eyes when they could no longer see him? My ears when they could no longer hear his voice? My heart when it could no longer feel him? The dull ache of a looming loss rose in my throat and the tears that followed were all for me. Poor me. He was dying and I had to somehow keep living without my life. I was, of course, aware that he was the one who had to do the actual dying, so *poor Max* was also present in my mind, but grief usually contains at least 70 percent self-pity and I was wallowing in it.

This devastating news meant it was time for hospice to step in. Hospice care is a type of health care whose main focus is to alleviate pain and suffering for people who have less than six months left to live. This meant my mother could finally get some help—not the kind of halfhearted help that a noiseless alcoholic and a bratty teen girl can offer, but real help.

Because Max's condition was worsening rapidly, the situation at home was becoming unsanitary and unsafe. Max didn't actually know he was dying, because we hadn't told him the doctor's grim reaper news yet, but his body knew and he started to lose control of more motor skills and bodily functions.

Upon entering our house, the smell of stale urine and physical exhaustion filled my nose. It was obvious that moving Max to a hands-on hospice facility that could actually care for him properly was now an absolute necessity. We didn't know how to tell him it was time for him to move to hospice though, because months earlier it had taken me over an hour to say "I love you," and now he had even fewer sensory receptors with which to receive communication.

The hospice my brother was going to move into was twenty minutes away from our house. As we drove my brother there, we were still trying to figure out how to tell him what was happening. We arrived at the single-story building and walked through the automatic sliding doors into a sterile lobby filled with drab furniture and tacky paintings of Floridian beachscapes.

My mom checked in with some nurses at the front desk while my brother and I waited nearby. Max had lost pretty much every ability except talking and he continued to talk incessantly. He was rambling on about a meal he had recently enjoyed—grilled grouper with tartar sauce—and I knew he was going to keep talking for a while, because my brother *loved* tartar sauce.

Imagine if you lost the ability to watch TV, read a book, listen to music, chat with a friend, go for a jog, watch the sunset, swim laps, or write in your journal, all the things that bring a human being peace and solace, all the activities that make us feel alive. There are many human beings who are not able do *all* of those things, but there are very few human beings who are not able do *any* of those things, and my brother was one of them. But he managed to replace his love of all the things he was no longer able to do with his love of tartar sauce. Taste was one of his few remaining senses, one of his few connections to the outside world. Toward the end of his life, he literally lived for food.

A few months before hospice, the three of us were crammed into a booth at a loud bar and grill. After our server placed my brother's fish tacos down in front of him, he immediately asked for tartar sauce. He said "tartar sauce" with reverence, like he was asking our server to bring him a Fabergé egg.

When our server informed us that they didn't have tartar sauce, my mom and I panicked. Max had already had everything taken away from him and he couldn't even have a ramekin of fucking tartar sauce? After some deliberation, my mom asked our server for a side of mayonnaise, some pickles, and onions. My brother again asked for tartar sauce because no one had answered him the first time. I signed "wait" into his receptive hand.

My brother asked three more times in the time it took for my mom to receive all the ingredients, chop them up, and mix them together. Finally, my mom presented my brother with her concoction. He slowly put it on his tacos and took a bite. He looked subtly pleased as a Zen smile formed on his lips and he said the thing he always said when he was eating something he enjoyed, "Mmm . . . Pretty good." My mom and I breathed a sigh of relief.

After my mom finished checking my brother into his death bed at the hospice front desk, she walked back over to us and Max was still talking about the many wonders of tartar sauce. Eventually, my brother began to instinctively realize we were somewhere he had never been before and asked where we were. *Uh oh.* We had no idea how to answer that.

He asked us questions more out of habit and didn't actually expect an answer because he knew he could only understand the word "yes" and the word "no." So the routine was, my brother would ask a complex question, then he would remember that we could only answer "yes" or "no" questions, so he would alter his previous question. For example: "What's for dinner?" *Oh, right I can't see or hear and I no longer have the cognitive ability to understand sign language.* "Are we having spaghetti for dinner?" Then we would quickly sign "yes" or "no" into his hand. If we signed "no," he would keep guessing what we were having for dinner, and this is how we lived our life.

So my mom and I were standing in the lobby of this sad hospice place, surrounded by the dying and the very recently dead, when my brother justifiably asked, "Where are we?"

We didn't know what to do. So we froze. Then my brother, as part of his process, adjusted his question.

"Are we at Freedom Village?" he asked, suddenly excited about even the slightest possibility that we were maybe standing in the lobby of his new assisted living apartment building.

My mom and I looked at each other. We had two options. We could sign "no" into his hand, and then spend the next few months trying to communicate to him *this building we are in is actually hospice and it's a super depressing place and you are dying.* Or we could sign "yes," and my brother would spend the last few months of his life thinking he had actually moved out of his mom's house and accomplished his dream of living on his own.

My mom pondered the options for about thirty seconds and then signed "yes" into his hand. Max lit up, happier than I had seen him in years. He was thrilled! The wait was over! He'd finally got his own place! He started cracking jokes about inviting ladies back to his bachelor pad. He couldn't wait to go sit in his new dope crib. As he rushed us down the hall, he asked all kinds of questions:

"Is the pool nice?"

Well, there was no pool, but what's the harm in one more lie. "Yes."

"Do any of my neighbors look like dicks?"

A quick glance around at all the near-death, elderly people shuffling around. "No."

"Are there any cute girls in the building?"

A quick glance around at all the decaying females clinging to their last breath. What's the harm in one more lie? "Yes!"

One of the nurses guided us to Max's room and we were relieved to discover it was quite large. There was a couch and a full bathroom and no reason for Max to suspect that it wasn't a real apartment, no reason except the old dying man who lay in a bed across the room from Max's bed. My mom panicked: "He has a roommate?! Why?!" The nurse explained that they were at capacity, so Max would have to share a room.

My mom pulled the nurse out to the hallway, although she could've just said it all right there, and explained the outrageous lie we had just told Max. The nurse empathized with our unorthodox situation. She told my mom she would do everything she could for us. She left and returned shortly afterward to inform us that the old man would be removed from Max's room. *Yay!* In one week. *Oh.* Somehow my brother had to share a room with this fatally ill man for a whole week without discovering he was there.

My mother told all the nurses what was happening and begged them to keep my brother away from the old man's side of the room. My mom lay awake at night for seven days, panic-stricken with the thought of my brother wheeling over to the other side of his room, touching this withering stranger, who wasn't supposed to be there, and then wheeling straight through the drywall and out into the street from sheer terror. But somehow, Max did not discover his secret roommate that first week and was perfectly happy in his new apartment.

Before we left him on that first day, he asked my mom for keys to his new pad. My mom looked caught, *right . . . keys*. Then she quickly slid a random key off of her key ring and handed it to my brother.

"What if he tries to use it?!" I asked, feeling overwhelmed by the lie, but also knowing there was no going back.

"I don't know, Laura! I've never done anything like this before!" She was banking on the fact that he was bedridden unless someone lifted him out of his bed and into his chair. He was never alone when he was in his chair and nurses always opened the door for him. So thankfully, he never had to use his fake key, but he always carried it in his pocket, immensely proud of his very own apartment.

Also, on that first day, my mom watched as they placed Max onto a machine that could lift and lower him into a warm bath. He hadn't had a bath in over a year; he could only take showers. My mom didn't have the strength to get him in and out of the bathtub, so that luxury went out the window. But there, in that magical hospice place, we were surrounded by machines that could make anything happen.

My mom said her whole body relaxed as she watched his whole body relax in that tub. Leaving him alone in hospice suddenly didn't seem so terrible. He was finally getting the care he deserved and my mom was finally getting the break she deserved. Max seemed genuinely blissful that entire first day. "Isn't Freedom Village fuckin' sweet?" my brother asked me after his bath. "Yes," I signed into his hand, and I meant it with my whole heart.

Free

I DON'T KNOW HOW I MISSED THIS, BUT SOMEHOW, IT TOOK A FEW VISITS TO that hospice place before I noticed there was a group of at least a hundred people standing outside the building. I think I was so distracted by the horror of losing Max that I didn't register the parking lot was filled with protesters. All these people were holding signs that expressed various exclamations of outrage about . . . something.

There were always at least ten news vans parked outside with forty-foot-high antennas sticking out of their roofs. Somber news anchors were frequently interviewing these outspoken people about . . . something. The crowd's emotions ranged from wild rage to deep sadness and I felt it every time I entered the building. On my third visit, a security guard was posted at the door. After I was patted down and my purse was searched, I finally asked my mom what the hell was going on.

As we walked down the ammonia-scented hallway, my mom explained that a woman named Terri Schiavo was inside this very building, and apparently, the whole country was in an uproar about her. The Terri Schiavo case was a heavily politicized, right-to-die legal battle. Terri was in an irreversible vegetative state and her husband argued she would not have wanted artificial life support without the possibility of recovery, so he decided to remove her feeding tube. But Terri's parents disputed her husband's claims and argued in favor of continuing artificial nutrition. So for seven years, Terri's husband and Terri's parents fought about whether or not she had enough brain activity to justify remaining on a feeding tube. And it all culminated right there in that building we were suddenly deeply connected to.

This family's very personal story became a media frenzy and our family's very personal story was being affected by it. Because some protesters were regularly making bomb threats, every time we pulled into the parking lot, we had to endure getting our car searched for bombs. We weren't allowed to bring cameras into the facility lest we sneak a picture of Terri and sell it to the media. Because of this rule, we have no photos of my brother's last months on earth. As I was walking into the building, a protester tried to thrust a bottle of water into my hands. "Bring this to Terri!" she begged. "They're gonna cut off her water soon." I respectfully declined.

As I was walking to McDonald's to get my brother a chocolate sundae (a rare treat because we limited his sugar intake after my dad read that sugar causes cancer), a protester asked me why I was visiting hospice. I told him my brother was dying inside the building.

"I'll pray for his recovery," he said.

"Oh—please don't," I blurted out. "He can't see or hear or walk. He doesn't even really know where he is or what's going on anymore. It's time for him to pass on." The protester just stared at me, baffled. I noticed he was wearing a cross around his neck. *Does he actually believe in heaven?* I wondered. *Does he actually believe that after death we go to a magical place in the sky to eat grapes and listen to harps? If so, why aren't my brother and Terri allowed go there? Why do they have to stay here?*

During those months, I walked past groups of young women sitting on curbs with red tape stuck over their mouths. The word "LIFE" was written on the tape in black Sharpie. I walked past semitrucks with images of chopped up babies on the side of them—somehow abortion was also being protested. I walked past men dressed like Jesus carrying giant wooden crosses. I walked past children as young as ten years old being arrested for trying to sneak into hospice with water for Terri.

Every day, I walked past hundreds of people fervently praying to God to save Terri. As I was trying to process the biggest loss of my life, I was watching all of these people process the loss of a woman they didn't know. But to some of them, it was very personal. There were people in wheelchairs holding signs that said, "I'm also on a feeding tube. Am I next?" These people were scared and they felt helpless. I related to that feeling.

We want so badly to control this life thing. We want to have some say over how it all goes down. We want to call the shots on our lives, but the universe has its own plans. My sweet, funny brother was dying and I wanted to protest it. I wanted to stand outside with tape over *my* mouth and an angry sign in *my* hands. I wanted to picket in front of God's house, demanding that my brother be spared, but I knew there was nothing I could do. I had to let him go.

There are physical signs that a person is close to passing on. Shortness of breath and yellowing fingers are two of them. When my brother started showing these signs, my father flew in from Los Angeles and thus began the most dramatic evenings of my young life. A hospice nurse would call us in the middle of the night, saying it looked like Max was going to pass away that evening. My mom and I would race to hospice, my father would meet us there, and we all would crowd around our handsome boy with bated breath.

On one of these nights, my father, who had clearly been drinking heavily in his motel room, broke down sobbing, screaming "my boy" into Max's chest. My mom and I sat on the couch holding space for my father's grief. It was agonizing to watch. My mother and I were swimming in the excruciating weight of grief but my father was drowning in it.

My mother had spent so much time with my brother in the past six years that she was able to have more peace with the thought of letting him go. My father hadn't had to go through the challenges of changing Max's adult diapers and holding him while he vomited from chemotherapy, but my father also didn't get to experience the deep intimacy and ultimate healing that can come from caring for someone in their final years.

Because there were so many false alarms during those weeks, the hospice nurse's late-night phone calls threatening that Max was about to die started feeling less and less urgent. Instead of running red lights to get to hospice, we started driving the speed limit and walking at a normal pace from the car.

On a Monday morning, a nurse called and again said today could be the day. We were eating breakfast and instead of throwing down our forks and racing out the door like we had done previously, we finished eating.

During our drive to hospice, I mentioned to my mom that I had a test to take in a few hours at my community college. I was still chipping away at my two-year degree and was anxious about missing an important Western humanities exam. "Do we think he's actually going to die today?" I asked; the number of false alarms had quickly made us jaded and callous. My mom sighed, "I don't know, honey. There's no way to know."

I looked out the window at the bright blue, cloudless sky. I heard birds chatting in the trees, I felt the warm sun on my bare feet as they rested on the dashboard. *There's no way he's gonna die on a day like this*, I thought. Death seemed reserved for nighttime or at least a rainy sky.

We met my father at hospice and the three of us walked through the parking lot. All the protesters were gone: Terri's husband had won his case. Terri's feeding tube had been removed once and for all and she had passed away four days earlier. That almost decade-long saga was over.

We anxiously crowded around my brother's bed for what felt like the hundredth time. The hour to go take my test was fast approaching, and both of my parents said they understood if I needed to go, but something made me skip it. Some unseen force made me stay by my brother's bed that day. I crawled in bed next to him. My dad sat on the right side; my mom sat on the left. And we just waited. All the drama had leaked out of us over the past weeks. There was no more energy for drama. We just calmly waited.

Time passed and nothing happened, then his already short and ragged breaths became noticeably further and further apart. A hospice doctor examined him and told us that it was happening right now. He was going. *Holy shit.* My heart started pounding, thumping like a drum in my throat. The doctor had to put a stethoscope on my brother's chest to hear to his heart's final beats, but I bet you could've heard mine from outer space.

Max would take a large breath and thirty seconds would pass. We would all look at each other . . . *was that it?* Then he would struggle to suck in more air. I started screaming, I don't remember what I was saying, just babbling into his chest, words like "No!" and "Please?!" My mom was yelling, "Go, Maxie, go! You can do it, we're here! We're all here! You can do it, Maxie!" My dad was weeping; loud, hacking sobs. My brother took another breath, short and fast, thirty seconds passed, then a minute passed . . .

I felt his laugh abandoning me. I felt his crooked teeth disappearing from my life. I felt his smell, that sweet salty boy smell that was only his and could not be replicated, slipping away from me. Finally, the doctor looked up from her stethoscope and said . . . "He's free." *Boom!* I felt an explosion, like the skies had ripped open. I felt him leave me, I felt him rip through the crown of my head. One of my soulmates was gone. The boy who taught me how to play and laugh and be a kid was gone forever. The word "never" radiated through me. I will never see him again. I will never touch him again. He will never speak again. He will never smile again. I will never have a brother again. Never is the worst feeling I have ever felt. Please not never. Anything but never.

When we were little, we had bunk beds. He was on the top bunk and I was on the bottom. We played a game every night when we were supposed to be sleeping; he would dangle his hand down from the top bunk and I would try and slap it.

I would whine, "Slow down, Max. I can't get you."

"You gotta be faster, Laurie," he would say, giggling. "You just gotta be faster."

He made me faster. He made me better. He made me stronger. He made me try. He made me grow. He made me me.

After my parents and I quieted, I looked down at Max's suddenly cold hand that I didn't realize I had been squeezing the whole time and was struck by the fact that we had the same exact hands. I had never noticed it before, but the hand I was holding was a larger, browner version of my own, down to the last crease and knuckle fold. *He'll always be with me*, I thought. *Whenever I need to see him, I can look at my own hands.*

When I finally looked up at my brother's face, I regretted it immediately. There is no lonelier sight in this world than a body without its soul. It wasn't his face anymore. It had hardened quickly; it was wooden and dull. His whole body looked like an empty shell, a husk I wouldn't have recognized as my brother if I saw it walking down the street. A nurse, mercifully, put a sheet over his face. Then I went outside to call Tori and tell her what had happened because I was still just a teenage girl.

Heartbreak

THE VIBE OF MY BROTHER'S FUNERAL WAS LOW-INCOME CASUAL. HOSPICE allowed us to use their outdoor area to celebrate Max's life free of charge. My mom served pizza and played loud hip-hop on a boombox. Everyone wore jeans and T-shirts—there wasn't a black dress or suit in the whole crowd. All of Max's old friends showed up and all of my friends did too. We chain smoked and caught up on each other's lives. It was like a mournful high school reunion.

Another friend had just recently overdosed on pills, so the group was mourning his loss as well as Max's. Tori arrived over an hour late, since she had been up until dawn doing cocaine the night before. She showed up hung over and guilt ridden. I assured her that her lateness did not offend me and I meant it. I thankfully had many other friends at that point in my life; Tori was no longer the one I leaned on. She could not be leaned on. Drugs had weakened her too much, and anyone who leaned on her would surely fall over.

My mom bought fifty helium balloons and asked everyone to write a message to Max on a balloon with a Sharpie and then release their balloon into the air. At the time, this was considered a beautiful gesture and not a horrific threat to the environment. We thought we were honoring my brother's memory with grace and elegance, not tarnishing his memory by inevitably murdering hundreds of sea turtles with our nonbiodegradable, plastic death balloons.

We released our hazardous waste into the air and watched them disappear into the clouds, filled with awe and hope that he would receive the messages from heaven or wherever. One of the balloons got caught in some branches and everyone pointed to it. "Watch over Laura" was written on the side. I felt incredible. This was even better than being famous for being sexually harassed at a concert. This meant that even though that day, like most days before it, was about my brother, it was *also* about me. For once, I was his costar. And as everyone talked about that beautiful message written on that balloon, I basked in the glow of momentary fame.

My boyfriend did not attend Max's funeral. That's right, I finally had a boyfriend. My first real boyfriend. His name was Jack and his beauty simply cannot be described in words, but I will try. He was six feet tall with inky black, curly hair, thick black eyebrows, and aquamarine eyes. The only other place I have seen his eye color is from airplane windows. During takeoff or landing, from my high vantage point I always notice backyard swimming pools, so bright and so blue that they stand out against any landscape, exactly like Jack's otherworldly eyes.

He was physically very fit. His chest and arms were covered in colorful tattoos. He was Black Irish, a term for Irish people that have darker hair and skin complexion than most other Irish people. He loved the ocean and was deeply tanned all year round from surfing and fishing. He had perfectly straight, white teeth, no matter how many cigarettes he smoked or how much coffee he drank. He hung out with a group of boys who were all so attractive it was hard to be around them.

I met Jack when I was twelve and he was sixteen. It was Halloween. Tori and I were trick-or-treating. We thought we were way too cool to wear costumes, but we really wanted free candy. So we got dressed up in our sexiest outfits and piled on makeup. When adults answered their doors and asked what we were dressed as, we said, "models," and struck a pouty pose. Then they filled our bags with handfuls of sweet, chewy goodness.

We had been running that scam for a couple of hours when we bumped into Tori's older sister on the street. She said she was going to hang out with some friends at a nearby apartment party and Tori begged her to bring us. She was four years older than Tori and never let us hang out with her, but for some reason she was in a good mood that night and let us tag along.

We arrived at a twenty-something-year-old's apartment: video games were being played, rap music was blaring, everyone was college age, but no one was a college student. Not one single person was wearing a Halloween costume and thank God we technically weren't either. Tori and I were sitting on a black leather couch under a large photograph of a tiger when Jack walked in. My heart swelled just at the sight of him. My eyes took him in like they were seeing beauty for the first time. He cracked open a bottle of Bud Light with his teeth and casually leaned against a cigarette-stained wall. My heart continued to expand until it pressed on my ribs, squeezing my lungs and cutting off my oxygen.

He was skinnier back then and didn't have any tattoos yet, but that hair, and those eyes, and his voice. He had the scratchiest voice, like a decrepit old man who had been drinking beer under the hot sun for fifty years. Not the sexiest image I know, but trust me his voice was so sexy that it startled me.

He didn't even acknowledge our presence. He was not a dirtbag and I'm sure he clocked out of the corner of his eye that we were basically ten years old and decided to leave us alone. But there were dirtbags in attendance and, after Tori and I sat there in silence for about an hour, one of them offered us a shot of tequila. We looked around for approval from Tori's sister, but she had disappeared. *Hmmm.* We didn't know where she went or if she was coming back, but we decided the smartest thing to do was . . . drink the tequila.

Tori took the first shot and didn't wince in the slightest. It was like she had been practicing at home for years, and she might've been—I wouldn't put it past her. Then it was my turn. I had been drinking beer since I was eleven, but this was my first stab at hard liquor. I picked up the shot glass and as soon as I did, Jack looked at me. When those eyes landed on me, my arm gave out and I almost dropped the shot glass. I couldn't breathe. I had to force the glass to my lips as every voice in my head was screaming, "Don't fuck this up, Laura! He's looking right at you!"

I put the shot glass to my lips and the harsh liquid felt like a bee sting on my tongue. I took a tiny sip and tried not to choke. Jack sort of chuckled. "Well, don't sip it, it ain't tea," he said under his breath in his raspy drawl and some kids around him laughed. I put the glass down, embarrassed. Then he smiled at me, a kind smile, like an older brother ragging on a younger sibling. I picked up the glass again. This time, I swigged the whole thing and held in the desire to gag. Through my watery eyes, I looked toward Jack to maybe collect another one of those devastatingly beautiful smiles, but he was gone. *Nooooo.*

I glanced out the window and saw him outside. I took in his whole body—he was shirtless, wearing board shorts and flip-flops, which to me at the time was the most seductive uniform a boy could wear. He was talking with some dudes in a pickup truck. I watched as he jumped into the back of the truck and drove away from me. I wanted to chase after the truck and beg him to spend the rest of his life with me.

Instead, I asked Tori who that perfect human specimen was and she told me. Of course she knew because she knew everything. "Oh, that's Jack, he's in tenth grade, he sells weed. My sister says he's cool as fuck."

Damn. Cool "as fuck" was as cool as it got and I immediately chucked him miles out of my league. But I didn't throw him so far that I couldn't still see him; he was hovering near the horizon, completely out of my reach but maybe, if I worked *really* hard on becoming cool as fuck, I could catch up to him someday . . .

And don't worry, shortly after Jack absconded with my uncool heart in his cool as fuck hands, Tori and I safely left that grown man's apartment. We drunkenly walked back to my house to dump our bags of Halloween treats on the floor and trade each other for our preferred candy brands, like the children we were. And I didn't see Jack again for several years.

But I kept tabs on him through small-town gossip. I heard he had a girlfriend: a very laid-back, white, straight-haired surfer girl, pretty much the opposite of me, which didn't give me much hope for my imaginary future with Jack. I heard he got arrested for breaking into someone's house and he had to go to a program for troubled teens for a year. I heard he proposed to his girlfriend while he was in the program; this news officially killed my imaginary future with Jack.

Sometimes at the beach, I'd lay on the sand with other teen girls while that disturbingly attractive group of guys would hang out on the pier above us. Every once in a while, Jack would be among them and I always knew when he was because I had placed a tracking device on him with my mind when I was twelve and that tracking device never malfunctioned.

When I was eighteen and freshly back from living in Los Angeles for that second time with my dad, I paid a visit to my favorite bar Greenbacks. I was wearing a hard cast on my broken wrist so I wasn't able to Jell-O wrestle, but the place was just as lively as it had been when I had left it.

I needed to get out and distract myself from my disintegrating self-esteem. I had just failed in my second attempt to live in Los Angeles. I was living with my mom again, my brother was undergoing yet another brain surgery, my wordless stepdad was always drunk and contributing nothing to our household beyond monthly mortgage payments. I had no idea what I wanted to do with my life. I had absolutely no future goals. So I threw on some ripped jeans, platform wedges, and a black T-shirt with the brand name bebe bedazzled on the front and headed out to downtown Clearwater.

At Greenbacks, I met up with Tori, who was high out of her mind on cocaine, and Zoe, who was drinking Bud Light and so relieved to be away from her two-year-old son for an evening. Zoe had officially called off the engagement with Beckett and returned her Kay Jewelers ring and I was delighted to have my friend back. I still had to share her with her toddler, but it was better than nothing.

As the evening went on, I proceeded to get extremely hammered. I wasn't driving, so I threw all my inhibitions to the wind. Somewhere between my fifth and sixth shot, the music abruptly stopped and everyone froze as Jack walked through the door. In reality, nothing stopped and no one froze; he just pushed his way through the raucous crowd. But in my mind, time stood still as he walked toward me. *He's here?!* I hadn't seen him in years. I figured he had married his girlfriend and they were off living some blissful existence that made me too jealous to think about. BLACKOUT!

The next morning, I woke up alone on a queen-size mattress on the floor. I blinked my eyes awake and realized I had never been in this room before. One of the walls was painted turquoise. There was a TV on a stand in front of the bed and a surfboard leaning against the wall. Where the hell was I? I was wearing my bebe T-shirt, no bra, and men's boxers. *Jesus Christ.* I had never had a one-night stand before and I always fought to keep my number of sexual partners low because the fake concept of a slut was one that still terrified me.

I called Zoe. Whispering on my flip phone, I explained everything to her, hoping she could help me figure out where I was. She told me that when she left Greenbacks, I was talking to Jack at the bar. *Jack?!* Suddenly the memory of him came flooding back to me. We had talked at the bar, shouting over the crowd. He told me he broke up with that girlfriend. That's all I remembered. *Oh God, I hope I didn't drunkenly tell him that I had been in love with him from afar for six years . . .*

I got off the phone with no clue what to do next. Then I heard someone approaching the closed bedroom door. I shut my eyes, and through my lashes I saw Jack enter the room, open the closet, and start changing his clothes. Jack was in the same room as me changing his clothes! I wanted to leap out of bed and go sing and dance in the street! I wanted to scoop twelve-year-old me up in my arms and yell, "We did it! We got him!" Instead, I pretended to be waking up for the first time.

He greeted me with a huge grin that essentially gave away what our evening had entailed, but I tried to casually suss out exactly what happened anyway. He looked surprised: "You don't remember?" He told me we had sex . . . a few times, and he was truly stunned I could've blacked it all out. He said after Greenbacks, Tori and I came back to his house and when Tori was ready to leave, I told her I wanted to stay.

Apparently Tori said, "Laura, you're really drunk. Are you sure you want me to leave you here?"

And I said, "Tori, I'm not drunk at all. I'm Laura. You're Tori. And that's Jack, I've known him since I was twelve, it's fine."

The moment he said that, I remembered all of it. As he filled in the night for me, pieces and chunks returned to my memory. I cannot stress enough how unsafe it is to drink excessively if you're a person who blacks out. Thankfully, Jack was someone I actually wanted to have sex with, drunk or sober. I called Tori and Zoe and asked them to meet me at a nearby diner for breakfast. Jack said he would drop me off, so we walked outside and got into a Spectrum cable van. Apparently, Jack was working as a cable technician and right then I decided that cable technician was the sexiest job a man could have.

I sat with Tori and Zoe and we dissected my evening over greasy bacon and fried eggs. Tori reiterated everything Jack had said. She too was shocked that I was able to seem so lucid while I was blacked out. Then Jack called my phone. I wanted to burst into tears. I can't explain why I loved him so much, for so many years, while knowing so little about him, but there was his number on my phone and dynamite went off inside my chest. I answered and tried to sound cool and relaxed while Tori and Zoe giggled in the background. He asked if I wanted to sneak into a fancy apartment complex and go swimming with him and I tried not to sob hysterically. It was the most romantic date proposal I had ever heard. He said he'd pick me up at my mom's in an hour.

He didn't pick me up in his cable van; he picked me up in his bright red pickup truck, with a large fish decal on the back window and Kanye West's first album, *The College Dropout*, bumping through custom speakers. He smiled at me when I got in his truck—that goddamn smile. "You look good," he said casually. I wanted to die. It was all too dream-come-true-y and I didn't know how to deal with it. Before I could say anything, he cranked Kanye, put his hand on my thigh, which was heavily exposed in my cutoff shorts, and we sped toward the beach. We spent days like this. Having sex. Going swimming. Watching movies. I was fully ready for him to propose, and I'm sure he was fully ready to keep doing what we were doing.

Meanwhile, I had to go back to LA to get my car. I had flown back to Florida so my broken wrist could heal for a few months, but I still had to fly back to my dad's and drive my car home. I told Jack my situation and mentioned how I had to drive across the country by myself because I had no one to drive with. Since that first cross-country trip had resulted in four speeding tickets and a resisting arrest charge for Charlene, she told me to go fuck myself when I asked her to drive with me again. But Jack offered to drive back with me. He said he had always wanted to see California and surf the Malibu coast. I was ecstatic. My mom even offered to pay for Jack's flight to LA since he was doing us the favor of safely getting me back to Florida.

I flew to LA and tied up my LA life, packed up my car, and prepared to move back to Clearwater. When I called Jack to arrange picking him up from the airport the next day . . . he didn't answer.

Days went by. He never returned my calls. I was devastated. I felt so silly and used. He just wanted sex, then he completely disappeared. Eventually I drove back to Florida by myself, nursing my aching heart with coffee and Red Bull.

My dad drilled into my head, pretty much my entire life, that the only thing boys want from me is sex. He told me they'll be nice and flattering and spend time and energy on me until they get what they want, and then they'll disappear. This kind of advice is helpful because it probably protected me from countless horny teens, but it's also harmful because it adds to the idea that all I am is a body and the only value men see in me is the potential for sex.

When I was sixteen, this very handsome, popular senior baseball player used to drive me home from parties. He was six-foot-four, the kind of guy who dated Jenny, or Gabby, or Haley, and I actually think he did date all three of them. His family was upper middle class. He probably owns a landscaping company now. Anyway, he used to drive me home from parties and before I got out of his car we would talk. He opened up to me about his family, his challenging mom, and his hopes for the future.

Eventually he started coming inside my house and we would lay in my bed and talk. Just talk. We did this dozens of times. I never thought he would actually date me because that would be like Thor dating a chimney sweep, but we really liked hanging out with each other. After several months, we were in my bed in the middle of one of our talks and we started kissing. Things started to heat up and he said, "Shoot, I don't have a condom." I thought, *Well, there's no way I was about to have sex with you, because slut-shaming is something I do to others and refuse to have done to me.* But I just said, "Okay."

We stopped kissing and he sort of laughed and said, "Man, when we first started hanging out, I always brought condoms with me, but then I gave up on the idea of us ever having sex." My mind was blown. He didn't think he was ever going to have sex with me but he kept coming over anyway?! I asked him when he stopped bringing condoms and he said, "two months ago." *Two months ago?!* I thought about this for days. For the past *two months* this boy had hung out with me for some reason other than sex? Was my dad wrong? Did I have other value besides sex? Did men maybe like talking to me? Thor changed the way I thought about men forever. I'm not saying my dad was completely wrong, because some men have been real pieces of shit, but not all men are the same. That's all I'm saying.

I survived my solo cross-country drive and I did everything I could to get over Jack, but I was completely hung up on him. I tried not to talk about him too much, because the whole thing was too humiliating, but I thought about him unceasingly and wrote at least five melancholy poems in his honor.

One night, Zoe and I were at a stoplight when Jack's bright red truck pulled up next to Zoe's window. Jack's ex-girlfriend waved at Zoe out of the passenger window. Zoe and the girl were casual acquaintances and they chatted. I knew Jack was driving, but I couldn't see him and he couldn't see me. As soon as they drove away, I cried. I correctly guessed that they had gotten back together and that's why he had disappeared from my life.

Zoe and I were on our way to the movie theater. If I had known what it was about, I would have chosen not to watch *The Notebook* while I was nursing a broken heart, but I had no clue what I was going to walk into. When I finally stopped crying in the car, we got out, walked toward the movie theater, and ran right into beautiful, blonde Haley. She was exquisite—really tall and had that glow that comes from a trauma-free childhood. She told us she was going to

University of South Florida and her parents had just bought her a condo on the beach as a high school graduation present. At my high school, the upper-middle-class girls either got condos or breast implants for graduation presents; some girls were lucky enough to get both. Zoe and I suddenly felt very short, very uneducated, and very poor.

Haley asked how Zoe's whole teen-mom thing was going. Zoe said, "Good, you know . . . hard."

Then Haley asked if my brother was getting better. "No . . . he's actually getting much worse."

Then, after tossing out a few words of pity, she walked away. Zoe and I laughed at the absurd difference between our lives and hers. As we headed toward the theater, a pickup truck full of random dudes drove past us and one of them yelled, "Whores!" It was a perfect evening. Made even more perfect by Rachel McAdams and Ryan Gosling reaching through the projector screen and ripping our souls from our bodies.

Boyfriend

SINCE I HAD NO OTHER REASON TO LIVE WHILE I WAS WAITING FOR MY brother to die, I decided to try and start an acting career in Florida. I bought a book that listed all the Florida talent agencies. I decided to submit myself to agencies in Orlando, Miami, and Tampa. I bought large envelopes and stuffed my terrible headshots inside them. Then I typed up a fake acting résumé. I claimed I had a small role in *Million Dollar Baby*, but my part was cut out of the final movie. I also claimed I had acted in some off-Broadway plays in New York. Then I looked up impressive acting schools like Stella Adler's and Lee Strasberg's, and I claimed I went to both.

Not surprisingly, all the agencies I submitted to wanted to work with me. They thought I was a highly educated teenage savant who had recently been in a major motion picture, not a Jell-O wrestling teenage alcoholic who'd recently had her heart broken by a cable guy. The theatrical rules in Florida allowed actors to have more than one agency represent them at a time, so I decided to work with every agency that asked. And to my astonishment, they started sending me on auditions for paying acting jobs. Most of them were terrible, but one was for a Levi's commercial in Miami; I didn't book the job, but just telling my friends I auditioned for a Levi's commercial in Miami boosted my self-esteem.

I decided to not share the part about how I'd only had one hundred dollars to my name and that money had to cover gas to Miami and pay for a motel, so I could wake up early and go to the audition. I also skipped the part about staying up all night in my extremely cheap motel listening to the sounds of prostitutes' heels clicking down the hallway as they led their Johns to their rooms, accompanied by the sounds of extremely loud sex work emanating from every wall. I just told everyone I went to a glamorous building in South Beach where I pretended to admire my amazing Levi's in an imaginary mirror in front of an important casting director.

I eventually booked my first paid acting job, a commercial for an online dating service. They paid me $500 and told me it was a local Clearwater commercial. It turned out to be a national late-night commercial that still sometimes plays around three in the morning (if you're lucky you'll catch it). But the most exciting opportunity my agents sent me was an audition in Orlando for an NBC Discovery Kids pilot.

The pilot was called *Vulture Island*. It was about a group of teens who sailed out to a deserted island to find treasure. I was eighteen and had abnormally large breasts, but the character was fifteen, so I wrapped a tight ace bandage around my chest and wore overalls to cover them up. Apparently, the boob vice worked because the producers believed I was fifteen and had me come back and audition two more times. By the third audition my breasts were like *Please, quit this acting stuff.* But it was all worth it when my Tampa agent called to tell me I had booked one of the lead roles! I was going to be a series regular in a pilot! I lived in an Orlando hotel for two weeks and got paid $3,000. My life was reaching a peak. A peak that rose beyond my imagination as I was driving home from Orlando after the final day of shooting.

My phone rang and I glanced at the caller ID. My eyes exploded when I saw Jack's number on my phone. I hungrily picked up, but forced the starvation out of my voice. "Hello . . . ? Jack who . . . ? Oh, hey, what's up . . . ?" Then he launched into the apology to end all apologies. He talked for forty minutes about how sorry he was and how ashamed he was of his behavior. He said he had recently become sober. He was currently in Alcoholics Anonymous and contacting all the people he had harmed in his life.

He said he felt terrible about abandoning me many months earlier. He said he was just too scared to go on a cross-country adventure like that. He was drinking and taking a lot of drugs at that time, then he got back together with his ex-girlfriend. She felt safe. She felt like home.

One night, while he was hammered, he got into a really bad car accident; injured his father, who was in the passenger seat; and lost his driver's license. That experience woke him up and he wanted to change his life. He broke up with the girlfriend and stopped drinking. AA led him to call me and try and make up for what he did. I had already forgiven him the moment I saw his name on my phone, but it was nice to hear all that other stuff.

We hung out a few times. I was tentative because I didn't want him to crush me again, but he was so solid and so trustworthy, my guard dropped quickly. The best word I can use to describe him at that time is clean. No drugs, no booze, no shifty behavior. He

worked out and took care of himself. But he didn't have a license so
I drove us everywhere; I even dropped him off at AA meetings every
evening.

He was working for a boat-cleaning business. He would strap
on scuba gear and scrub the bottoms of boats all day long. He paid
for all of our meals and minivacations; we would drive to the other
coast of Florida and stay in run-down beach motels. He taught me
how to surf. He took care of me and was there for me. He was mine.
My boyfriend. My very first actual real boyfriend.

Many months after my brother went into hospice, Jack and I
were sitting by Max's bed. Jack always came with me to visit my
brother. He would crack jokes and try to make me laugh in that
completely unfunny building. My brother was almost nonverbal at
this point. He called everyone "Mom" and had trouble describing
even the simplest things.

On this particular visit, Max was anxiously asking "Mom,"
a.k.a. me, for a beverage. I gave him water, but he didn't want
water. He was growing increasingly frustrated trying to describe
the beverage that he was intensely craving. "Give him the cake,"
Jack said and pointed to an untouched piece of chocolate cake on
Max's plastic dinner tray. But I refused to give him cake. I was
still stuck in the past, when we had kept Max off desserts, afraid
the sugar would feed the cancer and make him sicker. Max kept
asking for this mystery beverage. I gave him juice. *No.* Iced tea?
Nope. Coffee? *No!*

Jack said again, "Jesus, just give him the cake. He can't get any
worse." This finally snapped me out of it. I no longer had to worry
about trying to battle the cancer. He could've eaten all the sugar
in the world because the fight was over. The cancer won. I finally

picked up the cake and fed my brother a bite. He calmed down at once. That Zen smile spread across his face and after another bite, he said peacefully, "Mmm, that's pretty good." He forgot all about that elusive beverage. He ate the entire piece of cake and afterward his mood was completely changed. He told "Mom" how much he loved her and fell asleep. He never spoke or ate again. He died a week later. Because of Jack, I was able to witness my brother's last happy moment on this earth.

But after my brother died, Jack did not come to the funeral. He couldn't. His own brother had died several years earlier and he still had not processed it or dealt with it. According to Jack, his brother was an extremely gentle and kind young man. One evening, he was walking home from work when he stopped to chat with a few men. Jack's brother was gay and the men claimed he flirted with them, and in response they beat him to death. They kicked him and stomped him until his soul left his 120-pound body.

Jack told me this story several months into our relationship. He kept it close to him like sensitive, classified documents and talking about it agonized him. The men ended up going to jail for their hate crime. Jack's brother's murder changed Jack forever. Jack had a troubled childhood in many ways and he carried a great deal of pain around, but he masked it with that smile and his quick sense of humor.

When I asked why he wouldn't come to the funeral, he said, "I hate funerals, babe. I'm sorry, I just do." But the day after Max's funeral, Jack was near tears talking about how much he regretted not going and not standing by my side. He was very tortured. He didn't have a language to express his emotions. He would do things he wasn't proud of and couldn't understand why he did them. He was his own worst enemy and was constantly at war with himself.

A year after my brother died, I started to get very restless. I still wanted to someday move back to LA and Jack supported me. He also had a dream: he wanted to enroll in diving school and become a professional commercial diver. We decided to help each other accomplish our dreams and we began working really hard and saving all of our money. He was going to go to school in Louisiana and I was going to, for the third time, move back to Hollywood. We knew this meant we had to break up eventually, but we relished each other's company while we could.

He was my best friend and I would not have survived those years without him. He pushed me to go start my career in entertainment. He wrote me long letters, filled with simple words that expressed immense love: "If anyone I know can have a big life and a big career it's you, babe."

He'd remind me how smart I was and how I was capable of anything. He lifted me up in ways that no one ever had and I tried to do the same for him. Eventually we went our separate ways, he to diving school and I to Hollywood, where I actually stayed put this time. We kept in touch for fourteen years, always expressing our love for each other and rooting for each other to do well. I recently opened Instagram and saw a message from an old Florida friend:

"Hey, I was just curious. Do you know how Jack died?"

I stared at the message. Then my legs gave out and I fell on the ground. Apparently, my knees did not work in a world Jack was not in. *Not my Jack, please not him.* He still felt like my Jack. After fourteen years, he still somehow felt like mine. I wrote her back begging her to be talking about a different Jack, but I knew she wasn't. I learned he had died months earlier, but his family didn't tell anyone. No obituary. No funeral. No one knew how he died.

We eventually heard that it might have been a fentanyl overdose. He was still his own worst enemy and his dark side won out. He was trying desperately to relieve some of that pain he carried around and he closed those otherworldly eyes for the last time. Two months later, while I was still grieving Jack, I woke up to a text message from a different Florida friend:

> "Hey girl! I don't know how to tell you this, I have some terrible news. Please call me when you wake up."

Tori is dead, I thought. As soon as the thought moved across my mind, I felt the heavy weight of how true it was. Tori and I had lost touch over the years, but I knew drugs had never loosened their grip on her. Every instinct in my body told me the terrible news I was about to hear was that drugs had finally succeeded in destroying my oldest friend. I called my Florida friend back and she confirmed my instinct.

Tori had died the day before. Word was she also overdosed on opioids. I felt like my whole childhood was gone. The two people who had loved me, cared for me, raised me, and shaped me were gone. Their wisdom, laughter, beauty, and light were abruptly taken from this world. Their pain was too great and their stories were too short.

But on the good days, the days when I believe the universe has a beautiful plan for every soul and everything happens as it should, I don't believe their stories were too short. I believe their stories were told exactly as they should have been, their stories were perfect just like everyone else's and told in a way only the universe could understand. But on the bad days, I'm furious their stories are over. On the bad days, the universe can go fuck itself.

Los Angeles
One More Time

I WAS TWENTY YEARS OLD AND HAD JUST MOVED TO EAST HOLLYWOOD. I lived with a roommate. His ancestors were Chinese, but he was born in Jamaica. He had a vaguely Jamaican accent and was a phenomenal hip-hop dancer. LA was already racking up exotic cool points. We shared a one-bedroom apartment; I took the bedroom and he slept in the open loft above the kitchen. My rent was $625 a month. I would not have been able to make this third move to California without my father's generosity. He told me if I moved back one more time, he would give me $500 a month for one year while I got settled in my new life situation. That gesture, along with all of Jack and Zoe's emotional support, gave me the strength and courage to make the move again.

Also, a magical thing happened that made the lonely agony of transitioning to a new city much less agonizing: I made a friend.

We worked together at a late-night Hollywood bar. The first night I met her, I made some sardonic comment and she said, "Oh, we're gonna be *best* friends." That terrified me. Earnestness was not a language I spoke. I preferred tougher, colder, harder-to-get friends that made me work for it. This girl was friendly and warm in a way that made me feel uncomfortable.

When we first spent time together outside of work, she was asking me all kinds of questions to get to know me. She was so fresh-faced, openhearted, and kind. She had wealthy parents and grew up in Palo Alto. *She's so sweet and her skin is so clear because she's never really suffered*, I thought to myself, still wearing my pain as a badge of honor. *She's just like Jenny, and Gabby, and Haley.* But I was completely wrong. On that list of questions she rattled off to me during that first hang was "Do you have any siblings?"

"I have a half sister. And I had an older brother, but he died when I was nineteen," I responded.

"Shut the fuck up!" she said in genuine shock.

"Um . . . what?" I had gotten all kinds of weird reactions to sharing that news about my brother, but this one was a first.

"*My* older brother died when I was eighteen!" she said, staring at me like I suddenly had magical powers. *Whoa.* It was the first time I was speaking to someone who had been through exactly what I had been through at the same time in their life. And unlike Jack with his dead brother, my new friend was able and willing to talk about her dead brother.

It was also the first time I realized maybe Jenny, Gabby, and Haley had hardships too? Maybe my new friend was openhearted and kind because she worked hard to be, rather than because everything in her life had been perfect? And it turns out, she correctly predicted our best friendship, a friendship that remains to this day.

Soon after I arrived in LA, I bleached my hair blonde and my dad bought me new, scintillating headshots. I stuffed them in clear envelopes, along with my fake résumé, and mailed them to every agency in town, and eventually I landed at a boutique Beverly Hills agency. They sent me on one audition and I booked it. *Holy crap, I'm gonna be Julia Roberts in like six months*, I thought. The audition was for a horror movie about peaceful vampires who lived in the mountains, quietly drinking cow's blood to stop themselves from murdering humans. But when they accidentally drank a batch of cow's blood that had been infected with mad cow disease, they became evil zombie vampires. Very highbrow stuff.

My character was a sultry teen who wears a bikini in a lake and then wears a bikini in the shower. I was sitting in the makeup chair and the makeup artist started stressing about my zits. "Ugh, I don't know how I'm gonna cover this one. It's *so* big." I reverted deep into my head to try to avoid hearing everything she was saying, but there was no escaping it. "It's just that your skin is *so* textured, it's going to be hard to make it look smooth on camera. I'm gonna have to use airbrush makeup."

"Okay," I said, trying hard not to cry. I had been living with the acne for so many years, I had sort of pushed it to the background, but now it was front and center again. The girl next to me, the lead of the movie, who had recently been in an episode of *CSI* so everyone was treating her like a celebrity, turned to me and said, "You should really try tea tree oil. That's what I do whenever I get a zit." But one look at her face told me she had never actually had a zit in her life. Also, I had already tried tea tree oil! I had already tried everything! I thanked her for her thoughtful advice and as soon as I was able, sobbed inside my tiny trailer. I had to cry on my hands and knees so the tears would fall straight down to the floor and not smear my eye makeup.

On set, before the director called "action," a lighting guy approached him and loudly made a joke about how they were having trouble lighting my zit. The whole crew laughed and they nicknamed my giant zit "Doug." I laughed too. *Ha ha this is the most humiliating experience of my life, I just lost my brother, broke up with my first love, and moved to a new place, and I'm very vulnerable right now ha ha ha ha ha!* The crew joked about "Doug" for the rest of the two weeks, and every time they did, I shuddered in pain and laughed really hard.

I cried to my mom on the phone about that experience. Acting made me feel vulnerable enough; acting with a red, infected face was more than I could stand. I might've had a face for TV, but I felt like I had skin for radio, and I was willing to do anything to fix it. My mom told me about a website that sold cheap medication from India. We remembered how the Accutane had helped my face years earlier, but we chose to forget about the suicidal ideation that came with it. My mom ordered me a bunch of illegal Indian Accutane and mailed it to my apartment. Why didn't I just go to a dermatologist and get on Accutane with proper supervision? I didn't have health insurance. It was unthinkable to go to an actual doctor. The cost would've broken me.

The moment I got on Accutane again, my face cleared up. It was like magic. As my pores shrunk and my cysts healed, my self-hatred shrunk and my self-esteem healed. My agency was sending me on TV auditions and I started occasionally booking costars and guest stars. I was making about $8,000 a year from acting. Which was absolutely thrilling, but not enough to live on. To pay my bills, I was waitressing and working as a receptionist at a spa in Beverly Hills.

I also started nannying, and that is something I absolutely would not have done if I wasn't on Accutane. Historically, whenever my face was broken out, I refused to be around children. Countless times in my life, a young child has looked at me and said something like, "Oh, you have an ouchie?" and then pointed to my inflamed face. The nearby adult would look at their kid like, *shut the fuck up you idiot!* And then look at me like, *Well, shall we just go our separate ways and never speak again?*

Then I would have to lean down to the darling child and say something like, "Yes, sweetie, I have pimples."

"Pim-ples? Does it hurt?" the child would respond, so innocently.

"Yes, it does."

"Why do you have pim-ples?"

"Well . . . I don't know . . . that's part of the problem," I would respond. At this point, I usually would be drenched in sweat and slightly shaking.

Then the adult would grab their child roughly by the arm and say, "Okay, honey, that's enough questions."

Then the adult and I would smile at each other with the silent desire to commit a murder-suicide so the situation could be expunged from the world forever. One horrible afternoon, a child asked me if I had recently stuck large needles in my face.

"What do you mean?" I said with a big smile, masking my desire to kick the child through a wall.

"Well, you have holes in your cheeks," the little boy said, taking in my cheeks with his wide brown eyes.

"Oh, those are my pores. They're bigger than yours because I have a skin condition," I said with an even bigger smile and an even stronger desire to kick the boy. This kind of thing has happened to me so many times that I can sense the exact moment when a child notices the difference between my skin and everyone else's. I usually move away from them as soon as I feel their eyes landing on my skin, to avoid all the awkwardness. But since I was back on Accutane, I was free to nanny and my fear of curious children disappeared. And also, since I was back on Accutane, I became horrifically depressed.

Slowly those old feelings from my first round of Accutane came back, until nothing in my life seemed to bring me any joy. I would stand on my apartment balcony, lean over the edge, and fantasize about jumping off. The idea of feeling the cool wind on my face before I hit the ground became an obsession. My agents would inform me I booked a TV job and I wouldn't celebrate. I knew the job would entail me going to set, sitting in front of an actor in a cop costume, and crying about my friend who had just been raped, or crying about my husband who had just been murdered, or crying because I had just been the victim of a bombing. Acting, which had been my dream since I was three years old, suddenly wasn't fun at all.

After I had been on the Accutane for about six months, I read online that six months was the max amount of time one should be on it, so I quit taking it. I started to feel emotionally lighter, but I was still pretty miserable. I couldn't imagine this being the rest of my life: driving to auditions, getting a pass or fail grade from a casting director, waitressing to make ends meet, eventually booking a job, playing a victim on a show (lying in a pool of fake blood because a shooter was trying to hit the mayor but hit me by mistake), and then going back to waitressing.

Some of my friends had the same exact life, and they absolutely loved it. The lack of stability didn't bother them, and the rejection didn't weigh heavily on them. But my entire life up until that point had been so thoroughly unstable and so filled with loss and rejection, I couldn't take another year of it, much less make it my life-long career.

One night, a year into my new LA life, I met a man named Anthony Tambakis. He was a screenwriter and his first movie was about to go into production. I had never met a real screenwriter before and I gushed to him about how much I loved writing. I had actually been writing my whole life, keeping detailed journals and writing songs, poems, and short stories. My friends called me the group "historian," because I had been writing down all of our adventures and keeping track of our major life events since I was eleven. My parents didn't do much to nurture my inner writer, but my public school teachers did. They would notice I was drawn to writing and would enroll me in public writing programs or submit my essays to writing contests. But without a formal education, I never had the confidence to consider writing as an actual career.

Anthony told me he used to teach writing at a university and he'd be happy to give me some tips and guidance over email. I couldn't believe it. An actual, college-educated, real, flesh-and-blood writer was going to help me?

You might be thinking, this dude sounds super shady and he was obviously just hitting on you. *Or* you might be thinking, this dude sounds *legit*, he definitely was not attracted to you; you sound like you were violently insecure, had a raging skin disease, and were certainly not turning the world on. But I hope you're thinking, he was of course *very* attracted to you but resisted hitting on you because he saw how much potential you had. That way I get two compliments instead of none. But the truth is, he was just an extremely decent man who wanted to help a young person learn a craft he had mastered and loved.

A few days after I met him, he emailed me a college level writing assignment. After I turned in the assignment, he responded with glowing words of encouragement and crystal clear feedback for improvement. Then he sent me another assignment. And another. And another. I had no idea why I kept doing the assignments. The thought of actually becoming a paid writer was unfathomable. I didn't know what I wanted out of it, but something in me made me keep doing it. He sent me a long list of books to buy and kept sending me creative jumping-off points for various essays. What the hell was going on? Was I writing? "Of course, you're writing," my dad said proudly, after I told him about my new hobby. "You've been writing forever. I've always known you were a writer."

I was so distracted and happy with my new writing assignments that for the first time in my life, acting moved to the background of my desires. I started taking an online screenwriting class. I read every screenwriting book I could get my hands on. I wrote a short film and sent it to Anthony for notes. He said the story was pretty bad but the dialogue was good and he encouraged me to keep learning.

At this point my acne was fully back. Accutane didn't have much lasting power for me, and to soothe my agony over it, I let myself start imagining my life as a writer. In my imaginary life, I would never again have to stress about how to cover my zits for auditions, or worry about how a makeup artist or lighting person was going to be able to cheat that I had "normal" skin. I could maybe even write from home and avoid having to venture out into the world of curious children and pitying adults ever again. It was the first time I had ever considered a life where beauty wasn't intrinsically linked to my well-being. As far as I knew, I had always been an object, and the health, wealth, and safety of the object was completely dependent on the level of beauty the object possessed.

Writing was so different. I was thinking, I was learning, I was using my brain. I was allowed to write and have lots of zits at the same time! And even aside from freeing me from the hellish belief, fueled by advertisers, that women must always meet the impossible beauty standard or they have no reason to live, I simply loved the act of writing. I really, truly fell in love with words and with the creative freedom that comes from building a world and characters and deciding what they will say and do.

I had just finished writing a very dark short film about suicide when I asked Anthony what I should write next. He said, "Try writing something in the genre that you love to watch. What are you a fan of?" I hadn't really thought about it before, but it dawned on me, *all I watch is comedy* . . . I carried the DVD box set for the sitcom *Friends* around like an emotional support animal. I watched an episode every time I felt too sad or too lonely. Watching comedy was my respite from a painful life and it meant more to me than anything, but I had never considered myself funny. My first week back in LA, my sister asked me if I was going to sign up for classes at the Groundlings, a famous comedy school.

"Why would I do that?" I asked, genuinely confused.

"'Cause you're funny," she said. "I thought you'd want to get into comedy."

I was beyond insulted. I wasn't some fucking clown. I was a serious actress. As an actor, I was auditioning solely for drama television, and as I've mentioned, most of my acting jobs involved crying. But somehow without realizing it, I had become a huge fan of comedy and my sister knew me better than I knew myself.

After I became aware of what my favorite genre was, I enrolled in Upright Citizens Brigade and started taking improv and sketch classes. I couldn't afford the tuition so I interned at the theater. I would collect tickets at the box office, clean toilets, and pick up trash in exchange for free classes. There in that dark black box theater, while watching Sarah Silverman and Zach Galifianakis try out their new material, all the lights in my head flipped on at once. I knew what I wanted to do. I wanted to write comedy television.

I also wanted to win an Academy Award for Best Actress, be the airbrushed face of Lancôme, and direct my short film about suicide, but around this time in my life, someone gave me this advice: "When you're first starting out, pick one thing that you want to do and go hard at it. Tell everyone you meet that's what you want to do. Learn everything you can about that one thing. And your path will become easier."

Up until that advice, I had answered the "What do you want to do?" question with "I want to be an actress, but I also love writing, comedy makes me really happy, but I also, obviously, want to work with Martin Scorsese at some point." And my career wasn't exactly taking off, so I thought, *What's the harm in just going hard after one thing for a while?* All those rambling dreams and complicated goals became "I want to write comedy television."

Coinstar

I WAS STAGGERINGLY BROKE AT THIS POINT IN MY LIFE. NO MATTER HOW many random jobs I had, I was always one speeding ticket away from homelessness. Thank God for my parents. I knew I could call them in an emergency and they would give me what they could. But I absolutely hated asking them for money. They complained about not having enough money so often that I always felt like I was robbing from the poor to give to the poorer.

I was preparing to spend another depressingly lonely Christmas in LA when my mom told me she would buy me a flight back to Clearwater to celebrate the holiday with her and Joe. I was grateful for her generous offer and so relieved by the thought of spending the holiday with family that I didn't think to ask my mom if Joe was currently on the wagon or drinking profusely. He was drinking profusely.

A few months earlier, in a desperate attempt to not be sober, he drank half a bottle of rubbing alcohol and my mom took him to the emergency room. The doctor told him he would die if he didn't stop drinking; apparently this news stressed him out so much he just had to have a drink. Whenever his binges got too overwhelming for my mom and she couldn't stand watching him stumble around anymore, she would check him into a cheap motel so he could sober up in private. She would strip him of all his belongings and leave him in a motel room for several days.

I landed in Clearwater and learned this holiday season was going to involve driving with my mom to drop off hot meals at my stepdad's motel room and then watching my mom scream at him while she cleaned up all of his trash and vomit. After a few days, he was lucid enough to come home. He always expressed remorse to my mother after he sobered up from one of his benders, but he would never say anything to me about it. He would never say anything to me about anything.

But this year was different. My mom must have given him a very stern talking to, because Joe acknowledged me as a human being for the first time since I had met him ten years earlier. He still was not capable of speaking to me, but he did give me a typed note. In the note, he expressed his heartfelt regret for all of his past drinking and all of his shameful antics throughout my childhood. It was startling to read something so earnest and personal written by someone with whom I had yet to have an actual conversation.

On Christmas morning, the three of us sat down to open all the wrapped gifts tucked underneath Clyde. Clyde was the name my mom gave to her potted fir tree—she named all of her plants. I had yet to acknowledge Joe's letter, because I was still processing it, and I was scared to break our ten-year streak of never having had a full-length conversation, but the energy between us felt lighter.

I opened all the presents my mom gave me: two pairs of her old socks, two cans of beans, and four rolls of toilet paper. Those were actual Christmas gifts sitting under Clyde and wrapped by my mother. Reacting to those gifts was some of my best acting. "Wow . . . are these *your* old socks? They *are*? Oh my God. Thank you so much." Every Christmas prior to this one, my parents would actually buy my brother and me some pretty amazing presents. When we were little, we would sit under our tree ravenously unwrapping gift after gift. My bedroom looked like the Barbie aisle at Target. When I was six, I got an American Girl doll. When I was ten, I got a brand-new bicycle. For my nineteenth birthday, my mom asked Jack, Zoe, and my aunts to all chip in and they bought me my first laptop, a Dell. It weighed four hundred pounds and I lugged it around proudly wherever I went.

But after I turned nineteen, my mom's idea of what constituted a good Christmas or birthday present changed. Well actually, after I turned nineteen, my mom stopped remembering my birthday altogether. On my twentieth birthday, I waited for twenty-four hours for her to say something. Waiting all day for your mom to say "Happy birthday" is suspenseful; it would almost be exciting if it didn't hurt so much. The next day, I said in a shaky voice, "So, my birthday was yesterday . . ." My mom's pupils dilated and she looked like she had been shot.

"Oh my God. Yep, you're right. Oh, Laura, I'm so sorry. That will never happen again."

Then it happened again the next year. And pretty much every year throughout my twenties. I would always call her the next day and she would always seem stunned, as if she hadn't just forgotten *my* birthday but the whole concept of birthdays. But she would always

remember Christmas and that's when she started giving me very . . .
unique gifts. I think it was partly because my stepdad's drinking had
put a real strain on their finances and partly because I was over eighteen; she was legally allowed to give me jack shit for Christmas. But
instead of jack shit, she gave me beans and socks and I pretended to
love them. But before I could run to my room to go play with my new
beans and used socks, Joe handed me a present and I almost fainted.
He had never given me a present before.

"This is from me," he said, not looking me in the eye. My mom
looked giddy; I was finally going to see Joe's good side. He got me
a gift! The package was very heavy. I slowly unwrapped the paper,
almost scared of what might be inside. It was a large clear glass bowl
filled to the absolute brim with quarters. He got me a bowl of change.
I don't think he saw the irony in this gift. I don't think he remembered that time I took a cup of change from him when I was fifteen.

Joe had a habit of coming home from work and emptying all
the loose change from his pockets into this clear glass bowl on his
dresser. He did this for years and years. When he was drinking, my
mom took the bowl away from him; when he was sober, she gave
the bowl back. This thing had been collecting change for at least
five years before he gave it to me.

"There could be like a hundred and fifty bucks in there!" my
mom said gleefully.

"Thank you very much," I said to Joe, trying to make it sound
meaningful.

"Okay," he said back, which was his response to almost
everything.

The next day, Zoe drove me to a Coinstar, a machine that con-
verts change to paper money. My mom told me to call her as soon
as I found out how much the change was worth. She was excited

to see how much money Joe had given me. I was even more excited than she was since I owed my roommate rent money and my car needed new tires. After the machine swallows up all your coins, it prints out a little receipt telling you the value of your change. I dumped quarters into the intake slot for several minutes.

Zoe and I guessed how much money was in that bowl. I guessed one hundred dollars. Zoe guessed two hundred dollars. I waited for that receipt to print greedily, like I was standing at a winning Vegas slot machine. I watched as the Coinstar finally spit out the receipt and the number leapt out at me: Eight. Hundred. Dollars. I was in shock. I had won the lottery! Zoe screamed. We jumped up and down. I was rich! Joe had given me such a mind-blowingly huge gift. I loved him. I loved my mom. I loved everyone. It was a Christmas miracle! But what about my mom and Joe? How would they react when they found out how much money was in that glass bowl? Would they want some of it back?

"You were right, it was a hundred and fifty bucks," I told my mom afterward. I wasn't taking any chances.

When I returned to LA, I decided to write a response to Joe's kind letter. I felt so grateful for all the money he had just unknowingly given me and I wanted to heal our relationship. I wanted to let go of the past and finally get to know this man who had been married to my mom for almost a decade. While I was in the middle of typing up my forgiveness letter and fantasizing about all the stepfather-stepdaughter activities we were going to do together, my mom informed me that Joe had started drinking again, so I swiftly clicked and dragged that letter into the trash and that was the end of that.

Jaz

BACK IN LOS ANGELES, I STARTED DATING SOMEONE TWENTY YEARS older than me. He was forty-three and I was twenty-three. It was not lost on me that my subconscious was attracted to him on some kind of surrogate dad level. My stepfather wasn't exactly paternal and my actual father had just moved to Thailand. He was not a fan of the United States and decided to go full-on expat for the rest of his life. It felt like I had arrived in Los Angeles to finally live in the same city as my dad and he was like, *Goodbye forever!* I was mourning losing him for the fourth time in my life when this kind, stable, older man asked me out. My subconscious took one look at him and said, *Daddy? You came home?*

When I started dating this older man, I would have nightmares that my dad was my boyfriend. They weren't sex dreams; they were weirdly worse. I dreamed that my father and I would show up to parties, hand in hand, and everyone at the party knew we were father and daughter and also boyfriend and girlfriend. Everyone judged us and I felt humiliated, but I also felt very safe and taken care of by dad-boyfriend. I would wake up in a cold sweat next to this middle-aged man and think, *Hmmm, I should probably unpack all of this at a later date.*

My boyfriend was a screenwriter, a successful one, and because he was doing well financially, he exposed me to fancy things like basic medical care. When I was getting ready for bed one evening, picking at my face in the mirror and trying not to cry, my boyfriend said gently, "Do you want to go to a dermatologist? I'm happy to pay for it if you do." I still had never been to an American dermatologist. It was a combination of not being able to afford it and my mistrust of Western medicine that I inherited from my parents. But since he was buying, I agreed to go.

The dermatologist told me my teenage acne had transitioned into adult acne and if I didn't act aggressively, it could continue for the rest of my life. He prescribed me antibiotics, which if you came from my household, was like prescribing me Drano. My mom shuddered when I told her. "Oh Laura, that stuff is going to throw your whole body out of balance." But I was desperate and antibiotics were the only thing I hadn't tried. It worked quickly. Just like Accutane, except the antibiotics didn't make me want to kill myself. They also didn't make my skin flake off in chunks.

For a few months, I was flying high! My skin was cured. "I think I just had too much bacteria in my body or something," I said to my mom.

"Well, just get off of them as soon as possible," my mom responded, anxiously.

When I asked the dermatologist how much longer I needed to be on them, he said . . . "Indefinitely." *Huh?* He said I might need to stay on them until I was in my thirties and my hormones calmed down. That sounded scary. Being on antibiotics for ten years surely had to be harmful on some level, but he assured me it was not. And I believed him until my stomach started behaving wildly.

I was never the vomiting type. Even if I was very drunk, I could always hold my liquor, but suddenly I was throwing up once a week regardless of what I drank or ate. My stomach hurt regularly and my skin started getting very itchy. But man was it clear, *so clear* that I ignored all the other signs that my body was extremely unhappy. After a year, I felt so sick and weak, I was spending hours in bed every day, always complaining about a stomachache. Finally, I decided to get off the antibiotics. My dermatologist cautioned me against it, but I couldn't handle the stomach pain and vomiting anymore.

A week after discontinuing the antibiotics, my face exploded; it looked like I had switched faces with our Argentinian garage-dweller, Uncle Dog. I broke out worse than I ever had in my life. In an attempt to break into comedy writing, I was working as an assistant to producers on an Adult Swim show. I showed up to work on a Monday with clear skin; by Friday I had the most horrific case of acne in the history of acne.

People could not hide their shock at my sudden change in appearance. A crew member even made a joke about my skin in front of the entire cast, and I stood up for myself by running off set and weeping in my car. I was a wreck. My stomach stopped hurting and I stopped throwing up, but I looked like I had suddenly swapped faces with a greasy, hormonal teenager.

My boyfriend and my best friend sat me down and tried to stage an intervention to get me back on the antibiotics. They treated

me like a bipolar schizophrenic who was refusing to take her an-
tipsychotic medication. They pleaded with me because my mental
health was suddenly taking a downward spiral, but I couldn't do
it. I couldn't go back to feeling so sick. I started Googling and read
that treating acne with antibiotics is just a band-aid for something
underlying that your body is trying to process. I also learned that
long-term antibiotic use is extremely dangerous and hard on your
digestive system. Even short-term antibiotic use can damage your
natural intestinal flora, so mine probably looked like a war-torn
country. Google led me to trying a four-day apple fast, which is
exactly what it sounds like. I ate only red apples for four days. It was
extreme, but I had no other options and my skin actually calmed
down a little bit.

My mom sent me to a Los Angeles chiropractor. This chiropractor also did muscle testing and, just like the chiropractor ten
years ago, she told me I was allergic to all kinds of foods. But this
time I was an adult, so I did exactly what she said. She took me
off sugar, off fruit, off dairy, off gluten, and off grains of any kind.
I was only allowed to eat meat, fish, and vegetables. I had to take
probiotics and thirty other different kinds of vitamin supplements
every day.

To my shock, my skin improved a lot. If only I had stuck to the
diet when I was younger. It took about six months, and it wasn't
completely clear, but I no longer looked staggeringly broken out.
I was starving, but I ate all the time. Meat and vegetables don't
really fill you up though, and I lost a lot of weight. I stayed on this
very strict diet for years. I cut out desserts. I even cut out alcohol.
That's how much I wanted clear skin; *I gave up alcohol.* I finally
gave up my strongest addiction. The hardest part was, I continued to break out. Not as dramatically as before, but for all that

discipline and deprivation, it would've been nice to just finally have perfectly clear skin.

For several years, I spent most of my time writing bad scripts, getting notes on them from anyone who would read them, and learning how to make them better. Eventually, I had two decent TV pilots and I emailed them to every writer I knew asking if they would send them to their agents. A few months later, an actual TV literary agent emailed me. She told me she read my pilots and wanted to meet. I was in shock. She worked for a huge company and she seemed so passionate about my scripts. She told me she could probably get me staffed on a TV show right away and she kept her word.

About a month after agreeing to work with her, I landed my first television writing job. I started working on an NBC sitcom on the Paramount lot and earning a real living wage in the entertainment industry. Every morning, driving onto the Paramount lot, I felt like I was living someone else's life, someone who had graduated from college, someone who had grown up with wealth, discipline, and opportunity.

My new job meant I could join the writer's union and get health insurance. The holy grail. I stared at my shiny new health insurance card like it was the key to the city. I found a dermatologist in Pasadena who didn't believe in prescribing antibiotics for acne and I hastily made an appointment.

Meanwhile, my niece Jaz was living in Nashville with my sister. I hadn't seen her in a few months, but after going through some rough teenage years, Jaz seemed like she was doing really well. She called me one day to ask if she could borrow money to help pay for the registration and tags for her first car. She said she wanted to get a job and a car would help her do it. I was so excited that I actually had money someone could borrow, I sent her a check immediately. A few weeks later, she sent me photos of her new car. She was so proud of her twenty-two-year-old, black Nissan.

I woke up early one morning so I could go to my new Pasadena dermatologist and squeeze in a chemical peel before work. When I looked at my phone, I saw that my father had left me a voice mail. It was odd that he had called me in the middle of the night, but he was in Thailand, so I chalked it up to the time difference and listened to his voice mail:

"Hey . . . call me back, it's about Jaz."

Uh oh, I thought. *I hope she didn't get into an accident in her new car or something.* I got in my car and headed to my dermatology appointment, but I couldn't stop thinking about my father's voice mail. I tried calling him over and over, but I had no idea what time it was in Thailand. I called Jaz, but she didn't answer.

I was getting on the 110 Freeway, and I can't stress enough how dangerous this is so please don't do it, but something in my head told me I had to check Jaz's Facebook. The sun was still rising as I sped down the freeway. I glanced at Jaz's Facebook page on my iPhone and the words "RIP" leapt off the screen and into my brain. I started screaming. Involuntarily screaming. I exited the freeway saying, "No! What did you do, Jaz? What did you do?" I thought she had committed suicide. Nothing else made sense. She was twenty-one years old and healthy. Absolutely nothing else made sense. But things don't always have to make sense.

I parked my car and scrolled through all the "RIP" comments on my sweet baby niece's Facebook page. My lungs were rapidly expanding and contracting, trying to regulate my body. Finally, I

spotted a link someone had posted. I clicked the link and there was
a news article. The article was about a beautiful young woman who
had been murdered, strangled in the backseat of her black Nissan,
in the middle of the night.

I got out of the car and paced around saying "no" over and over.
My mind felt like it was also rapidly expanding and contracting,
trying to make sense of this. My niece's name was all over the article, but somehow, I still didn't believe it. Finally, my father called
me back. He was already crying when I answered, so he didn't need
to say anything. We both just cried. He'd lost his son and now his
granddaughter. My sister lost her daughter. Our sweet, loyal, unconditionally loving Jaz was gone.

They caught the man who took her life. He had just been released from jail a week earlier. He was intensely disturbed and had
been posting all kinds of demented claims that he was the second
coming of Christ on his Facebook page. No one knows why my
niece was with that unhinged man that night. She had just met him
that day and when she brought him with her to her friend's house,
all of her friends said, "Jaz, who is that guy? He's really creepy." But
Jaz wasn't like everybody else. She didn't judge. She saw only the
good in people. She was open and accepted everyone.

A few years earlier, Jaz and I were shopping in Hollywood.
I went inside Urban Outfitters and she stayed outside to finish
her cigarette. After a few minutes, I saw her through the glass,
smoking a fresh cigarette and chatting with a homeless man. Apparently, he had complimented her sneakers, then she gave him a
cigarette and they became fast friends. I, in all my neurotic glory,
ran outside, pulled her away from the man, and told her not to
talk to strangers. But Jaz didn't look around a city street and see
"strangers," she saw human beings who are "actually pretty chill,"

which is what she said about that unhoused man after I forced her to distance herself from him.

Her heart was so good. The world would be a better place if we were all more like her, open and accepting. I hate that her goodness and trusting nature made her so vulnerable to the darkness in this world, but it did.

New Age

IT MAKES PERFECT SENSE THAT I WOULD FIND OUT ABOUT MY NIECE'S MUR-der while I was driving to the dermatologist. My whole life I had been trying to just be left alone so I could quietly obsess about myself and the condition of my skin in private, but God kept forcing me to worry about other people and their far more serious tragedies.

After my niece died, my body started falling apart. I had been dealing with a dull tailbone pain for a few years and it suddenly became unbearable. I couldn't sit in a chair without a sharp pang in my lower back. I had to start bringing a donut cushion into the writers' room. And I don't recommend bringing a donut cushion into a room of fifteen comedy writers who have been training their whole lives to make fun of people.

I was twenty-six years old; I did yoga five times a week, I ate an incredibly clean diet, I slept eight hours a night and drank one hundred ounces of water a day, but my body was in agonizing pain and my face *still* would not stop breaking out. I no longer looked like I had full-on measles, but was it too much to ask to have Jennifer Lopez's silky complexion stare back at me in the mirror?

One day I was at work complaining about the only health problem I felt comfortable talking about socially, my tailbone pain (I still never talked about my skin in public), and a writer next to me leaned over and said almost in a whisper, "I know a woman who can heal the unhealable." He told me it would be unlike anything I had ever done before, but this woman had saved his life and healed a lot of his health issues. He wrote her number down and slid it to me, secretively, like he was committing a felony by sharing this sensitive information. *Maybe this woman can fix my skin too,* I thought, and I called her as soon as I got home.

Her name was Carol and the moment she answered her phone, I knew I was in over my head. She was brash in an aggressive East Coast kind of way, which would've been fine if she didn't also seem completely daft. She told me I was dehydrated. She said she could feel it over the phone. I almost hung up. I was in no mood for magic or bullshit. I had exactly zero tolerance for spirituality of any kind.

Six years earlier, I had decided to officially stop calling myself a Scientologist, and I never wanted to participate in anything religious or self-help-ish ever again. And all the death around me? For lack of a better way to put it, it made me hate God with a fiery passion. But that wasn't even it, because to hate God I'd have to acknowledge there was a God, and at that time, I wasn't even willing to do that.

Then Carol told me I was eating something that was poisoning my body. She told me to go to my fridge and touch all the things I was currently eating. I was furious. This woman was wasting my time. I reluctantly went to my fridge and started touching things.

"That!" she shouted over the phone. "That right there! What did you just touch?"

My hand was on a bottle of herbs I was taking to eliminate parasites in my digestive tract, because I had read online that parasites can cause acne. I told her that and she said, "Those herbs are bad for you. Stop taking them immediately." Then she gave me her address and told me she could see me for an appointment in one month.

Everything in me did not want to see this incredibly strange woman in person, but the current treatment for my tailbone pain was visiting a physical therapist once a week so she could put gloves on and stick her finger inside my anus to try and relieve some tension around my tailbone from the inside. My health insurance was paying for me to get my asshole fingered once a week, which is obviously awesome, but it wasn't helping with the pain at all. Months earlier I'd gone to an MD and they'd taken X-rays and told me my tailbone was completely normal and they had no idea why it was hurting so badly. They'd told me all they could do was prescribe me Vicodin.

"How long would I need to be on Vicodin?" I asked.

"Indefinitely," the doctor answered, fully prepared to turn me into an opioid addict without batting an eye. I, thankfully, declined. All those years of my parents repeatedly telling me how destructive drugs were and begging me to stay away from them saved my life yet again. Just like with the acne, I felt like I had already tried everything else to fix my tailbone, so I drove to my appointment with that ethereal woman out of sheer desperation.

I sat in a leopard print chair across from this strikingly beautiful older woman. Carol's hair was almost completely white and her eyes were so light blue they too were almost white. She looked to be anywhere from sixty-five to one thousand years old. She was somehow beyond age and beyond time. She dangled a small sterling silver pendulum from her hand and it seemed to move on its own as she asked me questions. I was very freaked out and wanted to run out of her cramped apartment. And that was before she started talking to the ghost of a dead doctor. Every few minutes she would consult this ghost doctor and, apparently, he would respond with sound medical advice.

Eventually, she sat in silence and took me in for a few minutes. I was looking at the floor, scared and overwhelmed. Then she said, "So you were ten years old when your dad left?" I looked up at her in complete shock. How on earth could she have known that? But before I could answer her, a tidal wave of emotion erupted from my body. Whatever this woman was doing to me with her metaphysical witchcraft was allowing me to suddenly open up and let out deeply buried emotions.

I was twenty-seven years old and still had not dealt with my parents' divorce. I'd made a lot of jokes about it, but I'd honestly thought, prior to this day, that since so many children have divorced parents, it wasn't really that big of a deal. The human ability to live in denial is impressively strong. I sat in that chair and cried harder than I had ever cried in my entire life.

"There's a box of tissues by your feet," she said casually, as if I wasn't in hysterics and barely able to breathe. I used more than half of the box during that first appointment. When I was done crying about my dad, she said, "Did your brother pass away?" *What in the literal fuck was going on?* I hadn't told her about my brother yet. I barely talked to anyone about this stuff. She knew things about me that some of my close friends didn't even know.

"He's here," she said. "Your brother is here and he wants you to know that he's not mad at you for being selfish while he was sick.

He forgives you and he's okay." I bawled. The human body is made up of 60 percent water, and I released most of that water from my eyes that afternoon, sitting across from that powerful woman. *She's a witch*, I thought, *an actual witch*. Her official titles were medical intuitive and hypnotherapist.

After I finished wailing, she put me under a gentle hypnosis. She filled my subconscious up with images of love and safety. I had never felt more at peace. As I drove home, I felt a sensation that was completely new to me: calm. I couldn't wait to go back for another appointment with Carol and Dr. Ghost.

But before my next appointment, my fear kicked in. *That was all bullshit*, I thought. *There are no such things as ghost doctors.* The thought of going back there filled me with dread. It was as if I sensed how much Carol was about to help me change my life and the old dark parts of me didn't want change. I knew who I was. I was a sarcastic, judgmental, self-deprecating comedy writer in her late twenties, who used humor to avoid dealing with anxiety and fear, who blamed her parents for all of her challenges, who always ended up in romantic relationships that were unsustainable, and who suffered from all kinds of random health problems for which there was no known cause or cure. Why would anyone want to give all that up?

If "scared animals return home, regardless of whether home is safe or frightening," then my inner scared animal was fighting to not be ripped out of its home, regardless of the fact that "home" was miserable and unhealthy. I could sense that Carol was going to rip me out of my old agonizing yet comforting home. *What would my new home be? Quiet and peaceful? Confident and secure?* The whole thing was terrifying.

But four appointments and several tissue boxes later, my tailbone pain was gone. It never came back. That left me with this undeniable proof that my body's health was intrinsically tied to my emotions. Carol never touched my back, she never gave me pills, she never gave me herbs, she just put me in a trance that allowed my walls to come down so I could finally let go. Whether or not she actually talked to my dead brother or a dead doctor I do not know, but I do know she is an incredibly gifted healer who facilitated my emotional transformation.

After my tailbone pain went away, I brought up my skin condition to this healing wizard woman and she told me my face was red and inflamed because my mind was red and inflamed. In other words, she thought I was very pissed off.

"Um, no, I don't think so," I responded, "I don't really get mad. 'Cause I, like, understand why people do the dumbass things they do, so there's no point getting mad about it or whatever." The human ability to live in denial is just *so* incredibly strong. She looked at me knowingly for a moment.

Then she said, "Grab that pillow next to you and punch it a few times."

I felt beyond self-conscious doing such a stupid, childish thing, but I gave the pillow a few obligatory punches. She watched me and then said, "Okay, you're not ready to let anger out yet, but you will be soon. When you feel it start to rise, punch pillows, scream and yell. Let as much out as you can. Don't judge it, just let it out." I felt annoyed at her, not angry, because I was apparently above the feeling of anger, but I definitely felt annoyed.

A few days later, after a yoga class, I got in my car and as I drove home, I thought about Carol accusing me of being a secretly angry person. Who the hell was she to accuse me of that? I don't get angry. I'm better than that! I don't stoop to the Neanderthal level of anger! I'm not a chimpanzee! I started screaming. "Fuuuuuuck youuuuuu!" I parked my car, ran inside my studio apartment, and started wailing on my bed; I worked up a sweat punching all of my pillows for over an hour. I called my mother a bitch. I called my father a monster. I called my brother an asshole. I called my stepdad a loser. I screamed about every person I had ever met.

Apparently, I hated everyone. I hated the man who killed my niece. I hated my niece for dying and leaving me. I hated the witch who was helping me heal. I hated all my childhood friends. I hated all my current friends. I hated every racist person in my hometown. I hated every misogynistic boy I had grown up with. I hated everyone. And I punched all of them in their dumbass pillow faces.

Then I turned on the worst person I knew. That scumbag, piece of shit I despised the absolute most: myself. I called myself every terrible name in existence. Then I turned on life itself, and I yelled about how much I absolutely hated being alive, how hard this place is, how agonizing all the loss and disappointment had been. My neighbors probably thought ten women were crammed in my tiny apartment, in the middle of a screaming fight club. But it was just one woman, beating the living shit out of her bed, finally allowing herself to feel her feelings.

Human beings are very emotional. We are told women are more emotional than men. This is not true. Gender is not an indicator of how much a human being feels. Gender is, however, an indicator of how much a human being is *allowed* to express those feelings and, in our society, women are obviously allowed to express their feelings more than men are.

But we pretty much despise when any person is emotionally expressive, regardless of gender. Especially the so-called negative emotions. Laughter is acceptable, if it is expelled from the lungs at a reasonable volume. But anger is shameful. Crying is embarrassing and weak. Guilt is probably the most tolerated "negative" emotion because it isn't really that loud or distracting. People can quietly express their guilt without drawing a bunch of attention to themselves. But in our quiet, repressed, puritanical society, most emotions are too messy and overwhelming.

When a child hits, they are told, "No, no, we don't hit our friends." When a child yells in anger, they are told, "Hey! That's enough!" When you were a child and you got angry, did your parents say "I understand you are very angry. And you are allowed to feel that. Let's go into your room so you can scream, punch some pillows, and let some of this anger out in a safe space"? If so, I bet you don't have acne.

Most of us were told to be quiet, no hitting, and enough with the crying. This is not our parents' fault; this is our whole damn society. We no longer light fires and chant and yell into the flames during a tribal dance. We barely dance at all (other than grinding on horny people in nightclubs). We never get a chance to let out all the complex feelings and energy burning inside of us. We medicate those feelings with drugs, alcohol, and pills. We distract those feelings with television and books, but we don't feel them, express them, and let them go. As soon as I started doing this, my skin started to heal. It was not easy and it was not instant, but it was working; finally something was really, undeniably healing my skin.

But, similar to antibiotics and Accutane, there were side effects to digging up deep-seated, old hurts and letting them go. The side effects were increased love of self, decreased terror of other humans, and newfound comfortableness looking other people in the eyes. My nervous tics and twitches went away, I stopped making jokes at my own expense, I stopped having suicidal thoughts, and I stopped being afraid of speaking in a writers' room. Every single part of my life improved; being alive became easier. We have to let those old feelings out. We cannot use logic to make them go away. We have to actually feel them and release them.

When dogs are upset, they growl or bark or rage-hump their stuffed animals. When humans are upset, they watch TV and drink whiskey. Give yourself space and time to growl or bark or rage-hump your stuffed animals, somewhere in private, somewhere where you won't harm another person. Let out all the screaming and hitting you weren't allowed to let out when you were a child. Your body will thank you.

Seeking

IBEGAN TO DELVE DEEPLY INTO THE METAPHYSICAL WORLD OF EMOTIONAL and energy healing. I went to Maui and visited a healer on Hale-akalā. When she brought some crystals out of a little back room, I rolled my eyes. Somehow even after all the miraculous experiences I was having back in LA, my inner skeptic was still alive and well.

Then this woman put those crystals all over my body and asked the crystals to offer me some wisdom on my healing journey. I thought, *Dear God, I'm letting a lunatic who talks to rocks put her hands on my body.* But before I could really judge it like I wanted to, the whole room started slowly spinning; I closed my eyes, went into a deep trance, and vividly imagined my mother when she was a little girl.

I felt the terror she felt. I saw her 1950s household, her angry, withholding dad who left her with a fear of all men and an inability to view herself as a strong and capable person. I flashed to my father as a young person and felt his childhood struggles, his overbearing mother who left him with a fear of powerful, controlling women and filled him with the desire to subjugate women to the role of caretaker and housekeeper so no woman would ever try to control him again.

All of my anger at my parents came to the surface, but suddenly I could see that all my anger was directed toward scared little children. Their adult bodies were still dealing with and acting out the terrors of their childhoods. Suddenly an idea popped into my head. We can only hold on to anger when we view life through a peephole. I was looking at my parents through a tiny hole. Through that hole they were two parents who neglected me, left me alone to raise myself, didn't protect me or parent me properly. When I expanded that hole and looked at their entire story, they were just people, with their own weaknesses and limitations, who loved me beyond measure and did everything for me they possibly knew how to do.

It also occurred to me that if I wanted to hold on to anger at my parents, I would also have to hold on to anger at their parents and their parents' parents. While I was at it, I would also have to be angry at our broken society that helped shape this Black man and this white woman all throughout the tumultuous latter half of the twentieth century.

If I was going to blame my parents for creating all my troubles, then I would also have to blame everyone and everything that supposedly created all *their* troubles, and did I really want to take on all that blame and anger? I could feel my anger trying to keep its footing in my mind, but it was slowly tumbling down. Did the crystals actually insert this wisdom into my mind? I have no clue. They just looked like pretty rocks, but I do know I felt amazing afterward.

After that trippy experience of hallucinating my parents' scary childhoods, I started thinking about my stepdad, Joe. He'd always been this ridiculous figure in my life, this drunk, this mute, this punchline. And I realized for the past fifteen years, I'd had such a busy schedule of hating him and judging him that I hadn't had time to learn anything about him. So in an attempt to understand him, I asked my mom about his childhood, and she told me that when he was growing up, he had—get ready for it—*a horrible skin condition.*

Apparently, Joe had overwhelming psoriasis. When he was a little boy, his whole body was covered in huge patches of what looked like flaky elephant hide. These painfully dry chunks of his body would crack and bleed, and he had to be covered head to toe in creams and wrapped in bandages. My mom said he went to elementary school looking like a mummy. On a good day, none of the other kids would speak to him. On a bad day, they would harass and bully him.

He developed a fear of speaking. He became intensely shy and withdrawn. He didn't make an actual friend until high school, and that's when he started drinking. The drinking made all that pain and loneliness go away, just like it did for me. Joe and I were more similar than I ever could have imagined. This information didn't take the anger away immediately, but it did help me begin to have compassion for him. I still needed to punch his stupid pillow face and release all that old energy, but then I began to really forgive him. I began to see him as a whole person and not just a villain from my childhood.

So when I judge a person's actions today, I try to take into account what they endured yesterday. That has permanently softened my heart and helped me forgive. And all I want to do is forgive everyone. It is *so* hard, but I want it so badly. Forgiving other people is so self-healing and self-helping, it almost feels like a selfish act. Especially now that I know forgiveness heals the skin! Now I forgive with a deep intensity and a passion. I take all the money, effort, and time I was putting toward microdermabrasion, facials, and benzoyl peroxide and I put it all toward learning how to forgive. I honestly wish I could bottle forgiveness and sell it; I'd put Proactiv out of business in a week.

I got so much out of all these New Agey experiences and they were so undeniably different from talk therapy, which I had been doing on and off for a long time. For years, I would sit in front of a therapist and cry about my brother. Then I would come back a week later and do the same thing. And I never felt anything shift or change. It was wonderful to be able to talk about my pain, but I couldn't get out of the pain. I don't understand the metaphysical world enough to be able to explain why it is so different from just talking, but the difference for me was vast.

Reiki, acupuncture, meditation, hypnotherapy, Neuro-Linguistic Programming (NLP), yoga, Neuro-Emotional Technique (NET), breathwork, somatic therapy, and Eye Movement Desensitization and Reprocessing (EMDR) are all different forms of moving stuck emotions and energy out of the body or subconscious, and they all helped me immensely. But what talk therapy did do for me was increase my awareness of the issues that were plaguing me, so I could figure out what feelings needed to move out of my body. Talk therapy allowed me to learn more about myself, so later when I was crying on the acupuncture table, I knew what I was crying about.

My advice to anyone who is embarking on this journey of self-discovery? Be open. Some things will work for you, some things won't, but just be open. I've sent friends to Carol. Some said she saved their lives, and some never went back. Just do what I did: roll your eyes, be skeptical, and maybe try it anyway. Humans have spent thousands of years creating all kinds of weird ways to make ourselves feel better and we might as well try them. But use your instincts; if it feels like a Ponzi scheme or if anyone offers you Kool-Aid, get the hell outta there.

Another thing that had a profound effect on my skin was inner child work. I started seeing an inner child specialist named Noah Rothschild, not to heal my skin, but rather to help me keep learning how to forgive my parents. My skin was at a stage where it actually looked pretty good with makeup on but a touch scary without it, and I had sort of just accepted the redness. But when I started seeing this specialist, one of the things he worked with me on was forgiving my teenage self, and my skin continued to heal. He told me to dig up photos of my sad, lonely teenage self and put them on an altar with pretty things like crystals and flowers. I really did not want to do this. Which told me I should probably do it.

After I dug up those painfully awkward photos and looked at them propped up on my pretty altar, so much anger at that teenager came rushing to the surface. My mom wanted help with my brother and that teenager didn't help enough. My dad wanted love and attention when he came to town and that teenager didn't give him enough. That teenager drank too much, smoked too much weed, stole jewelry from Claire's, and had sex in a Burlington Coat Factory dressing room, and my subconscious had labeled her a trashy loser. And this skin disease, which I couldn't seem to completely shake, started at that time in my life. At that time when I was peak angry at myself.

A lot of people would benefit from forgiving their teenage selves. Yes, your teenager was probably less attractive than you are now, they might've been a jerk, loud, obnoxious, they might've been culturally appropriating and pretending to be a race they were not, they might've been having sex with people they shouldn't have, or had an abortion or two, or had chlamydia, they definitely had HPV, but forgive them anyway. Chances are they were going through hard stuff and they deserve your forgiveness.

Some studies have shown that love is a necessary element like water or food. Newborn babies can die without someone there to give them affection and make eye contact with them. If love *is* a necessary element, that means many of us are literally *starving* for love. Even if you were lucky enough to have super loving, intensely present parents, our modern society is pretty lacking in the love department. Most of us did not grow up in large tribes of people whom we were all deeply and lovingly connected to. Our teacher's job was to teach us and discipline us, not love us; our coach's job was to encourage us and make us competitive, not love us. By the time a lot of us reached our teenage years, we were probably pretty desperate for love and human connection. If love were like food, most teenagers would look like emaciated famine victims, stumbling around desperately trying to feed their withering bodies with love.

And like a starving person, teenagers will do anything they can to try and get that love. Some overachieve to please their parents, or steal to impress their friends, or get tattoos on their face to fit in, or take copious amounts of drugs to medicate the agony of not feeling connected to humanity. We might look back in shame at some of our teenage antics, but the truth is *we were starving*. If we can have empathy for famine victims, we should have empathy for ourselves. So I worked hard on forgiving my inner teenage, love-starved famine victim and my skin responded.

I'm not saying emotional work is the answer for every skin condition. There are, of course, so many physical factors and every body is different. And I'm *definitely* not saying everyone with acne is angry. The last thing I want in the world is for people who are dealing with skin conditions to get even more unsolicited advice. "Hey, you should change your pillowcase more often and you're also secretly very angry." Please, God no. I'm just saying *my* condition was connected to emotional stress and finding the root of the stress helped me immensely, and I hope it helps you too . . . with whatever physical ailment you may be dealing with.

And if we want to strip away any magic or spirituality from the concept of emotional healing resulting in physical healing, a scientific approach might be this: when our bodies are stressed, we go into fight or flight and our hormones are thrown out of balance. Letting go of and releasing fear or anger relaxes our bodies and our hormones become balanced again. We can keep ourselves safe from all kinds of external toxins, but our bodies will keep producing *internal* toxins until we address the underlying stress that might be creating the imbalance.

Unicorn

ON MY DESPERATE QUEST FOR WELLNESS, I WENT TO BALI FOR A YOGA retreat. While I was there, I was determined to visit a local healer. I had read about all the famous healers of Bali and I made it my mission to go to one. I got up before the sun to stand outside a well-known healer's house. Every morning, a large group of both tourists and locals would line up outside this man's gates. I arrived and happily got in line with impossibly high expectations; I just knew this healer was going to fix all my issues. But my expectations began to waver as loud screams emanated from inside the gates.

The healings took place in the front yard, so I could hear the screams from the very back of the line. The healer was an elderly Balinese man and when I got close enough to the front of the line to be able to see him, he was stooped over a large Australian dude. The Australian was lying on his back and the healer announced that he had some "bad energy" inside of him that needed to be released. The healer took a wooden stick and pressed it into the pad of the Australian's big toe and this thick, muscular man let out a blood-curdling screech. He reacted as if this healer was slowly cutting off his toe with a butter knife.

My big toe looked up at me like, *We're waiting in line for this?!* I couldn't imagine how painful this was going to be for me. I knew I was riddled with "bad energy," and I felt the urge to run away. But I was so close to the front of the line and I had flown, crammed into a coach seat, for one million hours to get here. This massive Australian was writhing in pain from this old Balinese man's wooden stick. I didn't know what this healer was doing, but it was definitely more than just pushing a stick into the pad of this guy's toe. I watched him heal at least fifteen people ahead of me. Every single one screamed in pain and flailed about. I was getting nauseous with anticipation. After each session, the person who had just been wailing in agony seconds before looked very light, energetic, and smiley as they left the property and floated out onto the dirt road. Their faces made the whole ordeal seem worth it, but my big toe wasn't convinced.

When it was finally my turn, I was so scared about the upcoming pain, I could barely speak. The ancient healer looked up at me through his sagging eyelids and asked why I was there. I managed to croak out that I wanted to heal my skin. He examined my face and said, "Your skin is fine." I didn't know how to react to this. I was pretty sure I had seen a few zits on my chin in the mirror that morning. He had me lie down and he took out his dreaded wooden stick. I braced myself as he pressed it against my toe, but I didn't feel anything except the slight pressure of a wooden stick. "See?" he said, "You are fine. Your energy is good." Then he called for the next person.

I was very confused. I needed to get the "bad energy" out, and I was willing to deal with the excruciating pain. I wanted to grab his stick and jam it into my own toe, but I just slunk out, disappointed I didn't get the same treatment as everyone else. Then, on my million-hour flight home, it dawned on me that since I had been doing a lot of digging around for toxic emotions in the past few years, maybe I was finally ready to start living my life instead of just relentlessly trying to heal it. Maybe my skin had gotten a lot better, but I was so used to being hard on myself I couldn't see that. Maybe, when this mysteriously powerful man said my energy was good, he was right?

Then I went back to Carol and her colleague Dr. Ghost, because I wasn't fully ready to just be "good." But I stopped talking about my skin in those sessions and I started talking about my relationships. Up until that point I'd had a very fruitless love life; every relationship for one reason or another had an obvious expiration date on it from the very beginning. Whether they couldn't commit because they were afraid of serious relationships, or they weren't where they wanted to be with their career, or they were living on their mom's couch and dealing with their second DUI, every single one of them was a doomed prospect from the start. When I told Carol this, she watched her silver pendulum spin on its own for a moment and then said, "Do you ever think that maybe you're the one who is afraid of a healthy, stable relationship? Maybe the prospect of a lifelong marriage terrifies you, so you gravitate toward men who can't possibly lead you to that?" *Jesus, what a bitch.*

As much as I hated to admit it, I knew she was right. I was twenty-nine and all of my close friends were engaged or recently married, and I claimed I really wanted that, but the truth was, it absolutely terrified me. For one, I didn't think it was possible to be happily married. I had never seen a happy marriage, and I still carried my father's mantra that no man is capable of monogamy. For two, I didn't think I deserved to be loved in a real, long-term way and I only gravitated toward the relationships I felt worthy of, the unstable kind that were doomed to fail.

For the next several months, I worked on reprogramming these old beliefs with Carol. I dug up all my childhood programs about infidelity and divorce and filled myself back up with mantras like "I deserve to feel safe in my relationship" and "relationships can be healthy and good for me." I wrote these mantras down over and over again, slowly adopting these ideas as permanent beliefs.

Carol told me to write down exactly what I wanted in a partner. She told me to spare no detail. I spent weeks writing down every single quality that popped into my mind. I got greedy. I wanted him to be funny, and smart, and grounded, but I also wanted him to be spiritual, and open, and adventurous. And you know what? I wanted him to be handsome *and* have a really good job, because who says you can't have both?! I wanted him to be monogamous but not asexual. I wanted him to be strong and also sensitive. Every quality I wrote down contradicted the next. I didn't care, I was building a unicorn!

After Carol read all the attributes on my wish list, she asked me, "Do you believe this man exists?" Then all the fun I had been having writing down the qualities of my unicorn abruptly ended. "Yes," I said while tears streamed down my face, because although I did believe that man existed somewhere in this world, I did not believe my wonderful unicorn would want to be with me. We dug into self-hatred. We dug into self-disgust. We went very deep for several months and I was confronted with the truth of how I viewed myself. I always knew I viewed myself differently than other people viewed me, because when someone would comment on how confident I was, I would stare back at them confused as to how they could think something about me that was so wildly incorrect. Or after someone called me pretty, I would look in the mirror curiously like, *What are they seeing that I'm not?*

An interesting thing happened while I was brainwashing myself with positive messages about my worth and my value so I could eventually attract a man who would think I was full of worth and value. I stopped thinking about relationships. For the first time in my life, I stopped romanticizing the idea that somebody was going to swoop in and make me feel good about myself. I stopped daydreaming about being chosen. My craving for a long-term relationship began to dissolve. I was an empty cup who was learning how to fill itself. I cut myself free from any casual or short-term fling–type relationships, because I could feel them leaching my energy, but I also let go of the need for the husband-prince to ride in on his stability horse and take me off to self-esteem land.

In yoga class, I used to stare at all the girls on the mats next to me who were wearing engagement rings. I used to ache for that symbol on my finger. *See, world? I have value! I'm worth something! This ring is proof that I was chosen.* After years of forcing myself to see my own value, I looked over at a girl with her fingers spread wide in downward dog, wearing an engagement ring, and I thought, *Wow, that's a pretty ring.* I no longer saw it as a sign that she was better than me or knew something I didn't. My ring finger didn't feel empty anymore; it felt like my finger, my beautiful, healthy, worthy of being happy finger. I didn't feel jealous. I didn't yearn. I was still hard on myself about not having the upper body strength to do crow pose, so I wasn't completely cured, but it was a start.

All throughout this inner exploration, I was writing on a sitcom. Monday through Friday, I would pitch light, fluffy story

lines and silly jokes for wacky characters to say to each other inside their upscale houses. Then on Saturday, I would sit with Carol
and plunge into the depths of my self-hatred. In my fifteen-person
writers' room, we would all sit at a large conference table. There
was this thirty-three-year-old dude who pitched jokes and storylines
across the table from me. His name was Jared. He was kind and
mind-blowingly funny. We became friends. On the weekends, we
would go to the flea market and look at furniture or go to brunch.
Jared was Jewish. His dad was a doctor and his mom was a dental
hygienist.

One day, all the writers used Google Earth to look up their
childhood homes. I discovered Jared grew up in Connecticut, in
a giant house on a sprawling estate. I quickly learned it wasn't just
him. Every person I worked with grew up in similarly large homes
on rolling lawns behind picket fences. When it was my turn to look
up my mom's house, the entire room was shocked by how small it
was. I pointed out the garage where Uncle Dog had lived, the small,
dying front lawn where we sprinkled my brother's ashes, and the
charred lot next door where our neighbor had burned down her
house after murdering her husband. These joke writers were suddenly too uncomfortable to make jokes. The differences between
them and me were staggering.

I looked over at Jared, who seemed so wealthy, so stable, so solid.
Jared had attended an Ivy League university, while I had dropped
out of high school. Jared had two married parents who spent all
their time and energy securing his future, and I had two divorced
parents who wished me good luck and pushed me out the door.
Jared had all the things I didn't. He was all the things I was not. So
when one of our fellow writers told me Jared was in love with me,
I had trouble processing what she was saying. It was like my new

self-image and my old self-image were fighting with themselves. My new self-image said, "Of course, he's in love with me." My old self-image said, "Bullshit. In your dreams, ugly."

"Do you like him?" this cupid-playing writer asked me.

I had no words. Did I like him? Did I like this handsome, lean, six-foot-two Columbia graduate with the warmest blue eyes and floppiest brown hair? Did I like this hardworking genius who didn't abuse drugs or self-sabotage in any way? This mentally healthy man who meditated and loved to cook and travel? This man whose smile lit up even the bleak darkness of a comedy writers' room? This man who made me laugh harder than anyone else? This man who, when I thought about it, was kind of . . . a unicorn?

No, actually I did not. I did not like him at all. Because I would've never ever let myself like someone like that. Someone who was emotionally available, safe, and stable. That kind of guy, the marrying kind of guy, the kind of guy who would care for me and love me without question for the rest of my life, was just not the kind of guy I had hitherto ever considered spending time with.

He was in love with me? My head was spinning. *Am I worthy of that? Am I worthy of that type of guy? Of course, I am. Of course, I am worthy of everything good in this world.* My mind cracked open. My heart felt suddenly vulnerable, like it had been removed from its shell. *Oh my God . . . What if I'm in love with him too?* The feeling radiated throughout my whole body. I knew I loved talking to him. I loved laughing with him. I loved looking at him. I loved how tall he was. I loved when he wore sweaters. I'd loved hugging him that one time he had hugged me. I loved when he texted me or called me. I loved the sound of his voice. *What if I loved him?*

Hearing the way he felt about me, hearing that I was worthy of someone like that feeling that way about me, quickly knocked down every single one of my remaining walls. My old self-image could no longer lie to me. *Oh . . . I'm completely in love with him,* I realized. And I finally answered that other writer who had been curiously watching me while I had my internal world flipped upside down. "Um, yeah, I don't know, I haven't really thought about it," I said casually.

We began dating. There were no heavy talks about the difficulties of our relationship. There was no disclaimer about his fear of commitment. After a year, we moved in together. My friends became his friends, and his friends became my friends. I had never allowed this level of unity. I had always kept my life compartmentalized so, after the inevitable breakup, I could peacefully go back to my friends and my life. But this time, there was no breakup.

He was open to learning about all the different emotional healing methods I was practicing and he began to heal his own childhood issues and seek out answers to his own existential questions. Our union wasn't perfect because no part of this human experience thing can be perfect, but it was very solid and filled with love.

Four years later, we got married on the balcony of our home in East Los Angeles. My father flew into town from the Philippines, where he now lives. It had been years since I had seen my dad. My mother flew in from Florida. They hadn't been in the same room since my brother's death fourteen years earlier, but they both showed up for me. And they both walked me down the aisle.

My brother could not be there. My niece could not be there. But Jared's brothers were there and Jared's nephews were there. Jared's brothers were about to become my brothers. Jared's nephews were about to become my nephews. After releasing so much old pain, I felt like I had created space for more love in my life. Getting married didn't solve all of my problems, life continued to be unpredictable and sometimes painful, but I had the tools to deal with it. I knew how to not be a victim anymore. I knew how to heal.

I woke up on the morning of my wedding and immediately went into the bathroom to check out my skin in the mirror. Old habits really do not die easily. I was horrified to discover a small colony of zits on my neck and a *giant*, attention grabbing whitehead on my cheek. On. My. Wedding. Day. *Are you kidding me?!* I wish I could say I was above all that superficial, sexist, "the bride must look like a gorgeous virginal princess on her wedding day" nonsense, but I was very much not above it; I was one thousand feet under it and the pressure was intense. It was also the first traditional ceremony I had ever participated in. I never went to prom. I've never been to a graduation. *Can't I just have clear skin on this one fucking day?!*

I suddenly wasn't thinking about my dad who'd flown seven thousand miles to support me, or my mom who was confronting seeing her ex-husband after almost fifteen years, or my fiancé who I was about to vow to spend the rest of my life with. I was only thinking about these goddamn zits.

Something so small in comparison to everything else still loomed so large in my mind. My skin journey was not over. But I had seen all the healers, let go of all the anger, read all the books, and tried all the diets. When was this going to be over? When was I finally going to be the physical embodiment of human perfection?

I felt old self-hatred and panic rise in my throat. I sat on the cold tile floor. My need to be perfect was still controlling me. My fear of what others thought of me was still torturing me. I closed my eyes and took some deep breaths. I saw how much I still let the external world dictate my internal feelings. I felt how attached my ego still was to being flawless. *I have to let this go.* Whether it was clear skin, or an engagement ring, or black pubic hair, there was always going to be something someone else had that I didn't, some external thing that made me feel like I wasn't good enough.

And even if I never got another zit again, someday soon my face was going to change. Someday soon my face and my body were going to drastically change forever. Time would strip me of my attachment to the beauty standards, and that experience was going to be quite painful if I didn't let this obsession with the impossible goal of physical perfection go.

I could finally feel what this skin thing had been trying to teach me—vain, narcissistic, image-obsessed me: I had to find a way to be okay on the inside regardless of what I looked like on the outside. I had to find a way to *feel* beautiful no matter what. *Can I still feel beautiful today?* I wondered. *Can I still feel like a beautiful happy person and walk down the aisle with this flawed skin?* Yes, I finally decided, and I began mentally filling myself up with the *feeling* of beautiful as best I could. *Maybe my mother was right, maybe my skin is beautiful, maybe every single human being on this planet is beautiful and everything else is a lie.* Then I stood up in front of the mirror and looked myself in the eyes. I could be completely imperfect and still have a wonderful day. I can be completely imperfect and still have a wonderful life.

Acknowledgments

Oh boy, the whole idea of writing a book and getting a literary agent seemed like a far-off dream; I'm incredibly grateful to Doug Stewart for making that dream a reality. A giant thank you to my editor, Lauren Marino, who believed so much in this book and the stories I wanted to tell. Mollie Weisenfeld, Mary Ann Naples, Michelle Aielli, Michael Barrs, Michael Giarratano, Julianne Lewis, and everyone else at Hachette Books, your hard work is very appreciated. Mrs. Ladd, my fourth-grade teacher, signed me up for Florida Writes!, a publicly funded program that taught me rules about writing that I still use. Susie Fox, Oly Obst, and Josh Lieberman have helped me immensely and saved my life in immeasurable ways. Gail Lerner gave me my first writing job. David Wain and Ken Marino championed me when I was a scared, young TV writer. Laci Mosley, Jesse Dana, Nina Pedrad, and Aklia Chinn gave me the confidence to put this book out into the world. Talia Tabin has read everything I've ever written and told me it was good even when it wasn't, and every writer should have someone like that in their corner. Without all the years of advice and encouragement from the brilliant Anthony Tambakis, I would have never written anything. And without the life-changing friendship of Mircea Monroe, I would have never met Anthony. My parents have loved me unconditionally since birth and I am forever grateful to them for that. Jared Miller read every draft of this book. His wisdom and sense of humor make everything I do better and I am incredibly lucky to have him in my life.